Knoppix
FOR
DUMMIES®

Knoppix FOR DUMMIES®

by Paul G. Sery

WILEY

Wiley Publishing, Inc.

Knoppix For Dummies®

Published by
Wiley Publishing, Inc.
111 River Street
Hoboken, NJ 07030-5774
www.wiley.com

WILEY

About the Author

Paul G. Sery is a systems administrator employed by Sandia National Laboratories in Albuquerque, New Mexico. He manages and troubleshoots Unix and Linux systems.

When he's not beating his head against stubborn computers, Paul and his wife, Lidia, enjoy riding their tandem bicycle through the Rio Grande valley. They also enjoy traveling throughout Mexico. Paul is the author of *Linux Network Toolkit* and the coauthor of several other books. He has a bachelor's degree in electrical engineering from the University of New Mexico.

Dedication

To my wife, Lidia.

Author's Acknowledgments

It goes without saying — but I'm never one to shy away from stating the obvious — that Klaus Knopper made this entire project possible by inventing the powerful and great new way of using Linux called Knoppix. Klaus had the insight and possessed the engineering skill to create the most easily used, yet powerful, Linux distribution there is.

I want to thank the staff at Wiley Publishing, who make this book possible and provide outstanding support. Terri Varveris, Tiffany Franklin, and especially Pat O'Brien provided constant and essential assistance.

I also need to thank my wife, Lidia, for her patience, support, and good advice, all of which have made writing this book possible. Without her, I would still be the pocket-protector-wearing, busted-eyeglasses-fixed-with-tape-looking, *Star Trek*-costume-wearing, wrinkled-shirt-possessing, spaghetti-in-the-pot-over-the-sink-eating, Saturday-night-hacking sorry sorta guy. Well, I was never into *Star Trek,* but I *am* pecking at this keyboard on Saturday night so she still has more work to do.

Publisher's Acknowledgments

We're proud of this book; please send us your comments through our online registration form located at www.dummies.com/register/.

Some of the people who helped bring this book to market include the following:

Acquisitions, Editorial, and Media Development

Project Editor: Pat O'Brien

Acquisitions Editor: Terri Varveris

Copy Editor: Andy Hollandbeck

Technical Editors: Klaus Knopper, Jason Luster

Editorial Manager: Kevin Kirschner

Media Development Specialist: Laura Moss

Media Development Manager: Laura VanWinkle

Media Development Supervisor: Richard Graves

Editorial Assistant: Amanda Foxworth

Cartoons: Rich Tennant (www.the5thwave.com)

Composition Services

Project Coordinator: Maridee Ennis

Layout and Graphics: Andrea Dahl, Lauren Goddard, Stephanie D. Jumper, Barbara Moore, Barry Offringa, Lynsey Osborn, Heather Ryan

Proofreaders: Jessica Kramer, TECHBOOKS Production Services

Indexer: TECHBOOKS Production Services

Special Help

Emily Bain

Publishing and Editorial for Technology Dummies

Richard Swadley, Vice President and Executive Group Publisher

Andy Cummings, Vice President and Publisher

Mary Bednarek, Executive Acquisitions Director

Mary C. Corder, Editorial Director

Publishing for Consumer Dummies

Diane Graves Steele, Vice President and Publisher

Joyce Pepple, Acquisitions Director

Composition Services

Gerry Fahey, Vice President of Production Services

Debbie Stailey, Director of Composition Services

Contents at a Glance

Table of Contents

Introduction

* *

*K*noppix For Dummies describes how to get started with and use the new Knoppix distribution of Linux. Klaus Knopper invented Knoppix and designed it to be exceedingly easy to use — without sacrificing power — on almost any personal computer (PC). By *easy to use,* I mean really, really easy to use.

Unlike Microsoft Windows and nearly every other Linux distribution (Red Hat, SUSE, Debian, and so on), you don't need to install Knoppix on a computer in order to use it. You can insert a Knoppix DVD or CD-ROM and turn on the power. Instant Linux box. No muss, no fuss.

How is this possible? The *Knoppix For Dummies* DVD, sleeping peacefully in the back cover of this book, contains a live Linux version. Using a Live DVD means that you don't need to install any software to your hard drive. Instead, you boot — start the computer — directly from the DVD. This eliminates the complex and time-consuming process of making room on your hard drive, answering a lot of questions, holding your breath, and then installing the software onto your computer.

When you boot Knoppix on your computer from the DVD, you get a fully functioning Linux computer with all the bells and whistles. You get the powerful and easy-to-use KDE graphical desktop environment, Mozilla Firefox browser, Thunderbird e-mail, OpenOffice.org productivity suite, and many other tools and applications.

About This Book

Knoppix For Dummies is designed to be an easy-to-use and helpful resource. It tells you what you can do and then shows you how to do it.

Knoppix For Dummies is designed to work with the software contained on the companion DVD. We also describe how to use software packages not found on the DVD. Feel free to use other versions of Knoppix, but if you do, you should treat our instructions as general, but not specific, guidelines.

Foolish Assumptions

I want to make life as easy for you, the reader, as possible. To that end, I've made some — hopefully not too foolish — assumptions about what you want in a book like this. I assume that any or all of the following applies to you:

- ✔ **You want to use Linux as your workstation.** Knoppix provides all the applications, tools, and utilities that you want in a Linux workstation.

- ✔ **You have access to a computer.** Knoppix is indeed the next best thing to sliced bread, and may even rank higher. But you can't run it on a bread maker — even if the bread maker is computer controlled. You'll need a computer. You don't necessarily need your *own* computer; you can ask to borrow a computer from a friend or walk into a store and, with the sales clerk's permission, insert your Knoppix DVD and take off. (Knoppix's default mode of operation does not affect the computer's hard drive.)

- ✔ **You use a Microsoft Windows computer.** Most consumer computers use the Microsoft Windows operating system. Walk into any computer or consumer electronics store these days and you see row after row of such computers. There may be a few Apple Macintosh computers, but not many. Therefore, I assume that you use Windows — Windows XP in particular. Many instructions assume that you use Windows.

Knoppix For Dummies isn't for you if you want

- ✔ **Dog grooming information:** My dog Oso is currently reading *Dog Grooming For Dummies*. Stay tuned for his review.

- ✔ **A book that describes every aspect of Knoppix in minute detail:** I'm not in the comprehensive reference book business. I want to show you what Knoppix is, how to use it, and how to make your computing life better. To that end, I try to identify the essential topics and describe them in a way that's easy to understand.

Conventions Used in This Book

You don't have to go to a computer convention to understand this book's conventions. The following sections describe how you should interpret the instructions you find in this book.

Typing Universal Resource Locator addresses

Some instructions ask you to enter an address of a file or directory into a file manager. You also need to enter addresses in your Web browser. Such addresses are called _Universal Resource Locators_ (URLs) in Web-speak.

A full URL often includes the address protocol, such as Hypertext Markup Language (`http`), at the beginning of the address. For instance, the full URL of a Linux file is `file://etc/hosts`. Wiley, Inc., can be found at `http://www.wiley.com`. However, for the sake of brevity, I just use the shortened version, `www.wiley.com`, in any instructions. Most Web browsers, including Mozilla Firefox, which I talk about in Chapter 9, have no problems translating this shortened URL into the full address for you.

URLs are differentiated by monospace font, as illustrated above. For instance, the Web address `www.wiley.com` is entered in monospace type. The same goes with file or directory path names, such as `/etc/hosts`, entered into a file manager. I also print any text that you are expected to type in this same monospace font so there will be no question about which characters are to be typed and which characters belong to the surrounding text.

Entering commands

Knoppix For Dummies gives you two methods for interacting with your computer: the graphical user interface (GUI) and the command line interface (CLI). Using a GUI is the most familiar way of doing things on a computer — just point and click. But while the CLI is less familiar, it's sometimes the only way to accomplish a task. You can often use the CLI as an alternative to a GUI.

The CLI in Linux is roughly the same as the Microsoft DOS prompt. In the old days of MS-DOS, before Windows, you'd type a command at the `c:\` prompt and the computer would spit out some result. Using the Linux CLI works the same as far as your typing at the keyboard, pressing Enter, and getting a result. The CLI gives you a mechanism for manually interacting with your computer.

CLI commands embedded within paragraph text are given in monospace font. For instance, in order to get a directory listing, enter the `ls` command. Stand-alone commands are shown as follows:

```
ls
```

When giving CLI instructions, it's implied that you need to press Enter to complete the command execution.

Commands can be simple or complex. The previous `ls` command example was a simple command. You enter `ls` and no other information is required. However, sometimes you need to provide a command with options and parameters. In such cases, the command syntax is more complicated.

The following list summarizes my Linux command syntax:

- ✔ Command segments not surrounded by brackets [ ] or braces { } must be typed exactly as shown. For instance, if I say, "Enter `ls`," you should type `ls`.

- ✔ Text between square brackets [ ] is optional. For example, `ls [-l]` means the `-l` segment is optional. You can enter either `ls` or `ls -l`.

- ✔ *Italicized* text in a command indicates you should substitute your own parameter as necessary. For instance, if an instruction says "Type `ls` *somedir*", you should substitute something like `/etc/hosts` for *somedir*. That is, type `ls /etc/hosts`.

- ✔ An ellipsis (. . .) means to repeat the preceding command as needed.

If an instruction requires you to press a single key, it'll say, for example, "press the X key." The plus sign (+) is used to indicate multiple keys. An instruction, for instance, that says press Ctrl+Alt+Delete means that you should press the Ctrl key, Alt key, and Delete key simultaneously.

Clicks

Clicking mouse buttons is essential to working with any computer. Mice generally give you at least two buttons to click: the left and right buttons.

Linux GUIs work the same as Windows ones. You click the left button to activate or select an object. Clicking the right mouse button selects a context-specific pull-down menu.

So when you're directed to click on or select an object like an icon or menu item, that means to click the left mouse button. You'll be explicitly told when you need to right-click an object.

Meta versus detailed instructions

In order to provide the most balanced and helpful instructions, I provide both high-level — meta — and detailed instructions. The meta instructions give you an overview of what the steps of any process or system are. For instance, I provide a few simple instructions detailing the major milestones when installing, configuring, and using a system, application, or utility. I then proceed to provide detailed instructions that describe the exact process.

How This Book Is Organized

Wiley's *For Dummies* series books are normally organized into independent parts, and this one is no exception. You can just look for the parts you want and use them. You can even read the paragraphs backward if you're so inclined, although that might not be the best way to do so.

You can, however, read the book from start to finish. *Knoppix For Dummies* is organized in a logical fashion from the simple to the more complex. It's designed to help you get started and oriented before proceeding to more interesting topics.

The following sections describe each part.

Part I: Get Knoppix Now!

Part I shows you how to drop the *Knoppix For Dummies* DVD into a nearby computer and start using Knoppix without permanently installing the operating system. There's even a chapter that shows you how to save your Knoppix DVD configuration from session to session (or from computer to computer).

If you want only to *permanently* install Knoppix on a computer, you'll want to read through Chapter 1, but then skip the rest of Part I.

Part II: Permanent Knoppix

If you want a computer with a hard drive chock-full of Knoppix goodness, this is the place for you. This part shows you how to prepare your computer (either with or without sharing the computer with Windows), to install Knoppix on the hard drive, and to log in.

If you want only to run Knoppix directly from the DVD *without* permanently installing it on your computer, you can skip Part II.

Part III: Daily Knoppix

Chapters 7 and 8 provide you with the basic operational information you need to work with Linux and Knoppix.

Part IV: The Inevitable Internet Part

There's a chapter in this part just for you, whether you connect to the Internet with a dialup modem, a wired local network, or a wireless network. After you're connected, flip to the last chapter in this part to see how to use the Mozilla Firefox Web browser and Mozilla Thunderbird e-mail client.

Part V: Working (And Playing) with Knoppix

Part V helps you do actual work with Knoppix. The chapters cover subjects like using OpenOffice.org, printing, sharing files, and using multimedia applications. This is simple but necessary and even fun stuff.

Part VI: System Administration

Work is work, and even as easy-to-use as Knoppix is, it still requires work to manage. This part shows how to perform basic administrative functions, such as using Knoppix to troubleshoot and repair Linux and Windows computers, finding and fixing viruses, and figuring out what went wrong if you're hacked.

Part VII: Advanced Knoppix Devices

In Part VII, you see how to use Knoppix to provide advanced network services, such as diskless clients, a digital video recorder (DVR), and a server.

Part VIII: The Part of Tens

No *For Dummies* gets printed without The Part of Tens. The two chapters in Part VIII provide ten all-important general resources and ten security resources.

Icons Used in This Book

These icons amplify the discussion by injecting interesting or important information.

Tips provide additional information, shortcuts, and timesavers that don't necessarily fit neatly into the general flow of the book.

Danger Will Robinson, Danger! Be careful and read all warnings. Warnings provide tales of caution learned through hard experience. In all seriousness, you should pay extra attention to all such icons. (You've seen one already!)

Remember icons provide information that helps you recall information found elsewhere in the book.

Technical Stuff icons provide extra or advanced information pertinent to the current discussion.

Where to Go from Here

You're about to enter the world of Linux. If you've never been there before, Knoppix provides you with an easy and safe way to learn Linux without changing your current computer in any permanent way; start reading at Chapter 1. If you're already a Linux user, you'll gain access to the advanced capabilities that Knoppix gives you; pick a topic from the Table of Contents or Index and then dive right in!

Part I
Get Knoppix Now!

The 5th Wave   By Rich Tennant

"We're much better prepared for this upgrade than before. We're giving users additional training, better manuals, and a morphine drip."

In this part . . .

What's Knoppix? Well, you can find out in this part. You also start and use Knoppix and its graphical desktop environment *without* permanently installing it on a computer.

Chapter 1 introduces the basics of the Linux operating system and the Knoppix Linux distribution. Chapter 2 shows how to start and use Knoppix directly from the *Knoppix For Dummies* DVD — no installation needed. Chapter 3 shows how to create a portable memory unit that saves data and settings you create when you boot Knoppix from the DVD. (If you're ready to permanently install Knoppix on a PC, you can jump straight to Part II.)

Chapter 1

Knock, Knock, Knoppix on Bill's Gate

. . . .

In This Chapter

▶ Introducing Linux

▶ Understanding Linux distributions

▶ Introducing Knoppix

. . . .

*T*his chapter is designed to help you get oriented with the Linux operating system. This introduction sets the basis for the rest of this book.

If you want to start Knoppix without reading about the nuts and bolts behind the scenes in Knoppix and Linux, you can skip this chapter and either

✔ Run Knoppix directly from the DVD (see Chapter 2).

✔ Permanently install Knoppix on your PC (see Part II).

Peeking behind the Curtain: Understanding the Linux Operating System

Linux is both a word and a term:

✔ In its narrowest use, Linux is an *operating system* that interfaces between computer hardware and the processes and applications that utilize the hardware. This is called the *Linux kernel*.

✔ Linux can also mean the Linux operating system plus *supporting software,* such as GNU utilities (which are described in this chapter).

✔ In its most general sense, Linux means the total package of the kernel, GNU utilities, applications, and graphical interface plus configuration and installation utilities. This combination is called a *Linux distribution.*

The following sections describe the essential Linux capabilities and subsystems.

Introducing the Linux OS

From a nerd's viewpoint, Linux is a *multiuser, multitasking* operating system:

✔ **Multiuser** means that two or more people can use the computer at the same time. Each user account maintains a separate identity that is, in general, limited from accessing other user accounts and system resources (unless specifically allowed access).

✔ **Multitasking** means that many applications and tasks can run at the same time. Users can run multiple applications, as can the operating system itself.

Browse the following Web pages to find out more information about multitasking and multiuser computers:

  • www.webopedia.com/TERM/m/multitasking.html

  • www.webopedia.com/TERM/m/multi_user.html

Linux, and thus Knoppix, has the following advantages over other operating systems:

✔ Linux runs *efficiently* without much memory or processing power.

✔ Linux *networking* is efficient, fast, and reliable.

From its first version, Linux included networking, while networking on other operating systems was first inserted as a kludge. Those operating systems still have serious shortcomings.

The Linux operating system is patterned after UNIX. Ken Thompson, Dennis Ritchie, and others invented UNIX at the AT&T Bell Laboratories in the late 1960s. UNIX became widely used by universities because it provided the advanced capabilities that previously were available only on mainframe computers. Today, UNIX is widely used on server-class computers. Linux is overtaking UNIX as the operating system of choice.

A small biography of a humble giant

Linus Torvalds was born and raised in Helsinki, Finland. He was named after the famous Nobel Prize–winning chemist Linus Pauling. (*This* Linus won both a Nobel Peace Prize and a Nobel Prize in Chemistry. My father was an admirer of Pauling, too.) Linus Torvalds attended the University of Helsinki in 1988 and received a master's degree in computer science in 1996.

Torvalds was dissatisfied with the operating systems available during his early years at the university, so he designed his own. He started by modifying the UNIX-like Minix operating system but then started writing from scratch (although he used the Minix file system for certain functions). After he had the — pardon the pun — *kernel* of Linux working, he opened it up for public development. That act leveraged the talent, intelligence, and sheer raw energy of many people to create a powerful operating system. (Linux developers were among the first to use the nascent Internet to communicate and collaborate.)

The following excerpt is Linus's August 25, 1991, posting on the `comp.os.minix` newsgroup announcing his new operating system.

```
Hello everybody out there using minix -
I'm doing a (free) operating system (just
a hobby, won't be big and professional
like gnu) for 386(486) AT clones. This has
been brewing since april, and is starting
to get ready. I'd like any feedback on
things people like/dislike in minix, as my
OS resembles it somewhat (same physical
layout of the file-system (due to
practical reasons) among other things).

I've currently ported bash(1.08) and
gcc(1.40), and things seem to work. This
implies that I'll get something practical
```

```
within a few months, and I'd like to know
what features most people would want. Any
suggestions are welcome, but I won't
promise I'll implement them :-)

Linus(torva...@@kruuna.helsinki.fi)

PS. Yes - it's free of any minix code,
and it has a multi-threaded fs. It is NOT
protable (uses 386 task switching etc),
and it probably never will support
anything other than AT-harddisks,
as that's all I have :-(.
```

I always love reading this post because it's an amazing bit of history. This single e-mail heralded the introduction of both the software and the relatively young process of interacting over the Internet that changed the world. Linux is today the basis for a significant part of the world's economy and creative process. The amount of economic effect is impossible to measure, but Linux runs much of the world's servers, workstations, and embedded computers. (It brings back memories of my own struggles to find an inexpensive way to share files on my company's private network. I found and started using Linux to satisfy that need. It was a wonderful feeling.) Many, many people use Linux to develop software, products, and other intellectual endeavors. Today, Linux is like air that software developers and users breathe. Linus Torvalds acts as the gatekeeper of Linux development.

Linus Torvalds probably wouldn't like the title of this sidebar. He doesn't like words like *giant* and phrases like *changed the world* associated with him. However, it's the truth. And his humility about his accomplishments gives the Linux world even more good vibes.

Understanding Linux distributions

The Linux operating system isn't one huge chunk of software like Microsoft Windows. Knoppix and Linux are constructed from several subsystems. They are as follows:

- ✔ **The Linux kernel:** This is the fundamental piece of software that coordinates the interaction between the human user and the computer's subsystems. Note that the term *Linux operating system* can mean the kernel or the overall system.

- ✔ **Linux modules:** The Linux kernel uses modules to interact with your computer hardware. For instance, the Linux kernel needs a module to work with your computer's sound card. Linux modules are analogous to Windows drivers.

- ✔ **GNU software:** Linux distributions include GNU software that provides compilers, utilities, software libraries, and the general stuff that makes using the Linux kernel practical and possible. The GNU license allows you to copy, modify, distribute, and sell the software.

   The acronym GNU stands for "GNU's Not UNIX" — a nerd's acronym if ever there was one. GNU is a project of the Free Software Foundation, which develops and promotes free distributable software.

- ✔ **Open source software:** Most Linux distributions include applications, utilities, and other software that makes using your Linux computer easy and useful. Knoppix provides applications like Mozilla, OpenOffice.org, and the K Desktop Environment (KDE).

- ✔ **File systems:** Computers use media such as hard drives, USB memory sticks, and DVDs to store information in the form of files and directories, which are themselves stored on a *file system*.

   By default, Knoppix uses a ram disk as an alternative to hard disks for file systems.

- ✔ **Installation and configuration utilities:** Linux distributions combine pre-existing software and protocols to satisfy a need or a market niche. They also add their own value by creating installation systems and configuration utilities. The following chapters cover Knoppix-centric systems.

When someone puts all the "Linux pieces" together, it's called a *Linux distribution.* There are many, many Linux distributions in the world. Most do not distinguish themselves enough to become popular. Klaus Knopper, however, put the pieces together in a unique and useful way to create the extremely useful and popular Knoppix Linux.

The kernel

The Linux kernel (or simply the kernel) is the essential, basic system that keeps your computer tuned, organized, and working for you. You can look at it like

- ✔ An orchestra conductor (in this case, the Linux kernel) that keeps all the musicians (applications and utilities) in tune and in sync.
- ✔ A traffic cop keeping your computer's internal traffic flowing smoothly.

Coordinating all the pieces of modern consumer PCs requires the Linux kernel to deal with the following:

- ✔ **Programs and applications that you use to accomplish work**

    Programs can be either

    - User-level applications that humans interact with, such as word processors.
    - Utilities that help you configure the computer's subsystems, such as its graphical display and network systems.

- ✔ **Processes**

    The Linux kernel deals with processes by allowing them to start and stop and by scheduling them to access computer resources such as the CPU, memory, networks, and file systems. It also takes external signals to control the processes. For instance, the kernel takes input and output (I/O) from humans typing on their keyboards and helps processes display to the monitor. It also performs other functions, but you get the idea. The Linux kernel makes it possible for you to interact with your computer and keeps the computer organized internally.

Modules and libraries

The Linux kernel must know what hardware components a computer comprises and how to interact with them. Each hardware component has its own specifications and requirements that define how it interacts with other computer subsystems. *Kernel modules* are software that the Linux kernel uses to interact and control individual hardware components.

Linux kernel modules are similar in function to Microsoft Windows drivers. Kernel modules and drivers are software that the operating system uses to interface with computer hardware.

Early in its development process, Linux didn't use kernel modules. All the hardware-related software was built (*compiled* in software terms) directly into the kernel. Such kernels are called *monolithic*.

However, monolithic kernels tend to get very large as more hardware makes it to market. Such kernels can't deal with new hardware plugged into a computer without rebooting. Modules, however, let the kernel keep its svelte figure while simultaneously accepting new devices. Devices like USB memory sticks, for instance, would be impractical without kernel modules.

Kernel modules provide an elegant, relatively simple mechanism to let the Linux kernel interact with many different and varied pieces of hardware.

Libraries provide a convenient software mechanism to consolidate operating systems, applications, and other functions. They provide access to common functions, such as interacting with a keyboard or drawing a menu button on your screen. Libraries let operating-system and application software reuse common functions rather than writing from scratch.

File systems

File systems physically organize bits and bytes on a storage medium. The operating system must be able to find where the bits are located on the media in order to the read or write them. The most common storage medium is the hard drive, but it can also be old-style floppy diskettes, USB memory sticks, and RAM.

The file system is the structure that lets you easily interact with individual files or groups of files. *Directories* are a mechanism to organize similar files; Linux directories provide the same function as Windows folders.

GNU and open source software

The Linux kernel, GNU software, and many other familiar software are licensed as *open source software*. Open source software is both licensed and copyrighted. (Copyrighted open source software is sometimes called *copyleft* software.) The GNU General Public License (GPL) is the most common license for open source software. (GPL is often used as a verb. Open source software is often said to be *GPL'd.*)

The Free Software Foundation (FSF) designed the GNU GPL to be as unrestricted as possible. GPL'd software creates the following conditions:

✔ You can use and modify GPL-licensed software in any way you want as long as you don't restrict anyone else from using your modifications.

✔ You can give away or sell open source software. (You can even sell Knoppix if you want, but you'd better have a good marketing plan because it's easier to download it for free.)

Open-source software doesn't automatically mean free-of-charge software. The reason you can get such software for free is because the GPL creates a chain of unrestricted use.

Installation and configuration utilities

Linux distributors want you to use their products. Whether commercially based or not, it's in their interest to make using their distributions as easy as possible. Otherwise, their distributions don't get distributed and become very lonely.

To make life easier for you and to expand their market, Linux distributors provide tools and utilities to differentiate themselves. Knoppix provides network and other system administration tools to make your life easier. Knoppix adds value to Linux.

Live from DVD, It's Knoppix!

Knoppix is a Linux distribution that can run directly from a DVD (this is called a *live DVD*).

Chapter 2 shows you how to start Knoppix directly from the *Knoppix For Dummies* DVD without permanently installing Knoppix on your PC.

You can run Knoppix from a DVD on most PCs to

- ✔ **Use a full-featured graphical desktop and various applications, including Mozilla Firefox (Web browser) and the OpenOffice.org desktop productivity suite.**
- ✔ **Demonstrate Linux and commercial products.**
- ✔ **Troubleshoot and rescue a Windows computer.**

The full Knoppix distribution is included with this book on the companion DVD. You can download a "lite" Knoppix distribution that fits on a single CD-ROM from `www.knoppix.net` or `www.knoppix.org`.

Knoppix lets you boot from the DVD or CD without using or affecting the existing operating system at all; you don't have to install Knoppix on the computer to use it. This is the simplest way of getting access to the Linux operating system.

The default Knoppix operating mode boots directly from read-only media, using RAM (random access memory) to store the basic system files and your personal files. Part of your computer's RAM is set aside as *ram disk,* which emulates the function normally performed by a hard disk. The ram disk is faster than a hard disk but doesn't store information permanently — when you shut down your computer, its contents disappear.

Meet the man

Klaus Knopper created the Knoppix Linux distribution in 1999 to experiment with bootable Linux CDs. After he got his initial experiment to work, he started writing scripts and adding tools for his own use. He was also teaching computer classes at the time and found that being able to boot directly from CD-ROM made his life easier because he didn't have to worry about getting permission and taking the time to install Linux onto the classroom computers. He also found being able to use any available computer when traveling an added benefit.

Klaus's colleagues convinced him to publish the live CD at an early stage. He did so and got the feedback and software contributions that made the CD better and put it on a trajectory to success.

The rest is history. Klaus's project became a very popular and useful system. Klaus views Knoppix as a Debian system with the ability to boot off of DVD or CD. Knoppix can be and is viewed as a Linux distribution.

Klaus lives and works in Germany. He has a degree in Electrical Engineering (me too, Klaus!) and is a freelance consultant working in the open source field. You can learn more about the history and meaning of his project at www.knopper.net, www.knopper.net/knoppix/index-en.html (the English version), and www.knoppix.org. Eaden Mckee, from New Zealand, runs the great contributor's site www.knoppix.net.

Knoppix is based on the Debian Linux distribution. Debian is a widely used — especially in Europe — open source project. Debian is not developed by any single company but by the collective effort of many devoted individuals. Browse www.debian.org to find more information about the distribution and the Debian Project.

Ram disks store information as long as you maintain power to your computer. You can work around ram disk volatility (see Chapter 3) so it isn't much of a problem. Knoppix lets you store your *home directory* (like the My Documents folder in Windows) on *nonvolatile storage media* (such as USB memory sticks).

Knoppix can boot on many desktop and laptop PCs. I've successfully used it on nearly a dozen of them. So you stand a good chance of using it without problems.

Chapter 2

Instant Knoppix

• •

• •

*W*hen I started using Linux, it had to be installed from about a zillion floppy disks. (Ah, the good ol' days. I shudder thinking about the nights spent repeatedly removing one diskette, inserting the next, and pressing Enter.) It was a boring process, but the reward was great. I could use Linux on a cheap 386 PC as a server or even a workstation. With Linux, I could do things like create file and Web servers that were either *expensive* or *impossible* with a commercial operating system!

CD-ROM prices fell quickly and became the distribution media of choice. By 1994, I no longer swapped floppies, but installing Linux still took a lot of work. Later, when I started writing Linux "How-To" books, I described the installation process in detail over many pages. I figure a Linux book isn't very useful without a Linux computer.

Linux distributors worked hard to improve the installation process. However, you had to make room on your computer's hard drive to install Linux.

But how do you know if you want to use Linux before you even know what Linux is and can do? The installation process is still a hurdle too high for many people. Fortunately, there is a quiet revolution rolling through the Linux world — it's called *Knoppix*. While other Linux distributions' installation systems are evolving, Knoppix has leapfrogged the whole issue and lowered the hurdle. Knoppix is a Linux distribution that you can use *without* installing.

How is this possible? It sounds too good to be true! Well, it is true. In this chapter, I show that it's both possible and *easy*.

Introducing the Live Knoppix DVD!

You don't need to install Knoppix to use it. You can just boot your computer from the *Knoppix For Dummies* DVD and get Knoppix. As the shampoo commercials used to say: no muss, no fuss.

Booting Knoppix directly from the *Knoppix For Dummies* DVD is referred to as *live Knoppix*.

In this book, *computer* refers to the PC (personal computer) that you find in most offices and electronics stores. Most PCs use Intel-based processors, such as the Intel Pentium and the AMD Athlon. Such processors are sometimes called the *x86 architecture*.

Knoppix currently doesn't run on Apple Macintosh computers because they use PowerPC processors. However, work is being done by contributing developers to adapt Knoppix for the PowerPC, so stay tuned. (Debian itself already runs on the Apple PowerBook.)

If you try Knoppix from the DVD and like it, you can *permanently* install Knoppix on your computer. Part II shows you how.

"Installing" Knoppix

The following list shows what you need to boot Knoppix from the *Knoppix For Dummies* DVD on a computer:

✔ A computer with a CD-ROM/DVD drive.

Most computers manufactured since 2000 can read DVDs.

The computer you use to boot Knoppix can be your own or someone else's. However, you will leave no footprints, Grasshopper, so don't worry about harming the computer when you stop using Knoppix. (This assumes that you merely use the Knoppix DVD to boot the computer but don't use any of the available utilities to modify the hard drive. You should also obtain permission to use a computer not your own.)

✔ An Intel Pentium or compatible (for instance, AMD) PC with at least 256MB of memory.

Knoppix runs on older, "386" and "486" computers with less memory, but it's no fun. Klaus, for instance, has booted Knoppix on an old 486 PC with only 28MB! Yikes! However, you want the power of a Pentium to run a graphical environment and applications like OpenOffice.org.

✔ Keyboard, mouse, monitor, and power cords, plus some electricity.

Boot options

Make sure the computer boots from the CD-ROM/DVD drive. There are two ways you can direct your computer to boot from DVD:

✔ Most modern computers let you *dynamically change* the boot order without touching the BIOS configuration.

As your computer starts, watch your monitor closely to see whether there's a key you can press for access to the dynamic boot options. Dell computers, for instance, let you press the F12 key during the initial boot process and then select the boot device from a pop-up menu.

✔ Change the BIOS (Basic Input/Output System) boot order to look at the CD-ROM/DVD drive before the hard disk. Your computer saves any BIOS changes that you make. (If you use someone else's computer, make sure to return the boot order to its original configuration when you finish using Knoppix).

Be careful when modifying your BIOS settings. You can configure your BIOS so your computer doesn't work the way you intend it to. In general, you can reconfigure your BIOS to correct mistakes; you can also generally, but not always, restore your BIOS to its original, factory defaults. You're better off not changing settings other than the boot drive order. Go to www.webopedia.com/TERM/B/BIOS.html for more BIOS information.

Meta-view: Starting Knoppix

Here's a high-level view of how to start Knoppix:

1. Find a PC to use.

2. Boot the computer from the *Knoppix For Dummies* DVD.

3. Work on your instant Knoppix computer.

This short list demonstrates that using Knoppix is straightforward and much simpler than installing other Linux distributions.

Starting Knoppix

If your PC automatically boots from a DVD, you're ready to start using Knoppix. Follow these steps:

1. **Take the *Knoppix For Dummies* DVD from the sleeve on the back cover of this book.**

2. **Insert the DVD into your DVD drive.**

   • If your computer is *off,* just turn it on and press the DVD eject button.

   • If your computer already is *running,* reboot it.

   To reboot the Windows operating system, follow these steps:

   a. Choose Start⇨Turn Off Computer (or Shut Down)⇨Shut Down Windows.

   b. When the dialog opens, select the Restart option from the Turn Off Computer (or Shut Down Windows) dialog.

   Rebooting is the process of shutting down a running operating system and restarting it without actually switching the *computer* off.

   After the computer starts and passes through the BIOS configuration, the Knoppix boot menu appears (as shown in Figure 2-1).

3. **Press Enter when the Knoppix boot menu appears.**

   The Knoppix boot menu lets you select the Linux kernel version and options. Those options are described later in this chapter. You don't need to select any options at this point.

Figure 2-1:
The Knoppix
boot menu.

If your PC doesn't boot from the Knoppix 4.0 DVD, the computer's *BIOS version* may have trouble booting Knoppix. Here's the workaround for it:

a. Type the following option at the boot: prompt

```
knoppix acpi=off noapic pnpbios=off pci=bios
```

b. Press Enter.

Knoppix finds your computer's hardware, chugging along and displaying its progress. The progress takes the form of text that sometimes makes sense and most of the time does not. The senseless information deals with the very technical aspects of the Linux operating system. You can safely ignore the messages unless you want to become a nerd and spend your Friday nights (like me, d'oh!) delving into the finer aspects of Linux modules.

When the Knoppix DVD boot process finishes, the KDE desktop opens, as shown in Figure 2-2.

That's it! When the K Desktop Environment (KDE) desktop appears, you can use Knoppix for fun and profit. Click any desktop icon or menu to run applications and utilities.

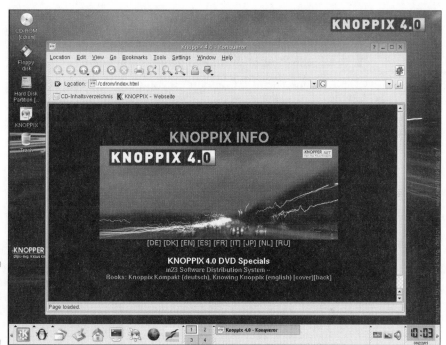

Figure 2-2:
The Knoppix KDE Desktop.

Introducing Knoppix boot options

Knoppix provides several boot options. The Knoppix boot options are divided into two categories:

⌐ **F2 options:** Press F2 at the `boot:` prompt to get to these options. These options let you supply the Linux kernel with various parameters, select a memory test, select various frame buffer modes to avoid problems with laptops, and open in a failsafe mode to avoid hardware problems.

⌐ **F3 options:** Pressing F3 at the `boot:` prompt shows a menu of examples using the options from F2. You can make your own variations to these examples. For instance, type `knoppix acpi-off noapic pnpbios=off` to avoid boot problems with ACPI board–based PCs.

Chapters 6, 7, and 8 cover the basics of Linux, Knoppix, and KDE.

When you run live Knoppix, you're automatically logged in as the `knoppix` user. (Chapter 6 explains Knoppix user accounts.)

You can shut down or restart live Knoppix:

1. **Click the K Menu and select Logout.**

   The End Session for "knoppix" dialog opens.

2. **Select the kind of shutdown process you want:**

   • Click Turn Off Computer if you want the computer to stop running.

   • Click Restart Computer if you want to reboot.

Chapter 3

Portable Knoppix

- -

- -

Knoppix is exceedingly easy to use. Power on your computer, pop the companion Knoppix DVD into your drive, and you're running Knoppix in a minute or two. Nothing could be easier!

One key to Knoppix's ease of use is the way it uses your computer memory as a *ram disk* to store files and directories. Using this mechanism allows Knoppix to work without touching your hard drive.

However, the one drawback that using a ram disk presents is its volatility. Any information stored on the ram disk disappears when you turn your computer off (or when it loses power).

But Klaus designed a system into Knoppix to account for this situation. Knoppix provides a "persistent Knoppix disk image" utility that takes advantage of the explosion of inexpensive external storage media. You can use USB memory sticks, external USB or FireWire hard drives, Windows FAT partitions, or even old-fashioned floppy diskettes (not recommended) to store your personal information and files, plus Knoppix's configuration settings.

Saving (Your) Private Directory

Knoppix provides the `Create a persistent KNOPPIX disk image` utility to overcome the limitations of ram disks:

✔ The utility saves specific files and directories, such as your personal home directory (folder), on nonvolatile storage media of your choosing.

✔ When you reboot your computer, Knoppix finds and restores your files and other system information.

This chapter describes how to use the `Create a persistent KNOPPIX disk image` utility.

Computer memory, called RAM *(random access memory)*, normally runs applications and stores temporary information. RAM is much faster than hard drive memory but is much more expensive. Your computer can read and write to RAM about 100 times faster than to your hard drive. However, RAM costs about *200* times more than a similar amount of hard drive space. Computers use a trade-off based on common-sense economics:

✔ Use expensive RAM to quickly run applications.

✔ Store bulky applications and data on inexpensive disk space.

The following sections describe how you can make a persistent home for your information.

Memory devices

A persistent home directory requires a memory device that you configure to store information from your home directory and your Knoppix computer settings.

Hardware

The storage device you need for a persistent Knoppix image depends on

✔ How you use Knoppix.

✔ How much space you need for your home directory and Knoppix settings.

I recommend at least 256MB of storage space for any persistent home directory.

Portable external devices

You need a portable memory device if you want to be able to *remove* your persistent Knoppix image and either

✔ Connect your persistent Knoppix image to a different computer.

✔ Securely store your data device.

This chapter shows how to securely *encrypt* any persistent Knoppix image.

I recommend one of these portable devices:

✔ USB memory stick

These storage devices are similar in function to floppy diskettes and hard drives. They're also known as

- USB flash memory

- USB pen drive

✔ External USB hard drive

✔ External FireWire hard drive

Internal hard drives

If you'll always use the same Windows computer to run Knoppix from a DVD or CD, you can save just your data and Knoppix system settings on the Windows computer's hard drive without actually installing Knoppix.

If your persistent Knoppix image is on your internal Windows hard drive, Knoppix requires

✔ A FAT (or VFAT) Windows partition on the hard drive

NTFS-formatted partitions found on most Windows XP computers *will not work* for your persistent Knoppix image.

✔ At least 100MB of free space.

There are a couple of ways to find or install a FAT partition on a Windows XP computer:

✔ Many Windows computers have a FAT partition, formatted with MS-DOS, to store disaster recovery files and utilities.

Knoppix can read and write to FAT/MS-DOS partitions to which it can save your persistent Knoppix image.

✔ The *QTParted* utility can shrink an NTFS file system and reformat the extra space as a Linux partition on which you can save your persistent Knoppix image.

Chapter 4 shows how to insert the *Knoppix For Dummies* DVD into your Windows computer and use QTParted to create a FAT/MS-DOS partition.

File systems

When you buy a removable storage device, it should be preformatted with one of these file systems:

✔ Windows file systems: *FAT, FAT32,* or *VFAT*

✔ Linux file systems: *ext2, ext3,* or *ReiserFS*

Meta-view: Creating a persistent home directory

A persistent home for your Knoppix settings and data is as simple as 1-2-3:

1. Prepare a storage device.

2. Open the `Create a persistent KNOP-PIX disk image` utility.

3. Save your home directory and settings to the storage medium. (You have the option of using *encryption* to protect your data from prying eyes.)

Every time you boot your computer, Knoppix automatically scans your hard drives for the persistent Knoppix image. If it finds the image, Knoppix asks whether you want to use it.

Saving a persistent Knoppix image

Using a USB memory stick, external USB hard drive, external FireWire hard drive, or even a Windows partition to mount your home directory isn't as complicated as it might seem, and it is very useful.

The steps to create a persistent Knoppix image depend on whether you want to *encrypt* your image for security. In this chapter, the sidebar "Encryption 101" explains the advantages and problems of encryption.

Using unencrypted persistent Knoppix images

The following instructions assume that you use an unencrypted persistent Knoppix image.

To save your home directory and Knoppix system configuration without encryption, follow these steps:

1. **Click the K-Menu and select KNOPPIX⇨Configure⇨Open the `Create a persistent KNOPPIX disk image` utility.**

   The Create a Persistent KNOPPIX Home Directory dialog opens.

2. **Click the Yes button.**

   The Create Persistent KNOPPIX Home Directory dialog displays the available partitions to use.

   Figure 3-1 shows a computer with NTFS and VFAT partitions on a hard drive and a USB memory stick partition.

Create persistent KNOPPIX home directory   _ □ ×

Please select a partition for creating the image:

○ /dev/hda1: IDE HD Partition [ntfs] (5020MB)

○ /dev/hda2: IDE HD Partition [vfat] (996MB)

⦿ /dev/uba: USB HD Partition [vfat] (247MB)

✓ OK   ✕ Cancel

3. **Click the button corresponding to the partition on which you want to store your persistent Knoppix image.**

   In Figure 3-1, for example, you could select either the /dev/hda2 or /dev/uba partitions; if you select /dev/hda1 (the NTFS partition), the utility tells you that it can't write to NTFS partitions.

4. **Click OK.**

   You're prompted to encrypt your persistent Knoppix image.

5. **Click No to skip encryption.**

   The dialog asks you to enter the amount of space on the storage device to use for your persistent home directory.

   The dialog defaults to 100MB but also shows the total available space.

   The amount of space you select for your persistent home directory depends on the size of the storage device. The larger the storage device, the more options you have.

6. **Enter the amount of space you want to use in the text box, and then click OK.**

   The dialog shows you its progress as it creates an image where it saves your home directory and system settings.

7. **Click OK.**

   Knoppix automatically starts saving your home directory and its system settings on your storage device.

   When you're ready to *restart* Knoppix with your persistent Knoppix image, the section "Booting from a Persistent Knoppix Image" in this chapter shows you how.

Understanding storage device names

Any *internal hard drive, DVD drive,* or *CD-ROM drive* can be `/dev/hda`, `/dev/hdb`, `/dev/hdc`, or `/dev/hdd`. However, Linux computers usually follow these rules:

✔ IDE hard drive: `/dev/hda`

✔ DVD drives, CD-ROM drives, and extra hard drives: `/dev/hdb`, `/dev/hdc`, or `/dev/hdd`

USB device names (such as USB memory sticks) depend on the order that USB devices are connected to your system:

✔ If no other USB devices are connected, your memory stick usually shows up as `/dev/uba`

✔ If other USB devices already are plugged in, your USB memory stick name usually uses the *next available letter* (`/dev/ubb`, `/dev/ubc`, and so on).

FireWire devices show up as SCSI devices. Like SCSI devices, FireWire device names are */dev/sda, /dev/sdb,* and so on. (I assume that you're using a typical consumer-type PC, so I don't cover true SCSI devices in this chapter.)

Partition names use the device name plus a number (such as `/dev/hda1`, `/dev/hda2`, and so on, or `/dev/uba1`, `/dev/uba2`, and so on).

Using encrypted persistent Knoppix images

An encrypted home directory can keep your data intact and private.

To create an encrypted home directory, follow these steps:

1. **Click the KNOPPIX menu button and select Configure⇨Create a Persistent KNOPPIX Disk Image.**

   An informational dialog opens.

2. **Click the Yes button.**

   The Create Persistent KNOPPIX Home Directory dialog shows the storage devices that are connected to your Knoppix computer.

   The "Understanding storage device names" sidebar in this chapter lists common devices.

3. **Click the button corresponding to the partition on which you want to store your persistent Knoppix image.**

4. **Click OK.**

   You're prompted to encrypt your persistent Knoppix image.

5. **Click Yes to encrypt your persistent home directory.**

   The dialog asks you to enter the amount of space on the storage device to use for your persistent home directory.

   The dialog defaults to 100MB but also shows the total available space.

6. **Enter the amount of space you want to use in the text box, and then click OK.**

   The Create Persistent KNOPPIX Home Directory dialog prompts you for an encryption password (also known as an *encryption key*).

7. **Enter your encryption password in the Enter text box.**

   Use a good password of at least 20 characters but not more than 68. A good password is complex — but not so complex that *you can't remember it.* At a minimum, don't use a dictionary word or other easily guessed phrase such as your birthday. But don't *forget* the password. You can't recover your data if you forget the password!

8. **Enter your encryption password a second time in the Again, Just to Be Sure box.**

   Knoppix displays a progress bar in the dialog as it encrypts your persistent home directory.

9. **Click OK when prompted.**

   Your persistent home directory is now encrypted. No one (including *you*) can access your data without the encryption password.

   Knoppix automatically starts saving your files on your storage device.

   When you're ready to *restart* Knoppix with your persistent Knoppix image, the following section shows you how.

Encryption 101

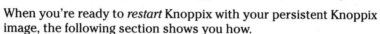

Knoppix lets you *encrypt* your persistent home directory so you can control who can see your information.

Encryption has a couple of *advantages:*

- ✔ **If you can lose your storage device, others can't look at your information.** Your information is secure from unwanted eyes whether you lose your memory stick or have it stolen by international spies.

- ✔ **Your data is safe while attached to your computer but unmounted.** Anyone hacking into your computer can't mount your encrypted file systems without the password.

Encryption also has a couple of *drawbacks:*

- ✔ **It slows down access to the file system.** The data is protected because it's encrypted; however, the computer must decrypt your own data in order for you to access it. This takes time, although not much time on modern, fast PCs (multi-gigahertz machines).

- ✔ **You must remember your password.** If you use encryption, you must enter your encryption password *every* time you open the drive.

Booting from a Persistent Knoppix Image

After you save your persistent settings, you can reboot from the *Knoppix For Dummies* DVD (or Knoppix "lite" CD-ROM that you download from www. knoppix.org or www.knoppix.net) and access any files you saved in previous sessions; your Knoppix computer also remembers previous configuration settings.

This section shows how to use persistent Knoppix image to boot your computer.

You must remount your USB memory stick, USB hard drive, or FireWire hard drive when you boot or reboot your computer. Knoppix provides a mechanism for doing this:

1. **If you saved your persistent Knoppix image on an external storage device, plug the device into your computer.**

   For instance, plug your USB memory stick, external USB hard drive, or Firewire hard drive into your computer.

2. **Power on or restart your computer.**

3. **If your *Knoppix For Dummies* DVD isn't already in the drive, insert it now.**

4. **Press Enter when you see the Knoppix boot: prompt.**

   Knoppix starts booting and automatically searches for a persistent Knoppix image. Knoppix displays the KNOPPIX-CONFIGURATION dialog if and when it finds an image.

   The KNOPPIX-CONFIGURATION dialog asks you whether to use the persistent Knoppix image.

   If you don't make a selection within 20 seconds, the dialog automatically defaults to *not* using the persistent Knoppix image.

5. **Press the Tab key to toggle to the OK button, and then press Enter.**

   If the image is *encrypted,* the AES256 encryption password dialog opens.

   The section "Using encrypted persistent Knoppix images" in this chapter covers the function and setup steps of encrypted images.

6. **If you're prompted for the encryption password, enter it.**

When the booting process finishes, your previous system settings and the previous contents of your home directory are restored to your Knoppix computer.

This is the coolest system since sliced bread! You get the best of both worlds: booting from DVD or CD-ROM with persistent storage. Wow!

Part II
Permanent Knoppix

The 5th Wave   By Rich Tennant

"I'm ordering our new PC. Do you want it left-brain or right-brain-oriented?"

In this part . . .

*I*f you're ready to take the plunge into a permanent Knoppix system, this part makes it a refreshing dip instead of a frigid belly flop. Chapter 4 shows how to ready your computer; then Chapter 5 installs Knoppix to a hard drive. Chapter 6 shows how to perform basic tasks such as logging in and out.

Chapter 4

Windows Gets a Roommate or Windows Gets Broken

*T*his chapter first shows how to prepare your existing Microsoft Windows computer for a Knoppix installation. This is called a *dual-boot installation*. You get the best of both worlds because you can use either Knoppix or Windows. (However, you can only use one at a time.)

The chapter also shows how to prepare your Windows computer for a Knoppix-only installation. *Preparing* is perhaps the wrong word because you completely erase your Windows operating system so you can install only Knoppix. You must be certain that you're through with Windows before you attempt this option.

Installing Knoppix on the hard drive is referred to as a *permanent Knoppix installation*. A permanent Knoppix installation is ideal if you

✔ Intend to use Knoppix frequently.

✔ Want Knoppix to boot faster.

✔ Intend to use Knoppix to provide services to your private network.

Preparing for a Dual-Boot Installation

Installing Knoppix alongside an existing Windows installation requires that you first make room for Knoppix on your hard drive. The process takes space away from Windows and gives it to Knoppix. This section describes the process.

You can install Knoppix side by side with an existing Windows operating system version and boot to either one. This chapter shows how to make room for Knoppix on a Windows system while avoiding disaster.

Meta-view: Preparing to install Knoppix alongside Windows

Before installing Knoppix alongside Windows to create a dual-boot environment, you need to prepare your computer. The following list outlines the preparation process.

1. Back up your computer.

Repartitioning your hard drive is a reasonably but not completely safe process. There's always some risk of failure whenever you modify or reconfigure your hard drive. Nothing is likely to go wrong, but just in case, it's best to make a backup of your system.

If you don't have a preferred tool for backing up your Windows PC, then this book shows you how to use the built-in Windows backup utility. You need someplace to store your information and the means to copy it. The section "Saving old information" provides an overview of how to use the Windows backup utility.

2. Defragment your hard drive.

Working with files on your computer tends to make a bit of a mess of its hard drive. Files appear to you, the user, to be well organized. However, the operating system stores information where it can. Sometimes, the information that makes up a file gets scattered around your hard drive. Your computer is a little embarrassed about its messiness, so it never lets on what's in the closet and under the rug, and you need to do some housecleaning before repartitioning your hard drive.

3. Repartition your hard drive.

This process makes space on your disk by making the Windows partition smaller. The new space is partitioned and formatted for Linux and, of course, Knoppix. You install Knoppix on the new space. (Repartitioning moves the end-point of the space (partition) occupied by Windows closer to its beginning point. Because Windows tends to grow from the start of the partition toward the end, you must move any far-flung file fragments back toward the beginning, which is why you defragment the hard drive before partitioning it.)

After you've repartitioned your hard drive, you're ready to install Knoppix in a dual-boot configuration. Chapter 5 describes how to install Knoppix alongside Windows.

Saving old information

You should regularly back up your Windows computer whether you're planning to install Knoppix or not. Protecting your data is important. Nothing is worse than losing hours, days, months, or even years of work and effort. Don't trust your data to fate!

I provide some general backup guidelines and describe one detailed method. (If you prefer another backup tool, that's fine.)

Here's the overall backup process:

1. Decide what you want to back up.

2. Obtain a large-enough backup medium to back up all necessary files.

3. Copy some or all of your Windows operating system and personal files and folders to the backup medium.

What follows is a brief, general explanation of each of these steps.

Selecting files and folders

The following list describes what you might want to back up on your computer.

✔ **Copy everything.** This is the easiest way to back up your computer.

This is also the most expensive way to back up your Windows computer. Right out of the box, a Windows XP computer usually consumes at least 3GB of disk space. So, before you copy any of your data and applications, you need at least 3GB of backup media space to back up your computer.

✔ **Copy only your personal data.** You can skip backing up your Windows operating system and third-party applications if you have copies on disc from which you can reinstall them.

You can obtain a copy of your Microsoft Windows installation media if you have the documentation, such as a sales receipt, proving your purchase. You can find out more information about Microsoft's replacement policy at: http://support.microsoft.com/default.aspx?scid=kb; [ln];326246.

By skipping software that you can reinstall from other media, you can concentrate the backup on your personal data. That saves time and space.

Getting backup media

Unless you intend to back up your entire Windows installation, I'm assuming you need between 100MB and 1GB of space to store your Windows configuration and personal data. If so, I recommend one of the following media:

✔ USB memory sticks between 256MB and 1GB

✔ Writable CD-ROM or DVD drive

Many home computers come with these devices. You can buy them for less than $100.

Your backup medium can be an external USB (universal serial bus) or FireWire hard drive; 80GB USB drives can cost under $100. You can also back up to another computer (if you have a network connection), a tape drive, a JAZ drive, or a second internal hard drive.

Saving files and settings

After you have your backup medium, you need to decide how to use it.

Many commercial backup packages are available. Norton's *Ghost* is one of the more popular and powerful systems. It performs full backups if you have enough space; I have used it a number of times and find it to be very good.

Short of purchasing commercial software, there are several ways to back up your Windows system with tools you already have.

File and Settings Transfer Wizard

You can back up your computer by using the built-in Windows facility that's designed to transfer data between old and new computers.

The utility is the File and Settings Transfer Wizard on Windows XP Home Edition. (It's called Backup on other Windows versions.)

The Windows utility saves the following objects to backup media:

✔ Your personal data and settings

✔ Other users' personal data and settings

✔ The computer's entire file contents

The following instructions use the File and Settings Transfer Wizard to back up your data and system settings on a USB memory stick:

1. **Start your Windows computer and log in as the administrator.**

2. **Insert or attach backup media to your computer.**

   USB memory sticks are relatively cheap and easy to use and store. (My device stores 256MB of data and is entirely adequate for my backups.)

3. **Choose Start⇨All Programs.**

   A menu opens.

4. **Select Accessories⇨System Tools⇨File and Settings Transfer Wizard.**

   The wizard dialog opens.

5. **Click Next.**

   The dialog gives you two options: Select New Computer to transfer data to or select Old Computer to save data from.

6. **Click Old Computer and then click Next.**

   The wizard offers you three transfer methods:

   - *Direct Cable:* Use this method if you back up to another computer and connect to it via a serial cable.

   - *Home or Small Office Network:* Use this method if you back up to another computer via a private network, such as you might use at home or your office. This method is very easy to use if your network has a Windows file server; you can use the file server to store your backup.

   - *Other:* Use this method to back up to a USB storage device.

7. **Click Other.**

   The Browse button appears.

8. **Click the Browse button.**

   The Browse to Folder dialog opens.

9. **Click the My Computer option.**

   A submenu to My Computer opens.

10. **Select your storage device.**

    In my case, I click Removable Disk (E:).

11. **Click OK.**

    The Browse to Folder window disappears.

12. **Click Next.**

    The Files and Settings Transfer Wizard offers you several backup choices.

13. **Select your transfer option and then click the Next button.**

    I suggest using the Both Files and Settings option (which is the default). This option saves your personal files and settings (such as Internet Explorer bookmarks).

    The wizard takes some time deciding what files and settings to save. After it finishes, it opens a dialog asking you to continue.

14. **Click OK.**

    The wizard starts backing up your files and settings to the storage device.

15. **After the backup finishes, click Finish.**

    Your files and settings are stored in a single file on the storage device. You can reverse the process to restore data to your computer. Redo these instructions but select New Computer instead of Old Computer in Step 6.

Copy

You can use the ubiquitous Windows copy function to back up files if you're using an older Windows version that doesn't include the transfer wizard or Backup.

Simply click the folder you want to save — such as My Documents — and drag it to the backup media icon. Release the mouse button and you have a backup copy of your important files and information.

You have to manually copy every folder that you want to back up in this way.

Knoppix tools

Knoppix provides a mechanism you can use to back up your computer: You can use the dd command to clone your Windows hard drive.

Chapter 17 shows how to clone your Window hard drive with Knoppix.

It's possible that you may have to restore the data you just backed up. For instance, you may encounter problems installing Knoppix on your computer and need to restore both Windows and your Windows data. In that case, you may need to restore Windows from your original media. You would then reverse the process you used to back up your data to restore the data.

Preparing your hard drive

After you finish your backup, you need to prepare your hard drive before installing Knoppix. This section describes how to get your hard drive ready for Knoppix.

Defragmenting

Defragmenting consolidates files, whose contents may be scattered across your hard drive, into contiguous blocks of data. This consolidation frees up space at the end of the Windows partition and makes repartitioning possible.

The following instructions show how to use the built-in Windows defragmentation utility. These instructions assume that you're using a computer with a single hard drive and one or two partitions. Many Windows computers use a second partition that holds Windows recovery software; this saves the manufacturer the expense of providing a Windows CD-ROM backup disc.

1. **From the Windows Desktop, choose Start⇨All Programs⇨Accessories⇨ System Tools⇨Disk Defragmenter.**

   The Disk Defragmenter utility opens and your hard drive is typically labeled as c:; the utility looks different in older versions of Windows. Its file system type is most likely NTFS unless you have an old computer. The disk size, free space, and percentage of free space are also displayed.

2. **If you have more than one hard disk, click on the disk you want to defragment.**

3. **Click the Defragment button near the bottom-left corner of the window.**

   Before the process starts, your disk is mapped. After the defragmenting process begins, the process status is shown in a progress bar in a corner of the window.

   You can pause or stop the defragmentation process at any time without hurting your disk.

   When defragmenting finishes, the Disk Defragmentation dialog opens.

4. **Click the Close button in the Disk Defragmentation dialog.**

   To see the details of the finished defragmentation process, click the View Report.

5. **Choose File⇨Exit to leave the utility.**

6. **Click the Start button and select Turn Off Computer.**

   The Turn off computer dialog opens.

7. **Click the Shutdown button.**

   Windows shuts down.

Repartitioning

When you finish the defragmenting process, you can create space on your hard drive on which to install Knoppix. The following sections describe how to

✔ Access your Windows hard drive from Knoppix.

✔ Use a utility to repartition your Windows hard drive.

✔ Permanently install Knoppix in a dual-boot configuration on your repartitioned hard drive.

The repartitioning process is summarized as follows:

1. Boot Knoppix from DVD and start the repartitioning utility.

2. Free up space by making the Windows partition smaller.

3. Divide the new space into a general-purpose and swap partition.

4. Format the new partitions.

Microsoft Windows XP, 2000, and NT computers use the New Technology File System (NTFS) by default to format hard drives. (Windows 95, 98, and ME computers used the File Access Table (FAT) file system, which isn't covered in this book.)

Freeing space on your hard drive

This section shows how to use the Knoppix QTParted utility to shrink the NTFS partition, which frees up space to install Linux. You format the new space with a Linux file system.

The Knoppix QTParted tool (and the behind-the-scenes utility `ntfresize` that QTParted uses) does a good job of shrinking NTFS Windows partitions. However, QTParted doesn't ensure that the resized Windows partition will have enough space for temporary files and Registries. You must make sure that there will be enough space. Space will not likely be a problem if your Windows partition is tens of gigabytes in size. However, you may not want to resize your Windows computer if you have only one or two spare giga-bytes of space.

1. **Turn on your computer.**

2. **While your computer is booting, insert the *Knoppix For Dummies* DVD into your DVD/CD-ROM drive.**

    The standard Linux graphical desktop — the K Desktop Environment (KDE) by default — loads.

3. **Select K-Menu⇨System⇨QTParted.**

    The QTParted window opens, as shown in Figure 4-1.

Figure 4-1:
The QTParted window showing a hard drive (hda) and CD/DVD drive (hdc).

4. **Click the `/dev/hda` disk in the left sub-window.**

    A progress dialog opens as QTParted scans your disk. Once finished, QTParted shows the disk you selected in its main window. An example is shown in Figure 4-2.

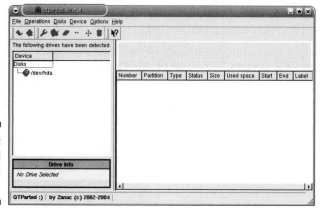

Figure 4-2:
A typical
QTParted
window.

The horizontal bar graph at the top-right section of the window shows the size and utilization of the selected hard drive; the black-and-white Figure 4-2 can't show the color detail of the graph, but a yellow bar shows the disk space in use. The little Microsoft flag in the upper-left corner of this graph indicates the file system type.

5. **Choose Operations⇨&resize.**

   The Resize partition dialog opens so you can select the new size of the old partition. You can either

   • Click the left end of the horizontal Minimum Size bar to select the space to free up.

   • Click the up or down arrows in the New Size or Free Space After text boxes.

   • Type new values into the New Size or Free Space text boxes.

6. **Select at least 3GB of free space.**

   You need at least

   • 3GB of space for the Knoppix installation

   • 128MB of space for the swap partition

   Klaus Knopper's definition of swap space is *an area on your hard disk that can hold program parts or data that are too huge for your computer's memory.* That way, you can start more and larger applications simultaneously without needing to buy more RAM for your computer. Even if you have enough RAM, swap space can be useful to hold data that is not permanently needed and thus keep your computer's memory free for performance-intensive tasks.

   • A few hundred megabytes for your files and applications

   Select more than 3GB so you can add applications and your own files to your Knoppix computer, if you have the space. You need elbow room.

7. **Click OK.**

8. **Choose File⇨&Commit.**

   QTParted does its work and the new free space is displayed as a new line below the original Windows partition. Figure 4-3 shows an example window.

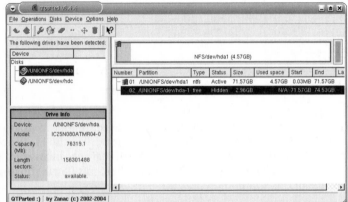

Figure 4-3:
The new
partitions.

Up to this point, you can undo any changes you've made. Click either the File or Device menu and select Undo to return to your previous partition.

The QTParted window remains open.

You still need to create two new formatted partitions from the newly created space. The next section shows how to do just that.

Formatting the new partitions

To install Knoppix, you must format the new partition you just created with a Linux file system. You need

- ✔ **A general partition**

   Knoppix is installed onto the general partition.

- ✔ **Some swap space**

   When Knoppix runs out of RAM to execute applications, it temporarily "parks" portions of the applications in the swap partition. Swap effectively extends your computer's memory from RAM onto your hard drive.

The following instructions show how to format the new space for your Knoppix installation:

1. **Click the new line showing the new free space, below the original Windows partition, in the QTParted window.**

   Figure 4-3 shows an example window.

2. **Click Operations⇨&Create.**

   The Create partition dialog opens.

3. **Make space for the Swap partition.**

   To make space for the Swap partition, shrink the size of free space by at least 128MB. You can type the new value in the Size text box or use the up/down arrows.

4. **Click OK.**

   Control returns to the QTParted window. The extra space you just created shows up as a new partition.

5. **Click the new partition.**

   This highlights the partition.

6. **Choose File⇨&Commit.**

   The QTParted Warning dialog opens. It tells you that the next step changes the partition permanently!

7. **Take a deep breath and click Yes.**

   A progress dialog shows the repartition progress.

8. **When finished, click OK.**

9. **Choose File⇨Quit to leave the utility.**

10. **Reboot your computer.**

Some hard disk controllers "remember" old partitions even after you successfully complete the repartitioning process. Therefore, you may not correctly "see" your repartitioning results until rebooting your computer.

You now have the file systems on which to install Knoppix. Chapter 5 shows you how.

Breaking Away: Preparing to Replace the Windows OS with Knoppix

You don't have to get along with Windows if you don't want to. You have the option of breaking the Windows habit and installing Knoppix as the only operating system on your computer. The process is simple: You reformat your hard drive, erasing everything on it, and then install Knoppix.

If you have *wireless networking,* you may need information and drivers from Windows before you remove the OS. Chapter 11 shows how to

- ✔ Identify your computer's *wireless NIC chipset* in Windows.
- ✔ Find whether Knoppix automatically supports your wireless NIC.
- ✔ Save your Windows system's *wireless NIC driver* for use with `ndiswrapper` (if Knoppix doesn't automatically support your NIC).

Now let's break some Windows.

Removing Windows partitions

Knoppix provides the QTParted utility. QTParted can perform many disk partitioning functions. The following instructions describe how to remove existing Windows partitions.

1. **Boot from the *Knoppix For Dummies* DVD (or Knoppix "lite" that you download from `www.knoppix.org` or `www.knoppix.net`).**

   Chapter 2 shows how to boot from the *Knoppix For Dummies* DVD.

2. **Click the K-menu and choose System⇨QTParted.**

   The QTParted dialog opens, showing your Knoppix computer's drives.

3. **Click the hard drive that you want to reformat in the left sub-window.**

   The dialog shows the existing partitions on the hard drive. Figure 4-4 shows an example configuration.

   If you're using a new or an unformatted hard drive, you won't see any Windows partitions. In this case, you can skip the following steps and go to the section, "Repartitioning your hard drive."

4. **Perform the following steps for each Windows partition you need to delete:**

   a. Click the Windows partition in the right sub-window that you want to delete.

   The dialog highlights the partition.

   For example, click the partition labeled as NTFS. The NTFS partition is where your Windows operating system is installed.

   b. Click the Operations menu and select &Delete.

   The dialog lists the partition type as Free.

You have not made any permanent changes yet. You can unwind any changes by clicking File and selecting &Undo; you can also simply exit the QTParted utility by selecting File⇨Quit. The following step, however, deletes the partition for all time. Please consider whether you want to proceed or not.

5. **Choose File⇨&Commit.**

The QTParted dialog opens, informing you about the finality of the step you're about to take.

The dialog also warns you to unmount all partitions before proceeding. You shouldn't have any mounted partitions because you just booted from the Knoppix DVD.

6. **Take a deep breath (you can still escape by clicking the No button) and click the Yes button.**

The Progress dialog opens showing the status of the deletion. The partition is erased and all data lost.

7. **Click OK and you return to the QTParted window.**

Repartitioning your hard drive

After you've deleted your Windows partitions, you need to partition the freed space.

1. **In the QTParted dialog, select the free space partition in the right sub-window.**

2. **Click the Operations menu and select &Create.**

The Create Partition dialog opens. It defaults to the Linux ext3 file system, which is good for our purposes.

3. **Click OK.**

Control returns to the QTParted dialog.

4. **Write the new partition to disk by choosing File⇨&Commit.**

The QTParted dialog opens, warning you about the consequences of what you're about to do.

5. **Click Yes to proceed.**

A dialog opens, showing the repartitioning progress.

6. **Click OK.**

7. **Choose File⇨Quit to leave the QTParted utility.**

You now have a hard drive with one partition. The partition is ready for Knoppix. Chapter 5 describes how to install Knoppix on a partition.

Chapter 5

The School of Hard Knoppix: Installing Knoppix to Your Hard Drive

In This Chapter
▶ Starting the installation utility
▶ Installing Knoppix on your computer
▶ Booting your Knoppix installation

*T*here comes a time to stop wandering and put down roots. That's why Knoppix can be a solid citizen on a PC. You can install Knoppix permanently on your computer so you don't need to use a DVD or CD every time you want to boot your computer.

This chapter shows how to install Knoppix on the hard drive.

A permanent Knoppix installation is ideal if you want

✔ A Knoppix workstation
✔ Faster operation

Before you permanently install Knoppix to your computer, you have to decide whether you want to keep Windows on your computer. Chapter 4 gives you the details to prepare your system for either

✔ A *dual-boot system* with both Windows and Knoppix
✔ A *Knoppix-only* system

Meta-view: Installing Knoppix

Knoppix comes with a utility that installs Knoppix onto a hard drive. The installation process is as follows:

1. Boot from the Knoppix DVD and start the Knoppix installation utility.

2. Enter information about your installation-to-be.

3. Install Knoppix on your hard drive.

This is the process of permanently installing Knoppix on your computer so it exists side by side with Windows.

4. Reboot to your permanent Knoppix installation.

The sections of this chapter guide you through these steps from start to finish.

To install Knoppix, you boot it from DVD and use a utility to transfer it to a hard drive partition.

Chapter 1 explains some of the technical details of the Linux operating system, but you don't need to know those details to install Knoppix.

Starting the Knoppix Installation

The following instructions show how to get ready to start an installation. You just open a terminal emulation window and enter a couple of commands. Follow these instructions:

1. **Click the Konsole Terminal icon in the "Start" bar at the bottom of the window (the "Start" bar is called the Kicker and is found along the bottom of the desktop).**

   The Shell – Konsole window opens.

2. **Start the installation script by entering the following command.**

   ```
   IGNORE_CHECK=1 sudo knoppix-installer
   ```

   A dialog opens describing what's going to happen.

3. **Press Enter to proceed.**

   A text-based menu opens.

The following sections describe how to use the knoppix-installer utility to install Knoppix.

Using the knoppix-installer Utility

After you start the Knoppix installation system, you need to navigate through it. You select several options that let you start using Knoppix after you finish installing it.

Follow these steps to install Knoppix on your hard drive:

1. **In the Knoppix installation menu, click OK.**

   The Choose System Type dialog opens and defaults to Debian: Debian-like System (Recommended) option.

2. **Click Next.**

   The Creating Knoppix Configuration Step (1/7) dialog opens. It shows the available partitions that you can install Knoppix to.

3. **Click on the partition you want to install Knoppix onto.**

   The Creating Knoppix Configuration Step (1/7)/Choose Filesystem-type dialog opens. This dialog defaults to the reiserfs option. This is the default file system used by Knoppix.

4. **Click Next.**

   The Creating Knoppix Configuration Step (2/7) dialog opens.

5. **Enter your name in the text box and click Next.**

   The Creating Knoppix Configuration Step (3/7) dialog opens, showing the username that it has created by combining the first letter of your first name with your last name.

6. **Click Next.**

   The Creating Knoppix Configuration Step (4/7) dialog opens.

7. **Enter a good password and press the Tab key.**

   Don't use dictionary words for your passwords. Simplistic passwords can easily be cracked. Think up simple phrases and then distort them. For instance, take the phrase "I love Knoppix" and change it to *iN0ppix*, using capitals and substituting numbers and special characters for letters; in this case, I shortened the password by five characters by deleting the spaces and replacing *like* with, which is a rough approximation — in my mind — of a heart.

8. **Confirm your password by typing it in the second text box.**

9. **Click Next.**

   The Creating Knoppix Configuration Step (5/7) dialog opens.

10. **Type the administrative `root` account password and click Next.**

    The Creating Knoppix Configuration Step (6/7) dialog opens, showing the default computer name `box`.

11. **Enter your computer name and click Next.**

    The final dialog, Creating Knoppix Configuration Step (7/7), opens.

12. **Select the default Master Boot Record by clicking Next.**

    Control returns to the knoppix-installer main menu.

13. **Click the Start installation menu.**

14. **Take a deep breath and click OK.**

    The Starting Knoppix Installation dialog opens and displays the installation options you've just selected.

15. **Click the Yes button to install Knoppix to your computer. (Select No to leave the installation process.)**

    The Starting Knoppix Installation dialog opens, showing a progress bar. The progress indicates how far along your Knoppix installation is. Sit back, have a drink, and bask in the glory of your soon-to-be Knoppix computer.

    The Creating Floppy Disk dialog opens.

16. **Click the No button.**

    The Installation successful dialog opens.

17. **Click OK.**

    The Knoppix installation is complete.

Finishing the Installation

After the Knoppix installation process finishes, you're almost ready to use your new (permanent) Knoppix computer. When the process finishes, use the following instructions to start your newly installed permanent Knoppix computer:

1. **Click the K-Menu and select Logout.**

    The End Session for "knoppix" dialog opens.

2. **Click the Restart Computer button.**

3. **Remove the DVD when it's ejected and press Enter.**

    Your computer restarts, and after the BIOS screen passes, you see the GRUB menu.

GRUB *(GRand Unified Bootloader)* is a tool to select which operating system to use.

If you're not running a dual-boot computer, skip to Step 5.

4. If your computer has more than one operating system, use the up-/down-arrow keys to select the operating system and then press Enter.

You can select one of these options:

- Knoppix

  Your computer boots into this option by default if you don't do anything.

- Your original Windows operating system

Knoppix boots and you're prompted for your username and password.

5. Enter your username and account password.

Knoppix opens the KDE desktop for your user account and you're ready to start using Knoppix. *Si, se, puede! Ahhhuuu!*

That wasn't very difficult — not as easy as running Knoppix directly from the DVD, but not bad. Knoppix provides a big leap in the ease-of-use and installation department. That makes my job and yours easier!

After you reboot your computer without the Knoppix DVD, it loads Knoppix from the hard drive and you get a login window. I discuss such basic Linux operations in Chapter 6.

knoppix-installer: Work in progress

The knoppix-installer utility is a work-in-progress and is developed independently from Knoppix itself. Sometimes Knoppix jumps ahead of knoppix-installer and the utility will not work correctly.

The knoppix-installer utility and Knoppix 4.0 on the *Knoppix For Dummies* DVD work correctly together.

Chapter 6

Starting and Logging Into Your Knoppix PC

· ·

In This Chapter

▶ Starting your computer

▶ Logging into and out of your user account

· ·

S o you have yourself a Knoppix computer? What can you do with it? Well, for one, you can turn it on and off.

Starting and stopping a Knoppix computer is not quite as exciting as watching paint dry, but it's close. Actually, it's not exciting at all, but it's an important, albeit basic, process to know, especially if you're running a dual-boot configuration. This chapter describes these basic processes.

Giving Your Computer the Boot

If Knoppix is permanently installed on your hard drive — whether alongside Windows in a *dual-boot system* or by itself — then Knoppix uses GRUB to boot. The *GRand Unified Bootloader* (GRUB) is automatically installed when you install a permanent instance of Knoppix.

GRUB lets you

✔ Boot to any installed operating system on your computer.

✔ Pick different versions of the Linux kernel and forward options to that kernel.

If you want to run Knoppix, just start your computer and wait for the GRUB boot menu screen to appear and disappear.

If you boot Knoppix only from a DVD (or CD-ROM) without permanently installing it on your hard drive, you can skip this section.

The following instructions describe how to boot Knoppix into its normal graphical (KDE desktop) and non-graphical modes, respectively.

Booting Knoppix into graphical and non-graphical mode with GRUB

Here's how you use GRUB to start Knoppix:

1. **Turn on or reboot your computer.**

   Your computer starts and displays the GRUB menu screen. The screen shows the following options if you're running a dual-boot configuration:

   - *Linux:* Boots the 2.6-1 Linux kernel.

   - *Linux (2.6)-1:* Boots the same Linux kernel as the first option.

   - *DOS:* Optional. Selects your Windows operating system if you installed Knoppix in a dual-boot configuration. (Chapters 4 and 5 describe how to create a dual-boot computer.)

   You don't see the DOS option if you're running a Knoppix-only permanent installation. (Chapters 4 and 5 describe how to install Knoppix as the only operating system on your hard drive.)

   - *Memory test:* Use this option to test your computer's memory.

   If you need to modify the PC's BIOS, enter the BIOS before the GRUB menu screen appears. Depending on the manufacturer, you can press a function key (typically F1, F2, F8, or F12), the Escape (Esc) key, or the Delete (Del) key to enter the BIOS. You should be able to skip modifying the BIOS unless you want to change the boot sequence. Some PC manufacturers allow you to select alternative boot devices without changing the BIOS; Dell, for instance, gives you a boot menu when you press the F12 key.

2. **If you don't want to automatically boot Knoppix, press any key but the Enter key while the GRUB boot menu screen is displayed.**

   If you don't press a key, GRUB waits 5 seconds and then automatically starts Knoppix.

3. **Use the up-arrow and down-arrow keys to select which operating system to boot and then press Enter.**

GRUB tells your computer to start booting the operating system you selected; you can select Knoppix or Windows (if available). After a minute or two, you're prompted to enter your username and password if you boot Knoppix. If you boot Windows, you may or may not be prompted for a username and password depending on the version you use.

The section, "Security," shows how to use the login menu.

Booting Knoppix into non-graphical mode

The following steps tell Knoppix to boot into the non-graphical (command line interface — CLI) mode:

1. **Start or reboot your computer.**

2. **Press the E key when you get to the GRUB menu window.**

3. **Press the A key and enter 2 at the prompt and press Enter.**

   Knoppix boots into non-graphical mode.

You can enter the `root` username instead of your own username. The `root` user — also known as the Super User — is all-powerful, and you need to be careful when using it. You're generally better off using the `sudo` command to run commands as `root` on a case-by-case basis. I discuss this in more depth in Chapter 7.

Default User Accounts

Knoppix (as well as all other Linux distributions) has *user accounts* so multiple users can work on the same computer efficiently and safely. User accounts let people share a computer without interfering with each other.

Knoppix (and other Linux distributions) has two levels of user accounts:

✔ **Regular** or **ordinary user accounts:** These accounts don't have special privileges.

A regular user account can access only its own files in its own home directory. However, you can modify an account's permissions to allow all or no interuser access. Regular users can also access system resources designed to provide restricted access if the root user gives them elevated access.

Running Knoppix "live" from the DVD provides a special case of user accounts. Live Knoppix provides the root user and one regular user named knoppix. When Knoppix boots, it activates the knoppix account and doesn't ask for a password.

✔ **Super User** (the root user account): The Super User account has unlimited access to all files and resources. Root is all-powerful. *All-Powerful!* Yikes! Never use the Super User account to perform normal work.

You can log in as the root user when working from a permanent Knoppix installation. You enter root in the Username text box at the login window. You then enter the root password you entered during the installation process (see Chapter 5).

You can't log in directly as the root user from a live Knoppix instance. Live Knoppix boots directly to the knoppix user account. The knoppix user is given all privileges via the sudo configuration. Any application or utility that you run gets Super User privilege if necessary.

You must be very careful when logged in as the Super User. You can do a lot of damage as root. Professional system administrators advise you to perform most, if not all, privileged tasks by using the sudo system. (When running a live Knoppix instance, the knoppix user can switch to root using the sudo command without entering a password. You should not allow access to the knoppix account without first deleting the /etc/sudoers file.)

Live Knoppix is easy to use yet secure. Because live Knoppix boots directly from read-only disc, it must use default accounts. Normally, you expect default accounts to have default passwords. However, taking that route would have eventually caused security holes because

✔ **You can configure Knoppix for network use from DVD (or the Knoppix "lite" version that you download from www.knopper.org or www. knoppix.net).** On a private network (or worse — the Internet) you'd be vulnerable to anyone who scans your system and determines it's using Knoppix.

✔ **Some people inevitably use the default passwords.**

Most single-function electronic devices, like wireless access points (AP), come preconfigured with default passwords. Many people never change their AP default passwords. This gives hackers easy access to many access points. Change your default password!

Knoppix can lock default accounts yet still makes them easy to use because the Knoppix initialization process circumvents the normal login process and starts your account directly. After Knoppix boots, you can connect your computer to a network, but no one can log in via the network unless you give the knoppix account a password. This is an effective and elegant configuration.

Security

To paraphrase Bill Murray in *Stripes,* "We zip in, we zip out. It's Czechoslovakia, not Moscow; it's like going to Wisconsin." He underestimated the difficulty of crossing the former Czech frontier, but he would have been correct if he had been talking about accessing Knoppix user accounts: *It's easier than going to Wisconsin.*

When you finish experimenting with Knoppix and get down to serious use, protect your system and personal information with passwords. Passwords are Linux's front-line defense against hackers and unauthorized access.

Logging in

You need to protect your personal and system information if you permanently install Knoppix to your hard drive.

The standard protection method dictates using an account that belongs to you and only you and that is password-protected.

You save files in your own dedicated "home" directory (similar to the Microsoft Windows My Documents folder) whose access permissions prevent access by other users.

Logging in and out on a permanent Knoppix computer takes just a little more work than using the default DVD mode. The process is simple but slightly more difficult than going to Wisconsin. Follow these steps:

1. **Turn on your permanent Knoppix computer.**

   The preceding sections show how to boot Knoppix with GRUB or the command-line interface.

   You're presented with the Knoppix login screen.

2. **Click the Menu pull-down menu and select Session Type⇨KDE.**

3. **Enter your username into the Username text box.**

4. **Enter your password in the Password text box.**

5. **Click the Login button.**

You are logged into your user account and see the KDE desktop just like if you'd booted directly from DVD.

When you install Knoppix permanently onto your computer, you must use passwords to access your accounts. The installation process described in Chapter 5 prompts you to set passwords for your personal account and the `root` (Super User) account.

Logging out

Logging out is a straightforward process:

1. **Choose K-Menu⇨Logout.**

   The K-Menu icon looks like a small *K* and can be found in the lower-left corner of the window.

   The End Session For dialog opens.

2. **Click End Current Session.**

You log out of your account and return to the Welcome to Linux At . . . window. You can log back in as another or the same user at this point.

The End Session For dialog provides other shutdown options. You can also

- ✔ **Halt your computer.** Click the Turn Off Computer button and Linux gracefully shuts itself down and powers down the computer.

- ✔ **Reboot your computer.** Clicking the Restart Computer button shuts down Linux and sends a *reset* signal to the computer, which reboots.

Part III
Daily Knoppix

The 5th Wave   By Rich Tennant

WHAT DO YOU MEAN
THERE'S A UNIX
OPERATING SYSTEM
IN THE LOBBY?

In this part . . .

After you're logged into a Knoppix computer, you need to operate it. Knoppix gives you the power and convenience of Linux interfaces and environments. Chapter 7 guides you through the Knoppix interfaces, and Chapter 8 introduces the powerful K Desktop Environment.

Chapter 7

Housekeeping

Knoppix is a great and powerful Linux distribution. It's a wonderful place to live and work. However, even the best homes require housework to keep going. This chapter introduces some of the basic Knoppix housekeeping chores that you need to perform.

Now is a good time to learn about the utilities and processes that underpin many of the examples described in this book. It's the type of information that's basic and not particularly interesting, but you gotta know it and you gotta do it — just like housekeeping chores.

Anyway, I have only a handful of good habits, and most have to do with housekeeping. (One is sweeping my floors; another is doing the dishes. I can't think of any others, so maybe it isn't even a handful.) So I'll play to my talent and show how to do some of those chores that ultimately make your Knoppix experience easier.

The setup steps in this chapter are designed for a permanent Knoppix installation. You can use these instructions when running a live Knoppix instance, such as when you boot from the *Knoppix For Dummies* DVD (or a CD you download from www.knoppix.net or www.knoppix.org). However, you must *repeat* the steps every time you reboot the PC unless you use a persistent home directory, as described in Chapter 3.

Using Interfaces

Don't just stand there, do something! That's the cry from you, a new Knoppix user, wanting your Knoppix OS to jump through some hoops by . . . doing something. But what?

That's up to you. Knoppix provides lots of tools, games, and applications. So now that you're an expert logger-inner, you can start doing stuff.

But wait! You could aimlessly click and peck away at the KDE desktop icons if you want. However, the following list offers quick, basic information about two methods for running applications, programs, and utilities:

- ✔ **Click an icon:** This starts a *graphical user interface* (GUI). You can also refer to the GUI as just a *graphical interface*.

  You're probably familiar with the graphical interfaces of Windows and Macintosh computers.

  You use the mouse (and sometimes the keyboard) to control the GUI.

- ✔ **Open a Linux shell and type commands:** This is called a *command line interface* (CLI).

  If you've used Microsoft's MS-DOS (or an MS-DOS prompt window in Windows), you've used a CLI.

  Linux shells have the basic functionality of MS-DOS but are very different internally. The UNIX shell provides a real programming language and is much more powerful than the old DOS command line. Most of the Knoppix utilities and configuration tools are written in the UNIX `bash` shell.

The following sections describe using the CLI and GUIs.

Using a GUI

GUIs have stolen the show from the CLI in much the same way that mammals replaced dinosaurs.

Here are two philosophical observations about the use of GUIs:

- ✔ GUIs generally make life easier for both inexperienced and experienced computer users.

  GUIs are often described as *intuitive* interfaces, but that isn't always true. GUIs are often difficult to use and confusing without practice.

- ✔ What GUIs do best is

  • Reduce the number of decisions you need to make.

  • Reduce every action to a few decisions or options.

  • Organize decisions and choices into logically consistent groups.

    The available options are also grouped into logical menus.

Neal Stephenson's *In the Beginning . . . Was the Command Line* (Harper) provides great insight into the weaknesses of the GUI. Check it out.

With your options limited and organized, using the system is more intuitive.

GUIs are generally easier to use than CLIs, but GUIs isolate you from the underlying operations they perform. You need to know a little more about what's going on underneath the surface if

✔ You depend on computers for a livelihood.

✔ You want to understand and work more closely with your computer.

Using the CLI

Using the command line interface (CLI) is simple: You type commands from the keyboard and see the resulting output, if any, on your monitor. No drags, drops, clicks, or pretty pictures — just clacking on your keyboard and text on your screen.

Using this simple interface lets you work more directly with your computer. Working with the CLI takes out the GUI middleman between you and the computer. Sometimes you need to use the CLI to get work done.

Open a CLI by clicking the Terminal Program icon — it looks like a computer monitor — on the K-Menu. The Shell – Konsole window opens. This window houses a *terminal emulator,* which interacts with a Linux shell.

To understand terminal emulators, you need to know how computing was done in the past, before the Apple Macintosh (and before that, Lisa; and before that, experimental Xerox computers — Xerox invented the mouse) and Microsoft Windows came along. In prehistoric times, before the advent of cheap PCs and GUIs, people used simple text-based terminals that were hooked directly to computers via serial data lines. They were called *computer consoles* (or just *consoles*).

After PCs became popular, someone devised a program that would emulate the old-style terminal. The program is called a *terminal emulator.* Terminal emulators let you work through a Linux shell and directly tell the computer what to do.

Shells are programs that act as an interface between you and your computer. They interpret the text you enter through the keyboard and send parsed commands to the operating system to execute. Shells also perform other functions that are beyond the scope of this book. Suffice it to say that shells are the workhorses of the Linux world.

The most popular Linux shell is Bash. *Bash* stands for *Bourne again shell*. This, in typical GNU-speak, is a play on words. Bourne isn't a post-modern 007. It's an older, shaken-not-stirred UNIX shell. Bash combines the best of the Bourne shell and the C shell. Therefore, it's Bourne-again. Anyway, it's probably an acronym that only a computer nerd could love. *(¡Me gusto!)*

Open the terminal emulator and you see a prompt that combines your user and machine name plus some other information. For instance, I see the following Bash prompt.

```
psery@box:~$
```

If you're running a live Knoppix instance (from the companion DVD or a CD that you obtained from www.knoppix.net or www.knoppix.org), you see the following prompt:

```
knoppix@0[knoppix]$
```

This prompt is made up of the following items:

- ✔ **Your username:** The username depends on who you're logged in as.

   The username is knoppix when using the live Knoppix instance mode. My username is psery.

- ✔ **The @ symbol:** This symbol separates the username from the hostname.

- ✔ **The hostname:**

   - If you boot live Knoppix from the companion DVD or from a CD, the default hostname is 0.

   - If you install Knoppix on your hard drive, the hostname is the name you gave your computer during the installation process (as described in Chapters 3 and 4). The default hostname is box.

- ✔ **The tilde symbol (~):** In this case, the tilde stands for the user's home directory. If you move to another directory, the tilde changes to the appropriate name. For instance, if you move to the /etc directory, the prompt changes to knoppix@1:[/etc]$. The default live Knoppix home directory is /home/knoppix.

- ✔ **The dollar sign ($):** The dollar sign means that I'm working as a regular user. If I log in as or switch user (su) to root, the symbol changes to the pound (#) symbol.

You enter commands from the prompt. For instance, to list your current working directory contents, enter the command ls. The listing is displayed in your terminal emulator window.

Knoppix provides shells other than Bash. You can use the Bourne Shell (sh), the C Shell (csh), the A Shell (ash), and the Stand Alone Shell (sash). You can also open other CLIs by clicking the K-Menu and selecting System⇨Shells⇨ Bash (Bash), System⇨Shells–Csh (Csh), or a number of other versions. The shells correspond to the most popular Linux shells and terminal emulators.

Throughout this book, I show you how to use both the GUI and CLI:

✔ I use the GUI more often because it's the easiest and most concise way to accomplish tasks.

✔ I show the CLI when no GUI is available or when I think it necessary to understand how to perform a configuration process.

Sudo the Super User

The sudo (pronounced "SUE-dough") system lets regular users run commands as the Super User. It's middle ground between *root* and *regular* users.

Klaus Knopper makes the following insightful point about using the sudo system:

> *Some programs refuse to work as root, and using the root account for some GUIs may break your system because root is in no way "secured" via permission restrictions. So, the root account (via sudo) should only be called if absolutely necessary, which is for: Changing the global system configuration, installing drivers and programs. Nothing more. The job of the administrator is to make the user accounts as comfortable and easy to use as possible, without them needing root permissions.*

The sudo system has two parts:

✔ The sudo program executes commands for a regular user as root if allowed by the /etc/sudoers configuration file.

✔ The /etc/sudoers configuration file tells the sudo program which users can run what commands as root.

For instance, when running a live Knoppix instance, the knoppix user can execute any command as root. This line in the /etc/sudoers file gives the knoppix user its power:

```
knoppix ALL=NOPASSWD: ALL
```

The simplified `sudoers` syntax is as follows:

```
user machine = options commands
```

The command syntax breaks down as follows:

- **User:** The user(s) whose access is defined.
- **Machine:** The machine(s) that the user can operate on.

  The `sudo` system can be used across a network.
- **=:** The equal sign separates the user/machine from the command(s).
- **Options:** You can define many options that affect `sudo`'s behavior.
- **Commands:** Command(s) that the user can execute as `root`.

You can insert comments into the `/etc/sudoers` file. Characters after the pound (#) symbol are *comments*. They don't affect the operation of the sudo configuration.

The `/etc/sudoers` file says that the `knoppix` user can execute any command from any machine without having to enter the destination user's password. Normally, you can execute the command that you've been given access to after entering your user account (not `root`) password. The `NOPASSWD` option removes that requirement.

Using sudo: A simple example

You can test the sudo system by trying to read the `/etc/shadow` file as the `knoppix` user. Normally, an unprivileged user like `knoppix` can't access the Shadow file. However, sudo allows access. Follow these steps:

1. **Start a live Knoppix instance.**

2. **Open a terminal window by clicking the Terminal Program icon on the K-Menu.**

3. **Run the following command:**

```
cat /etc/shadow
```

A "permission denied" message appears because the `/etc/shadow` file is owned by `root` and doesn't give either read or write access to regular users.

4. **Enter the following command:**

```
sudo cat /etc/shadow
```

Success! You see the contents of the file even though you don't own or have access permission. The `sudo` system provides access.

You must be careful using `sudo`. By using `sudo`, the `knoppix` user can execute any command as `root`. You can erase your entire file system by running the `sudo rm -rf /` command.

You can't erase your file system by using `sudo` when running a live Knoppix instance. Live Knoppix runs from the companion DVD or CD-ROM, whose contents you can't erase even if you wanted to because they're read-only media. However, Knoppix doesn't configure `sudo` to give the `knoppix` user *carte blanche* when you install Knoppix permanently to your computer. The configuration `knoppix ALL=NOPASSWD ALL` parameter is commented in that configuration. If you want to use the `sudo` command, you're forced to manually modify the `sudoers` configuration file.

Configuring sudo

You should use the `sudo` command to perform system administration functions when working in a permanent Knoppix installation. The following instructions describe the process of configuring the `sudoers` configuration file to allow a regular user to run commands as the root user.

1. **Log in as a regular user.**

   Chapter 6 shows how to create a regular user.

2. **Open a Terminal screen by clicking the Terminal Program icon.**

3. **Enter the following command:**

   ```
   su -
   ```

   This runs the switch user (`su`) command, which makes you the Super User.

4. **Enter the `root` password when prompted.**

5. **Enter either of the following commands depending on whether you want to require the user to enter a password:**

   • If you want the user to enter his or her password, enter the following command:

   ```
   echo "myusername ALL= ALL" >> /etc/sudoers
   ```

   • If the user shouldn't need a password, enter the following command:

   ```
   echo "myusername ALL=NOPASSWD ALL" >> /etc/sudoers
   ```

6. **Enter the `exit` command to leave the root account.**

   You return to your regular user account.

7. **Try to access the `/etc/sudoers` file as yourself.**

   ```
   sudo cat /etc/shadow
   ```

Success! You can execute privileged commands from a regular user account.

Creating User Accounts

Creating user accounts is simple. Knoppix provides a couple of utilities for creating new accounts and modifying existing ones.

The following instructions add users on a permanent Knoppix computer. These instructions are valid when using a live Knoppix instance. However, your configurations are lost when you turn off your computer unless you save them using the persistent home directory settings described in Chapter 3.

You can make and modify user accounts with either

- ✔ A GUI-based account tool
- ✔ A CLI account tool

  Use the command line tool if you boot into the non-graphical text mode (using the knoppix 2 cheat code at the boot prompt). The KDE User Manager utility needs to run as root because it has to modify files owned exclusively by the Super User. The CLI instructions are easier than the GUI instructions in that case.

GUI steps

You can use the GUI and the KUser utility to create a new user account in a permanent Knoppix installation.

The following instructions work for a live Knoppix instance, but you must use the persistent home directory utility to save them:

Follow these steps to create a new user account:

1. **Log in as a regular user.**

   This is the user account that's created when installing permanent Knoppix, as described in Chapter 5.

2. **Choose K-Menu⇨System⇨KUser (User Manager).**

   The Run as root – KDE su dialog opens.

3. **Enter the** root **password and click OK.**

   The KDE User Manager – KUser window opens.

4. **Click Add.**

   The KUser dialog opens.

5. **Enter a username and click OK.**

    The User Properties – KUser dialog opens.

6. **Enter any other information, such as the user's full name, that you want to add to the account setup.**

7. **Click the Password button and enter the password (twice) in the Enter Password – KUser dialog that opens.**

8. **Click OK.**

    Control returns to the User Properties window.

9. **Click OK.**

    Control returns to the User Manager window.

10. **Click File⇨Quit to exit from the User Manager window.**

Your computer now has a brand-new addition to the family. Use the User Manager to modify the various settings of the account, such as its default shell or home directory; you can also delete or add users.

Command line steps (CLI)

You can use the command line interface (CLI) to add, delete, or modify users on a permanent Knoppix computer. (The commands are also valid on live Knoppix instances, but you must use the persistent home directory utility described in Chapter 3 to save them.)

The following instructions use a CLI to create, modify, and delete a user account:

1. **Open a terminal emulator window by clicking the monitor icon on the KDE Kicker.**

2. **Type the following command to create a new user account named** joe.

    ```
    sudo useradd -m joe
    ```

3. **Set the account's password by typing the following:**

    ```
    sudo passwd joe
    ```

4. **Enter** joe**'s password twice when prompted.**

5. **Modify the account by adding a comment describing the user's human name, like this:**

    ```
    sudo usermod -c "Joe Blow" joe
    ```

6. **Delete the account — but not the home directory.**

    ```
    sudo /usr/sbin/userdel joe
    ```

Use the commands `man useradd`, `man userdel`, `man usermod`, and `man passwd` to display usage and option information about those commands. `usermod` modifies accounts.

The Linux file system tree

Trees? File systems? Linux? What do any of them have to do with one another? Linux stores information in *files*. Files interface with devices; store data, programs, and graphics; and even provide views into the Linux kernel itself:

- Files are stored in directories.

- Directories can store other directories, which are called *subdirectories*.

  A directory that houses subdirectories is called the *parent* of its *child* directories.

When you draw lines between directories and multiple levels of subdirectories, the diagram resembles a *tree*. The figure shows a fragment of the Linux file system tree.

Linux sees all objects (except certain network functions) as *files*. By viewing every resource as a file, Linux simplifies its internal logic. For instance, Linux uses its disk drives as if they were files. The `/dev/hda` and `/dev/sda` files mentioned in Chapter 4 are *abstractions* for the disk drives they represent.

One central directory is called the `Root` directory (because all other directories descend from it). The `Root` directory is denoted by a single slash (`/`) — you don't see the word *root* anywhere. All directories always have the `Root` or a descendant directory as a parent.

The following list describes some subdirectories of `Root`:

- The `home` directory, in which all user account directories are stored by default, is a descendant of the `Root` directory. The `home` directory is designated as `/home`.

- The `log` directory stores log files. Its parent is the `var` directory, whose parent is `Root`. `log`'s location is written as `/var/log`.

- The `/usr` directory and its subdirectories store system files and libraries. For instance, the `/usr/bin` directory stores user-accessible programs, `/usr/sbin` houses system administration programs, and `/usr/lib` stores library files.

- The `/etc` directory stores system configuration files.

- The `/dev` directory stores files used to access computer hardware.

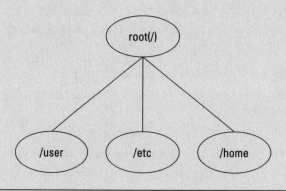

Chapter 8

Navigating the KDE Desktop

Knoppix (and other Linux distributions) lives in a modular world, combining many different parts to form a complete computer environment. Knoppix uses a separate kernel, GNU utilities, a graphical system, and an open source application to do its job. Microsoft Windows, on the other hand, is one big monolithic operating system. It's a big blob that combines most of its operations in one piece. The advantage that Knoppix has over Windows is that each piece can evolve, leaving only the best at the end.

This chapter describes the parts that make up the Knoppix graphical environment.

The K Desktop Environment What?

Knoppix supplies the easy-to-use, powerful, and attractive KDE graphical environment. KDE provides Knoppix (and other Linux) users with the same capability and refinement you find in other operating systems. In fact, KDE provides *more* innovation than other commercial operating systems.

KDE just stands for the *K Desktop Environment*. Initially, *K* stood for *Kool*, but now it's just the letter *K*. You can also make something out of the fact that *K* precedes *L*, which is the first letter in *Linux* — bit of a stretch maybe . . . well, a lot, but who cares? (I should be the last person to question a verbal stretch.)

The X Window System

The X Window System isn't part of the X-Men of the Marvel Comics universe. Nor did *X,* as it's frequently called, emerge from the creative mind of Stan Lee. No, X comes from the much more mundane yet very creative MIT (Massachusetts Institute of Technology). It's intended to provide a platform-independent graphical system for UNIX and Linux systems (such as Knoppix), not graphic novels for middle-aged kids like me.

X provides the graphical framework for desktop environments like KDE. KDE uses X as its base, while X uses Knoppix (or any other Linux distribution) as a base. The relationship forms a pyramid: KDE sits on top of X, which sits on Knoppix.

The X Window System comprises the following subsystems:

- **X server:** The X server displays *graphics* on the computer. When you're sitting at your Knoppix computer, the graphics you see come through the X server. It also takes input from the mouse and keyboard.

  The X server interacts with your video display drivers. It processes requests from other sources and produces simple graphics objects, such as rectangles and shaded areas.

- **X clients:** X clients are applications that use the X server to accept input and display graphical output. *Mozilla* is an example of

an X client. The X client and the X server can run either on the *same* physical machine or on *separate* machines that are networked together. The X client is a graphical application that sends its output to the X server.

- **Graphical libraries:** The X graphical libraries enable Clients (as mentioned above) to interact with the X server.

X is designed to work in a networked environment. The common graphical clock (xclock) can illustrate the relationships in the X clients and X server systems. As an example, start with a private network of two Knoppix computers, Homer and Marge:

1. Sit at Homer and log in. (Homer is the *X server*.)

2. Connect to Marge from Homer over the network with Secure Shell (SSH).

3. Run xclock from the CLI on Marge. (xclock is the *X client* but is displayed on the X server Homer.)

   xclock is displayed on Homer's display. (The X server on Homer displays the output from the X client on Marge.)

This is different from most client-server relationships, in which you use the *client* to work on the *server.*

Whatever the acronym means, KDE is an excellent graphical environment.

The K Desktop Environment is multifaceted, with four primary parts:

- **Desktop**

  Figure 8-1 shows the default Knoppix KDE desktop.

- **Panel (also known as the Kicker)**

  Figure 8-2 shows the Kicker, found at the bottom of the desktop.

✔ **Taskbar**

Figure 8-3 shows the Taskbar (which exists in the Kicker).

✔ **KDE Applications and Utilities**

Each part performs a function that makes your Knoppix computer an effi-cient, pleasurable place to work.

KDE provides the following features to make your Knoppix experience more productive and enjoyable:

✔ KDE provides the look and feel that you want when you work on a com-puter. It provides the background (or simply the desktop), menu system, icons, applications, and a help system.

✔ KDE is available in more than 50 languages, so you can use it no matter where in the world you live.

✔ KDE is configurable, is reliable, and works well within a networked environment.

✔ KDE provides an extensive and useful help system. The help system pro-vides an extensive KDE glossary and table of contents. Each subject is discussed in simple and easily understood terms.

Figure 8-1:
The KDE
desktop.

Figure 8-2:
You find the
Kicker at the
bottom of
the KDE
desktop.

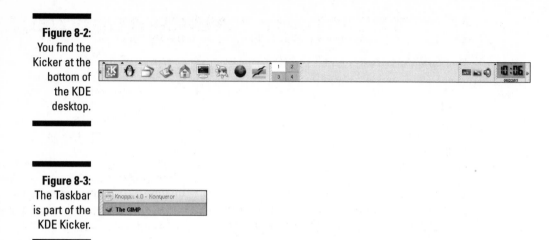

Figure 8-3:
The Taskbar
is part of the
KDE Kicker.

Introducing the desktop

The KDE desktop, or simply the desktop, is the most anonymous part of the K Desktop Environment. The desktop is the background or backdrop that you work from. It's like the surface of your desk, where you place files, folders, pictures of your kids, and whatever else you need to work. I don't think about my office desk's desktop much when I'm using Knoppix, but I sure would if it didn't exist. Likewise, the KDE desktop does its job without much publicity.

The desktop's primary function is to help you organize your work. Use it for such jobs as creating icons and opening windows. For instance, you may edit a spreadsheet with your spreadsheet application and browse the Internet with your Web browser simultaneously. Clicking on either window brings it to the top of the desktop.

The desktop is also the platform for objects like icons and the Kicker (also known as the Panel). The Kicker is the horizontal bar along the bottom of your screen that houses various buttons and icons. The following section describes the Kicker (Panel) components.

The Panel

The Panel is nicknamed the Kicker. The Kicker houses menus, the Taskbar, and applet icons — like OpenOffice.org and Mozilla Firefox — that make working in the KDE easier. (I'll refrain from suggesting you try kicking the Panel's tires or anything like that.)

The Kicker is an environment within the KDE. It contains a wealth of helpful menus and shortcuts. The Kicker has these components.

- **K-Menu:** The icon with the big *K* on the left end of the Kicker. Clicking it opens an extensive menu system from which you can access almost every application and utility. The K-Menu is similar to Microsoft's Start button.

- **KNOPPIX menu:** The cute penguin provides access to a reduced K-Menu. Clicking it opens a menu that provides access to configuration, networking, and system service utilities, plus a Root shell.

  You don't have to enter the Super User password when you run from a live Knoppix instance and start administrative programs and utilities from this menu. However, you're prompted for the `root` password if you're running from a permanent Knoppix installation.

- **Hide buttons:** The small arrows at either end of the Kicker. Clicking either arrow hides the Kicker, sliding it to one side or another until it disappears. Clicking either button again restores the Kicker.

- **Application icons:** Knoppix installs several general applications by default, such as Firefox and terminal emulator. It places icons on the Kicker for the applications. Click an icon to start an application.

- **Pager applet:** Maps your desktop into many virtual desktops.

  Imagine an infinitely large monitor that you could use to really spread your work out. KDE can't create such a device, but it can make an effectively large virtual workspace that's just as good.

  By default, the Pager applet gives access to four virtual desktops. Clicking any virtual desktop switches you to that virtual workspace. You can divide your work between the workspaces to create an uncluttered environment. This is the type of innovation you don't find in other operating systems. Windows, where's your virtual windows?

  Applets run programs that have an icon on the Kicker. The KDE clock on the right side of the Kicker is an example of an applet.

- **The Taskbar:** The applet in the middle of the Kicker that looks like a numbered grid. Clicking a numbered block switches the workspace to the corresponding virtual desktop.

- **KDE applets:** The right side of the Kicker shows icons that look like a flag, a speaker, and a clock. These applets perform simple functions.

The Taskbar

Starting a graphical application opens a window on the desktop and places a button in the Taskbar.

If you minimize an application by clicking the Minimize button in the upper-right corner of the application window, it disappears from the desktop, but its button remains in the Taskbar. Clicking the Taskbar button returns the window to the desktop.

Applications and utilities

KDE provides numerous applications for you to use. It provides an extensive office productivity suite consisting of a word processor, spreadsheet application, presentation manager, and related utilities.

Konqueror is a lightweight browser. *Lightweight* means that it provides the bare minimum of functions compared with a full-fledged browser like Mozilla. Konqueror starts up very quickly. You primarily use it as your Knoppix computer's file manager, but you can also use it to navigate file systems on your private network and as a simple Web browser.

KDE provides numerous system-management and other utilities. You can manage your entire Knoppix computer by using KDE utilities. I introduce and describe Knoppix configuration utilities as needed throughout the book.

Navigating the K Desktop Environment

If you're familiar with Microsoft Windows, you can work in KDE very quickly. The concept of using a mouse to navigate through a desktop environment is universal. KDE is easy to use and to customize.

Clicking the Kicker

The Kicker is the KDE Panel. Using the Kicker is straightforward. It basically involves clicking. Click the Kicker.

K-Menu

Click the Kicker's K-Menu icon and you see the KDE menu, which is shown in Figure 8-4.

Figure 8-4:
The
K-Menu.

Desktop fundamentals

The following list describes the various KDE desktop components:

✔ **Objects:** In KDE, an *object* is an icon, applet, menu, or window.

✔ **Mouse cursor:** The arrow that you see on the computer screen. It's positioned by moving the mouse. The cursor becomes *active* when you position it over a button, menu, or icon that performs some action or function.

These are the basic actions that you can perform with a mouse:

✔ **Clicking:** Clicking the left mouse button selects, activates, or executes whatever the mouse cursor is touching. Clicking doesn't do anything if the cursor isn't active.

✔ **Right-clicking:** Clicking an object with the right mouse button generally activates a pull-down menu. The pull-down menu actions depend on the object selected.

✔ **Double-clicking:** Opens or executes an icon or a file in a file manager that you find on the Desktop. (Icons found in the Kicker are single-click-to-start.)

✔ **Dragging and dropping:** Selects and moves object(s) with the mouse. Position the cursor on an object, click and hold the button, move the cursor to another location, and release the button. The resulting action depends on what object(s) you select and its (their) function.

For instance, if you drag and drop an icon on the desktop, you just *move* the icon. Its function and contents remain unchanged; you don't execute any application.

The K-Menu contains nearly every utility and application you can access on your Knoppix computer. The menu provides access to the following categories:

✔ **Recently Used Applications:** The last five applications that you've opened are shown in this section. Use this service to easily reopen stuff.

✔ **All Applications:** This heading groups the majority of functions found in the top-level KDE menu. You access almost every application that KDE is aware of. This section mostly contains links to submenus that contain either the application or further submenu links.

The All Applications section of the K-Menu includes five special links, described below:

- Control Center (a KDE configuration utility)
- Find Files (a file searching utility)
- Help (a help system)
- Home (your home directory)
- Wine (a system that allows you to run Windows applications)

✔ **Actions:** This heading section groups the following special actions:

- **Bookmarks:** Use or edit the bookmarks for Konqueror and Mozilla. Clicking an *existing bookmark* opens Konqueror and then opens the URL. Clicking the Edit Menu option opens a dialog in which you can modify the bookmark's name and location (the URL it points to) and add a comment.

- **Quick Browser:** Opens your home directory or the Super User (`root`) home directory in the Konqueror browser or a terminal window.

- **Run Command:** Opens the Run Command dialog. It can run commands like the CLI without using a terminal emulator.

- **Lock Session:** When running a permanent Knoppix installation, sets a screen lock on your current KDE session so that you (and anyone else who happens by) can't access your KDE session without entering your user account password. This function is not enabled when running a live Knoppix installation.

- **Logout:** Opens a dialog that lets you log out, halt, or reboot your computer.

Chapter 6 shows how to log into and out of your KDE session.

Panel

The default Knoppix Panel contains icons for the following applications and functions:

✔ **Window list:** Opens a menu with a list of all open windows. Click any menu item to select the open window.

You can access options to rearrange open windows on the desktop.

✔ **Show desktop:** Minimizes all open windows, revealing the desktop.

Clicking the icon a second time returns the windows to their previous positions.

✔ **Personal files:** Shows the contents of your home directory in the Konqueror window.

✔ **Terminal program:** Opens a terminal emulator window.

Chapter 7 covers the terminal emulator.

✔ **Web browser:** Opens Konqueror for browsing.

✔ **Mozilla Web browser:** Opens the Mozilla browser.

✔ **Pager:** Allows you to switch between virtual KDE desktops.

✔ **Taskbar:** Gives you access to every KDE application, utility, and menu.

✔ **Applets:** Small programs that KDE uses to start other applications.

Working with windows

Knoppix users work *with* windows, not *in* Windows. Put another way, it costs money to work in (Microsoft) Windows but nothing to work with KDE windows.

A *window* is a graphical object that houses running applications. The application might be a browser, word processor, or terminal emulator. The window provides a uniform platform to display the application.

The uniform platform has these parts:

- **Title bar:** The thick, solid-color border along the top of the window.

  Use the Title bar to drag and drop the window. Click and drag the *edge* to resize the window. The Title bar also gives a window visual continuity and someplace to situate the window buttons.

- **Border:** The thinner solid-color bar that wraps around the rest of the window.

  Resize the border by clicking and dragging it.

- **Menu button:** The downward-pointing arrow at the upper-left corner of a window.

  Clicking the Menu button opens a drop-down menu that gives you such options as resizing the window or moving it within a desktop.

- **Minimize button:** Clear workspace for yourself with the Minimize bar (a single, horizontal bar) in the upper-right corner of a window.

  Minimizing a window removes a window but doesn't close it from the desktop.

  Click a window's icon in the Taskbar to return a minimized window to the desktop.

- **Maximize button:** Expands the window to fill the entire desktop.

  This button is designated by an upward-pointing arrow on top of a horizontal bar.

- **Close button:** Closes the window and shuts down any associated applications. X marks the spot.

Managing your files

Conquer your files with Konqueror! However, Konqueror doesn't want to be another Genghis Khan; it just wants to help you manage your files.

To start Konqueror, click the Personal Files icon (it looks like a house) in
the Kicker; you can also click the K-Menu and select Home (Personal Files).
Konqueror opens and displays the contents of your home directory, as
shown in Figure 8-5.

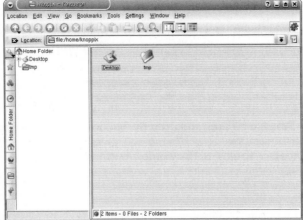

Figure 8-5:
Konqueror
showing the
default
Knoppix
home
directory.

The Location text box shows that it is displaying the contents of the /home/
knoppix directory. You see the default Knoppix user directory contents,
which is the tmp directory.

You can use Konqueror to open, move, and copy files and folders (directories)
from one location to another.

Customizing Your Desktop

You can customize your KDE desktop in many ways. The KDE Control Center
gives you one-stop shopping when it comes to configuring your desktop. It's
easy to start; just click the K-Menu and select Control Center.

You can customize the KDE desktop when you run Knoppix from the *Knoppix
For Dummies* DVD (or a CD if you download one from the knoppix.org or
knoppix.net Web site), but you must *repeat* the steps every time you reboot
the PC unless you use a persistent home directory. (Chapter 3 shows you
how to use a persistent home directory.)

The Control Center modifies the following types of KDE elements:

✓ **Appearance and themes:** Change the desktop background settings,
   colors, fonts, icons, screensaver, and an animated picture shown
   when KDE is starting up.

✔ **Desktop:** Change the behavior of the desktop, the number of virtual desktops, the layout of the KDE panel, the behavior of the Taskbar, and window (containing open applications) behavior. For example, you can change the mouse button functions or whether moving a mouse over an icon displays a short description of the application.

✔ **Internet and private networks:** Set your Internet and LAN (local area network) options here. See Chapters 10 and 11 for more information.

✔ **KDE components:** KDE is highly configurable. This section lets you

- Choose which components handle services, such as the e-mail client, by default.

- Set KDE to execute applications when encountering certain file types.

- Modify the file manager and spell checker behavior.

✔ **Peripherals:** Use the functions found here to configure such devices as digital cameras, printers, video display, keyboard, mouse, and joystick. Chapter 15 shows how to use and configure printers.

✔ **Power:** Show a laptop's battery level.

✔ **Regional and accessibility:** Change the behavior and layout of your keyboard, plus its language.

✔ **Security and privacy:** Change cryptographic options used by the Secure Sockets Layer (SSL) protocol. SSL is typically used to

- Encrypt communications to and from Web sites over the insecure Internet. (Encrypted browsing is essential for e-commerce.)

- Secure e-mail.

- Create digital signatures.

This section also changes such security settings as your Knoppix password.

✔ **Sound and multimedia:** Modify your computer's sound settings.

✔ **System administration:** Change your general Knoppix settings, such as the KDE directory defaults.

Part IV
The Inevitable Internet Part

The 5th Wave   By Rich Tennant

"We have no problem funding your web site, Frank. Of all the chicken farmers operating web sites, yours has the most impressive cluck-through rate."

In this part . . .

One of my favorite *Simpsons* lines is Homer saying "Hmm, they have computers on the Internet now." Well, when you think about it, Homer makes a lot of sense. Sometimes it's difficult to differentiate between computers and the Internet. An Internet connection is almost as important these days as flowing water and electricity. This part shows how to connect to the Internet and use its two primary functions: browsing and e-mail.

However you prefer to connect your computer, there's a chapter that shows how to use Knoppix with the Internet. Chapter 9 shows how to connect your Knoppix computer with a dialup modem. Chapter 10 shows you how to connect Knoppix to a wired local network, and Chapter 11 helps you set up Knoppix for wireless networking. Chapter 12 introduces the new and powerful Mozilla Firefox browser that's causing Internet Explorer to play catch-up. It also describes how to use the Mozilla Thunderbird e-mail client.

Chapter 9

Dialup Modems

• •

In This Chapter

▶ Setting up a simple firewall

▶ Connecting to the Internet with a dialup modem

• •

Knoppix makes connecting to the Internet easy by providing network configuration utilities. This chapter describes how to use Knoppix to configure old-fashioned dialup analog modems to connect to the Internet.

If you connect to a *private network* for your Internet connection, Chapter 10 covers wired LANs and Chapter 11 covers wireless LANs.

You can use the setup steps in this chapter when you run a live Knoppix instance from the *Knoppix For Dummies* DVD (or from a CD that you download from www.knoppix.net or www.knoppix.org), but you must *repeat* the steps every time you reboot the PC unless you use the persistent settings utility to save your configuration. (Chapter 3 shows you how to use a persistent home directory.)

Protecting Yourself with a Firewall

When you connect to the Internet, you also plug into an ocean of potentially nasty viruses, worms, spyware, and hackers. Before making any potentially harmful connections, you should build a firewall.

Firewalls are an important defense against the harmful aspects of the Internet. They block some, but not all, hackers and *malware* (malicious software such as worms) on the Internet from connecting to your computer or network.

Meta-view: Connecting with a modem

Using a modem with Knoppix takes a few basic steps:

1. Configure a host-based firewall.

2. Obtain an Internet Service Provider (ISP) subscription.

3. If necessary, buy a modem and connect it to your computer.

4. Configure the modem.

5. Drop the dime and connect to your ISP.

This chapter explains each step in the process.

Firewalls are good but they are only a single piece in your security universe. There's no single security "silver bullet" out there. Your only reasonable protection comes from "defense in depth." You must layer one security mechanism on top of another to protect yourself. Even then, you're still vulnerable to the unexpected security werewolf.

Linux provides an excellent firewall system called Netfilter/iptables:

- Netfilter is the kernel-based IP packet filtering system.

- iptables is the interface to Netfilter. I refer to the whole system as just iptables.

iptables is your first line of defense to filter out unwanted connections. iptables filters incoming and outgoing network traffic based on the following parameters of a connection:

- **IP address:** IP addresses make the Internet world go round by acting as addresses.

- **Port number:** Ports direct Internet connections to find the right application or service.

- **Connection state:** iptables can allow or deny network traffic depending on whether it belongs to an existing connection. This powerful capability allows you to better prevent hackers from deceiving your firewall and gaining access to your private network or computer.

Use the following instructions to build a firewall that allows you to make outgoing connections on your Knoppix computer but doesn't allow anyone or anything to make incoming ones.

1. **Open a** `root` **shell by clicking K-Menu and selecting System⇨ Root Terminal.**

   The Change User dialog opens.

2. **Enter the** `root` **password.**

3. **Start by denying all traffic. Type the following:**

```
iptables -P INPUT    DROP
iptables -P OUTPUT   DROP
iptables -P FORWARD DROP
```

4. **Type the following commands to open the** `loopback` **(lo) device.**

```
iptables -A OUTPUT -j ACCEPT -o lo
iptables -A INPUT -j ACCEPT -i lo
```

Linux uses the `loopback` device for internal communications. It isn't a physical device.

5. **Type the following commands to allow all outgoing communication from your computer.**

```
iptables -A OUTPUT -m state
   --state NEW,RELATED,ESTABLISHED -j ACCEPT
iptables -A INPUT -m state
   --state RELATED,ESTABLISHED -j ACCEPT
```

Connecting to the Internet is a two-way process. For instance, you connect to a Web site and the Web site sends information back to you. The second rule in this step allows the return traffic from your outgoing connections.

6. **If you want to allow secure shell (SSH) connections into your computer, add the following rule to your firewall script.**

```
iptables -A INPUT -p tcp -m state
   --state NEW,ESTABLISHED -j ACCEPT --dport 22
```

You can modify this rule to allow any other service by modifying the `--dport` parameter as appropriate. For instance, add the following rule to allow access to your Web server.

```
iptables -A INPUT -p tcp -m state
   --state NEW,ESTABLISHED -j ACCEPT --dport 80
```

7. **Save your changes and set the firewall to turn on when you boot.**

```
/etc/init.d/iptables save active
update-rc.d iptables defaults
```

You now have a firewall that provides enough protection to connect to the Internet. The firewall also starts up when you boot your computer.

You can manually start and stop your firewall by using the `/etc/init.d/iptables` script:

✔ Start the firewall by typing either

```
/etc/init.d/iptables start
/etc/init.d/iptables restart
```

✔ Stop the firewall by entering `/etc/init.d/iptables clear`.

Connecting to the Internet with a Modem

New technology, like high-speed wireless and broadband Internet connections, gets all the attention these days. Let's face it, it's sexy compared to old, stodgy, analog modem technology. But many people still use plain old telephone system (POTS) dialup modems to connect to the Internet.

This section describes how to connect to the Internet with a modem. Modems aren't cutting edge, but they're effective and cheap.

The instructions in this chapter work whether you boot Knoppix from the companion DVD or from a permanent installation on your hard drive. The exceptions are the instructions to permanently save your firewall.

Connecting a modem

Most new computers have a preinstalled modem. That sounds great, but, unfortunately, most of the modems are *WinModems*.

WinModems aren't real modems. They use the computer's sound card and software drivers. They use the Windows operating system to perform the functions that "real" modems do themselves. WinModems are cheaper than regular modems because they essentially don't exist.

But the lower cost doesn't help Knoppix users. Knoppix (as well as other Linux versions) generally doesn't work with WinModems. The situation is getting better — Linux works with more WinModems as time goes by — but you probably need to buy a non-WinModem modem.

Fortunately, regular modems are relatively cheap. You can buy external modems for between $40 and $100. Internal modems run between $10 and $40. The difference in cost arises because external modems require extra parts in the form of an enclosure, connector, cable, and power supply. Internal modems plug into a connector inside your computer and don't require the extras.

Don't confuse dialup analog modems with digital broadband ones. Dialup modems work over your telephone line and are generally called *Data/FAX* or *analog* modems. They're much slower than broadband modems because the old telephone lines they use were designed only to carry the human voice with low fidelity. Broadband modems were designed for speed. They're called *cable modems* or *DSL modems,* depending on whether they use your cable TV or modified telephone connections.

Subscribing to an ISP

Finding and subscribing to an Internet Service Provider (ISP) boils down to whether you want to use a local or national ISP. Both types have advantages and disadvantages.

Consider these issues when considering a local ISP:

✔ **Personalized service:** ISPs work in a tough business because it's hard to compete with the advantages of scale the big boys at national ISPs have — and they have to give you a reason to give them your business. My ISP — www.swcp.com — provides fantastic service, and I can speak to the owners if I need a tough question answered.

✔ **Reliability:** Being closer to your ISP allows it to more precisely tailor its service to your location.

✔ **Price:** This important area is pretty much a wash. Local ISPs tend to charge roughly as much as the big boys. However, local ISPs rarely, if ever, provide free limited service like Access4Free. Count on spending between $10 and $25 per month for local service.

✔ **Local service only:** Obviously, local ISPs provide local service. They generally provide mechanisms for making out-of-town connections, but you have to jump through hoops to do so. So trying to access your e-mail while you're out of town can be a pain.

Consider these issues when considering a national ISP:

✔ **Price:** The national services compete mostly on cost. The competition drives down prices — even to zero. Access4Free — www.access4free.com — provides up to ten hours of free monthly access at no cost, and additional hours cost only $10 per month. And they work with Linux.

✔ **National service:** National ISPs provide local dialup numbers across the nation. European-based ISPs and ISPs in other parts of the world provide the same.

✔ **Call-bank/e-mail service:** National ISPs provide varied customer support service. If you have a problem, you have to call them and hope for the best.

External modem

Connect your external modem to your computer with either a serial or USB cable. The type of cable you use depends on the modem's connections:

✔ **USB connectors and cables** use either a square or rectangular connector.

✔ **Serial cables** use either

- 9-pin connectors (DB9)
- 25-pin connectors (DB25)

Serial connections are disappearing. Your Knoppix computer may not be able to use an external modem that has only a DB9 or DB25 connector.

Manually finding your modem

If Knoppix doesn't detect your modem, you can use the following steps to manually find it.

1. Click the Terminal icon in the KDE Kicker.

2. Type the following command:

   `dmesg | grep tty`

   The result you see on your screen should be `ttyS0` or `ttyS1`, and possibly `ttyS2` or

`ttyS3`. This is a device file that points to your modem.

3. Scribble down the result on some scratch paper, a blank spot on the desk, or the back of your hand.

4. Click Session⇨Quit to leave the shell window.

Internal modem

Internal modems plug into your computer's PCI (peripheral component interconnect) bus. Unfortunately, most are WinModems and don't work with Knoppix.

Turn off the power and unplug the power cable before removing the computer's case.

Configuring your modem

Configuring your modem is a two-step process, which I describe in the following two sections.

Locating your modem

By default, Linux doesn't necessarily know where to find your modem. "But my modem is right in front of me!" you might say. It's so close, yet so far. Linux needs to know to which *port* the modem is connected. The following instructions show you the location of the modem, which you then communicate to Knoppix to make the connection:

1. **Click the K-Menu and select KNOPPIX⇨Network/Internet⇨ /dev/modem Connection Setup.**

   If you're working from a permanent Knoppix installation, the Run as Root – KDE su dialog opens.

2. **Enter your `root` password if prompted.**

   The Connection Type dialog opens.

3. **Click OK.**

   The next dialog shows the modem that Knoppix detects.

4. Click OK.

Knoppix creates a link to your modem.

You need to use the modem's location in the following section.

Configuring your modem

When you finish configuring Knoppix to connect to your modem, you're almost ready to connect to the Internet. Find the dialup and connection information your ISP gave you and use the KPPP utility to configure your modem to dial and connect to your ISP and the Internet:

1. Click the K-Menu and select KNOPPIX⇨Network/Internet⇨ Modem Dialer.

The KPPP dialog opens.

2. Click the Configure button.

The KPPP Configuration – KPPP dialog opens with the Accounts tab active.

3. Click the New button.

The Create New Account – KPPP dialog opens. You can use this wizard in almost any country other than the United States. The dialog, however, doesn't include a U.S. setting, so you must use the manual configuration utility.

4. Click the Manual Setup button.

The New Account – KPPP dialog opens, as shown in Figure 9-1.

Figure 9-1: Entering your account information into the KPPP dialog.

5. **Enter a name for your connection in the Connection Name text box (I suggest you enter a name that's descriptive of your connection, such as** `my dialup isp`**) and click the Add button.**

   The Add Phone Number – KPPP dialog opens.

6. **Enter your ISP's phone number and click OK.**

7. **Back in the New Account – KPPP dialog, click OK.**

   Control returns to the KPPP Configuration – KPPP dialog.

8. **Click the Modems tab and then the New button.**

   The New Modem – KPPP dialog opens.

9. **Type any arbitrary name for your modem, such as** `mymodem`**, in the Modem name text box.**

10. **Click the Modem Device pull-down menu and select the modem serial device that you obtained in the section "Locating your modem" and then click OK.**

11. **Back in the KPPP Configuration – KPPP dialog, click OK.**

    You return to the KPPP dialog.

12. **Enter your username and password in the appropriate text boxes.**

    You're ready to connect to the Internet!

Dialing the Internet

When your Knoppix dialup Internet connection is configured, you can connect with KPPP.

Follow these instructions whenever you dial up an Internet connection:

1. **Start the KPPP utility, if you haven't already, by clicking the K-Menu and selecting KNOPPIX⇨Network/Internet⇨Modem Dialer.**

   The KPPP dialog opens.

2. **Click the Connect button.**

   The modem dials your ISP, screeches the familiar weird modem noises, and eventually makes the connection. When the connection is established, a terminal window showing your ISP's login prompt opens.

3. **When you're finished using your dialup connection, click the Disconnect button.**

   Your modem closes its connection.

If your connection fails, try the following steps to manually enter your authentication information.

1. **Click the Configure button in the KPPP window.**

2. **Click Edit in the KPPP Configure – KPPP dialog.**

   The Edit Account: dialog opens.

3. **Click the Authentication pull-down menu and select the Terminal-based option.**

4. **Click OK to return to the KPPP Configure – KPPP dialog.**

5. **Click OK.**

6. **Click Connect.**

   The modem dials your ISP. After it makes the connection, a terminal emulator window opens.

7. **Enter your username and password when prompted.**

Manually entering your authentication information helps avoid authentication problems. For instance, you can see whether the password you enter is accepted or not.

Chapter 10

Getting Wired: Connecting to Wired Networks

In This Chapter

▶ Preparing your network connection

▶ Configuring your network connection

▶ Installing a firewall on your Knoppix computer

*Y*our private network may be a simple consumer-level Ethernet switch that connects a couple of computers. Or, your network might be a much larger and more extensive one like you find in a big business, university, or other large organization.

Either way, connecting your Knoppix computer to a wired private network is simple: You plug one end of a cable into its Ethernet port and the other into the network switch. Once connected, you configure Knoppix to work on the network. That configuration is also simple to make, and this chapter describes the process.

The setup steps in this chapter are designed for both

✔ Permanent Knoppix installations

✔ Live Knoppix instances (as shown in Chapter 2)

With a live Knoppix instance, you must repeat the steps in this chapter every time you reboot unless you use a *persistent home directory* (shown in Chapter 3).

Meta-view: Connecting to a wired LAN

The following steps provide a general idea of the process of connecting your computer to a private network:

1. Install (if necessary) your Ethernet *network interface card* (NIC) in your computer.

2. Physically connect your NIC to your private network. (Connect your computer to an Ethernet switch or hub with a Cat5 or Cat6 cable).

   I assume you are connecting to a network that provides DHCP. DHCP makes configuring Knoppix computer networking very easy.

3. Give your NIC an IP address and network mask; set your default gateway router and domain name servers.

   Most consumer Ethernet switches and gateway routers provide the *dynamic host configuration protocol* (DHCP) service. DHCP automatically provides clients with an IP address, a network mask (`netmask`), a default gateway IP, and a domain name service (DNS) address. Many, if not most, organizations also operate networks that provide DHCP.

4. Optionally, install a firewall on your Knoppix computer.

Preparing Your Ethernet Adapter

Connecting to a wired network doesn't require lots of coffee or all-nighters. Wired LANs are easy to work with, and Knoppix provides the utility for doing the task.

The following instructions describe how to attach and configure your Knoppix computer to work on a private network. The following steps may be required to connect your Knoppix computer to a wired private network:

1. **Install an Ethernet NIC, if necessary.**

   Most modern computers — laptops and desktops alike — include an embedded Ethernet NIC by default. Look in the computer's manual or, alternatively, on the computer itself, to find out whether you already have an NIC installed.

   Ethernet is a standard or protocol that defines how multiple networked devices communicate on a single bus. Ethernet connectors look very much like *telephone* jacks. If you look inside the jack, Ethernet NICs have *eight* little copper pin connectors. (Telephone modem connectors have either *two* or *four* pins.)

2. **Connect your Knoppix computer to the private network via a network cable.**

   A network connection requires a network cable, which should be rated category 5 (Cat5) or higher. Plug one connector into your computer's Ethernet NIC and the other into your network hub or switch.

Wired networks use either *copper* or *fiber optic* cable. Consumer-level LANs always use copper cable. Copper cables are categorized as either

- Cat5
- Cat6 (which can handle faster Ethernet NICs than Cat5 but is also more expensive)

Configuring Your Network

With a working NIC connected to a private network, you're ready to configure Knoppix to communicate on the network. Knoppix networking depends on whether your network has a *DHCP server*.

Knoppix automatically configures itself to work on your network if your network runs the DHCP service. All you have to do is connect your Knoppix computer to the network and boot Knoppix. Knoppix sends a DHCP broadcast, and the DHCP server provides the Knoppix computer with its network configuration.

If your network doesn't provide DHCP, then you have to manually configure Knoppix networking as described in this section.

DHCP (dynamic host configuration protocol) automatically sets such network parameters as the IP address and gateway for your computer.

If you don't know whether you have DHCP capability, ask your network administrator (if you have one). Alternatively, you can simply configure for DHCP and see if it works. The configuration process is very simple, so failure *is* an option. If DHCP fails and your Knoppix computer doesn't connect to your network, you can use the manual configuration steps described later in this chapter.

Using DHCP

Follow these steps to configure your Knoppix computer to work with DHCP broadcast:

1. **Click the KNOPPIX menu (a subset of the K-Menu) and select Network/ Internet⇨Network Card Configuration.**

   - The Xdialog window opens, asking if you want to use DHCP broadcast.

- The netcardconf dialog — contained in a terminal emulator window — also opens. This window shows the progress of your network configuration.

2. Click Yes to use DHCP broadcast.

DHCP provides your computer with its network configuration. Your network connection is established and you're finished with the setup. When you leave the configuration utility, you can use your network.

Open a browser and browse away. If you have problems and your network doesn't appear to work, try manually configuring your connection. The following section describes the manual configuration process.

Without DHCP broadcast

If your network doesn't have DHCP service, you must manually configure your connection.

The sidebar "Introducing Knoppix network defaults" explains the networking parameters that Knoppix sets by default. These parameters are normally set by DHCP.

Follow these steps to configure Knoppix networking without DHCP broadcast:

1. Click the KNOPPIX menu (a subset of the K-Menu) and select Network/ Internet➪Network Card Configuration.

The Xdialog window opens, asking if you want to use DHCP broadcast.

The netcardconf dialog — contained in a terminal emulator window — also opens. This window shows the progress of your network configuration.

2. Click No when asked whether you want to use DHCP.

You're prompted to enter an IP address.

3. Enter your *IP address* in the Xdialog window and then click OK.

4. Enter your *network mask* value in the Xdialog window and then click OK.

Unless you know you need a different network mask value, just click OK to use the default value, `255.255.255.0`.

5. Enter your *broadcast address* in the Xdialog window and click OK.

The default value is `192.168.1.255`, which works if you selected the default network mask value in Step 4.

6. **Enter your *network gateway IP address* in the Xdialog window and click OK.**

    The default gateway address value is `192.168.0.254`. This value might not be correct for your LAN.

7. **Enter DNS server addresses and click OK.**

    • Your ISP gives you at least one DNS IP address to use.

    • If you have two addresses, separate them with a space.

    The netcardconf dialog shows the progress as your NIC is set up.

After you finish setting up your network connection, you can use your network. Open a browser and browse away.

Introducing Knoppix network defaults

To connect your Knoppix computer to a network without DHCP broadcast, you need to specify parameters manually. The following list describes the default parameters that the network configuration utility provides.

✔ **An IP address:** IP addresses are like telephone numbers or street addresses. They allow one network device to find and communicate with another. IP addresses are set dynamically when using DHCP. However, you must set a static IP address if you're not using DHCP.

When setting a static IP address, I use the range `192.168.1.200` through `192.168.1.240` on my home network so it doesn't interfere with the common DHCP range. I suggest you use any value in this range; alternatively, you can select values between `192.168.1.2` and `192.168.1.99`.

Xdialog provides a default IP address of `192.168.0.1` to your NIC.

✔ **A default gateway IP address:** Computers route their communications through the default gateway IP address when connecting to other devices outside the local network.

Many network switches and routers use `192.168.1.1` as their Internet gateway address. They typically use the address range `192.168.1.100` through `192.168.1.150` for DHCP.

✔ **Network mask:** IP addresses are divided into network and host sections. The network section is specific to your private network, and the host identifies your device. The network mask — also known as a *netmask* — defines the division of the IP address.

The Knoppix network utility uses a default value of `255.255.255.0`, which works for almost all home, small, and medium-sized networks.

✔ **Broadcast address:** Network interfaces often need to find other devices. They find each other by broadcasting requests to an entire private network. Broadcast addresses define how a network device performs a broadcast.

The Knoppix network utility uses a default value of `192.168.1.255`, which should work for you.

Chapter 11

Wireless Networks

. . . .

. . . .

*W*ireless networks make the world much easier and more pleasurable to work in. Wireless network interface cards (NICs) — commonly referred to as *WiFi* (wireless fidelity) *cards* — free us from the constraints of time and space . . . well, maybe just space. You no longer have to find a network connector to plug into, which makes traveling around with your laptop immensely easier. Many airports, hotels, businesses, and even parts of whole cities — such as Albuquerque, New Mexico — provide WiFi network access. WiFi also makes it easier to work in your own home because you no longer have to physically plug in.

You can use the setup steps in this chapter when you run Knoppix from the *Knoppix For Dummies* DVD (or the Knoppix Lite CD that you download from www.knoppix.org or www.knoppix.net), but you must *repeat* the steps every time you reboot the PC unless you use a persistent home directory. (Chapter 3 shows you how to create and use a persistent home directory.)

Many wireless access points also have built-in connections for *wired* networking. Chapter 10 shows how to connect a Knoppix computer for wired networking.

WiFi Chipsets

Wireless network performance, security, and convenience with a Knoppix PC depend on your system's protocol and hardware.

Network protocols

There are two common wireless networking protocols: 802.11g and 802.11b.

Table 11-1 lists the key attributes of both protocols.

Table 11-1	Wireless Network Protocols	
Feature	*802.11g*	*802.11b*
Transfer speed (maximum; megabits/second)	54Mbps	11Mbps
Works with both 802.11g and 802.11b access points	Yes	No
WiFi Protected Access (WPA) encryption	Compatible	No
Wired Equivalent Protocol (WEP) encryption	Compatible	Compatible

WEP is *less secure* than the WPA encryption protocol.

Protocols are standards that the Institute of Electrical and Electronics Engineers (IEEE) has devised so wireless network equipment from different manufacturers can work together.

NIC hardware

Wireless NICs come in two general flavors:

- **Add-on.** If your PC doesn't have a wireless NIC, you can add a wireless 802.11b or 802.11g NIC:
  - *PCMCIA:* Insert a PCMCIA WiFi card into your laptop (or your desktop machine with a PCMCIA adapter).
  - *USB:* Attach a USB-based NIC to any USB-equipped computer.
  - *PCI:* Insert a PCI-based NIC into the motherboard slot inside your desktop machine.

    If you're shopping for a wireless NIC for your Knoppix computer, look for an *802.11g* NIC that uses a *chipset* listed in Table 11-2.

- **Built-in.** You don't need to insert a device in a computer with a built-in WiFi NIC.

  Most laptops built since 2004 include an internal WiFi 802.11g NIC.

Finding hardware information in Windows

In Windows, the *Device Manager* contains plenty of information about Windows and the PC that runs it. If you can't find the NIC chipset in the hardware documentation, follow these steps:

1. **Boot Windows.**

2. **Open the Control Panel.**

   The Control Panel may be directly visible in your Start menu or under Settings. If you can't find it, search your Windows partition for control.exe.

3. **Open the System item and then click the Hardware tab.**

4. **On the Hardware tab, click the Device Manager button.**

   The Device Manager window organizes the system information into a list of hardware types.

5. **Click the plus sign next to Network Adapters.**

   Your system's wireless NIC is listed in the window, as shown in the following figure.

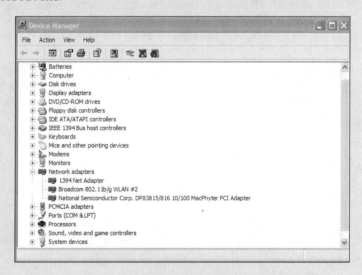

Table 11-2	Knoppix-supported Wireless NIC Chipsets	
Chipset	*Network Protocol Capability*	*Knoppix Device Name*
Amtel	802.11b/g	
Atheros	802.11b/g	ath$X$ (X=0, 1, etc.)
Centrino/ipw2*00	802.11b/g	

(continued)

Table 11-2 *(continued)*

Chipset	Network Protocol Capability	Knoppix Device Name
Orinoco	802.11b/g or 802.11b-only	ethX (X= 0, 1, etc.)
Prism I and II	802.11b-only	ethX (X = 0, 1, etc.)
Prism54	802.11b/g	
Ralink ra2*00	802.11b/g	raX (X = 0, 1, etc.)
Wavelan	802.11b-only	ethX (X = 0, 1, etc.)

Essential wireless networking parameters

You may need some network information to install the wireless kernel module in your Knoppix system. If your wireless network won't work with the Knoppix default values, you can get the correct values from either the network administrator or from the equipment, such as your home network's access point.

The most common method for connecting wireless NICs to a LAN is an *access point* (AP). To configure a WiFi NIC, you need the following information for your AP at your fingertips (unless you leave items *blank* to accept the Knoppix default value or action).

✔ **root password**

Don't write your root password in the book!

✔ **SSID (service set identifier):** _____

Leaving the SSID value blank connects your WiFi NIC to the AP with the strongest signal (usually, the nearest AP).

The SSID identifies the wireless network name. (Some network vendors call this an *ESSID*.) Every AP has a default SSID; for example, the default SSID for Linksys APs is linksys.

✔ **Encryption key:** _____

If your network doesn't use encryption, leave this value *blank*.

Encryption keys are binary numbers that WiFi NICs and APs use to encrypt their communication. The binary encryption key can be formatted as either a hexadecimal number or a text string.

✔ **NIC chipset:** _____

You need to know your NIC's chipset to use native Linux drivers, encryption, or the generic ndiswrapper.

There are a couple of ways to find your wireless NIC's protocol and chipset:

✔ Consult the WiFi NIC documentation that comes with your wireless NIC.

✔ If your computer can run Windows, look for the name of your wireless NIC chipset in Device Manager. The sidebar "Finding hardware information in Windows" shows you how.

The challenges of using Knoppix over a wireless connection depend on your chipset and network security:

✔ **Easy: Using supported NICs with an unencrypted network**

Knoppix does a good job of automatically connecting supported NICs to unencrypted APs. You can simply plug such NICs into your computer and start working on the wireless LAN.

✔ **Work, Work, Work: Encryption and unsupported NICs**

This chapter shows you the manual configuration steps for

• NICs based on unsupported chipsets

• Wireless networking to encrypted APs

Whether you're on Easy Street or clocking in for work, the following sections guide you through the steps to connect your NIC to a wireless network.

Wireless NIC Configuration

The steps for using wireless NICs depend on whether Knoppix supports your NIC's *chipset* (the microchips that make wireless NICs work):

✔ If your wireless NIC uses a supported chipset (listed in Table 11-2), Knoppix can automatically install the wireless kernel module (driver).

✔ If your NIC uses an unsupported chipset, you must use the `ndiswrapper` utility to install the wireless kernel module and use a Windows driver.

Knoppix-supported WiFi NICs

Knoppix makes using certain WiFi NICs easy. You can plug in a supported WiFi NIC and Knoppix configures the NIC and automatically connects to unencrypted APs.

Meta-view: Connecting to a wireless access point

Ya gotta do what ya gotta do. Here's what ya gotta do to make your wireless connection. I assume that you already have an access point (AP) running in your home or business. (This book doesn't cover all the steps of running an AP or a whole wireless network.)

The following steps connect your Knoppix computer to an AP:

1. Beg, borrow, or buy a WiFi card and install it in your computer.

   This may not be necessary if you're using a recently manufactured laptop. Laptops built since 2004 increasingly include built-in WiFi NICs.

2. If necessary, install the wireless kernel module (driver) using the `ndiswrapper` utility.

Knoppix automatically installs the wireless kernel module for the NICs listed in Table 11-2.

3. Configure the WiFi NIC for DHCP.

   Knoppix automatically connects to unencrypted APs. If Knoppix finds an unencrypted AP, it can automatically obtain an IP address for 802.11b-based networks. Otherwise, you can manually run DHCP to obtain an IP address for 802.11g networks.

4. Connect using encryption.

   Knoppix provides wireless network configuration utilities that help you easily connect using the WEP encryption protocol. You can use the `ndiswrapper` utility to connect using WPA encryption.

5. Use your wireless network.

Table 11-2 lists NIC chipsets that Knoppix directly supports. Compatible NICs and APs depend on their wireless protocol:

- ✔ **802.11g NICs** connect to *both* 802.11g and 802.11b APs.
- ✔ **802.11b NICs** connect *only* to 802.11b APs.

To configure supported WiFi NICs to connect to unencrypted and WEP-encrypted access points, follow these steps:

1. **Click the K-Menu and select KNOPPIX⇨Network/Internet⇨ KWiFiManager (Wireless Manager).**

   The Run as Root – KDE su dialog opens if you're running from a permanent Knoppix installation.

2. **If prompted, enter the `root` password and click OK.**

   If you don't want to re-enter the `root` password when you reopen the utility, click the Keep Password button.

   The KWiFiManager dialog opens, as shown in Figure 11-1.

   The sidebar "KWiFiManager parameters" describes the information in the KWiFiManager dialog.

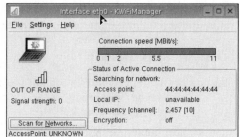

Figure 11-1:
The KWiFi-
Manager
dialog.

3. **Click the Settings menu and select Configuration Editor.**

   The Configure – KDE Control Module dialog opens, as shown in Figure 11-2. It gives you the choice of selecting any of four possible configurations by clicking the tabs at the top of the dialog.

   The Config1 tab is selected by default.

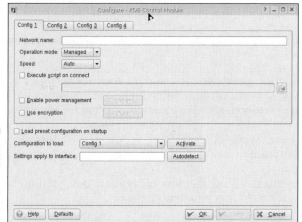

Figure 11-2:
Configuring
your
wireless
NIC.

4. **Type the SSID of the AP you want to connect to into the Network Name text box.**

   The wireless network SSID is in the KWiFiManager dialog.

5. **Click the Autodetect button.**

   KWiFiManager determines the network interface your WiFi NIC uses. For instance, 802.11b NICs tend to use the eth0 and eth1 interfaces, while 802.11g Atheros-based NICs use ath0.

6. **Click the Activate button.**

KWiFiManager parameters

The KWiFiManager dialog offers the following parameters:

✔ **AP SSID:** The *Connected to network:* line shows the SSID (or *name*) of the AP.

✔ **AP MAC address:** The *Access point:* line shows the MAC (machine access control) of the AP.

✔ **Channel number:** *Frequency [channel]:* shows the channel your NIC is connected to on the AP.

✔ **Connection speed:** The *Connection speed (MBit/s)* activity bar shows the maximum speed at which your NIC can communicate with the AP.

✔ **Connected/not connected:** If the *Connection speed (MBit/s)* activity bar is *green,* you're connected to the AP.

✔ **Encryption:** This shows whether you're using encryption.

✔ **IP address:** The *Local IP:* line shows the IP address that the AP has assigned to your WiFi NIC. The IP is assigned automatically if you connect to a nonencrypted AP.

✔ **Signal strength:** The signal strength that your WiFi NIC sees from the AP. The value is displayed in both graphical and numeric form on the left side of the dialog. The numeric values range from 0 to 100.

The following section guides you to the right security options for your system. After you set up a wireless NIC with Knoppix's automatic configuration utility, you're ready to set up *wireless encryption* for network security.

If your network uses wireless encryption, set up your Knoppix system for the most secure encryption you can use:

✔ **WPA encryption:** This is the best encryption, but it requires a network that uses only 802.11g equipment.

If you've configured an NIC for an 802.11g wireless network, jump to the step-by-step guide for WPA configuration at the end of this chapter.

✔ **WEP encryption:** This is the only encryption option if your wireless network uses any 802.11b equipment. The sidebar "WEP: Weak Exposed Protection" shows you how to set it up on your Knoppix system.

For the best practical protection, upgrade to 802.11g NIC and use WPA, not WEP.

If your wireless network uses an *unencrypted* AP, your NIC automatically connects to the AP and you're ready to go.

WEP: Weak Exposed Protection

The 802.11b protocol uses the *wired equivalent protection* (WEP) encryption, which provides only weak encryption; 802.11g protocol can use either WEP or the newer, more secure WPA encryption. Anyone can break a WEP encryption key by using widely available tools. WEP is better than nothing, but it doesn't ensure your privacy. WEP comes in two strengths:

- ✔ 128-bit WEP is preferred if you must use 802.11b networking. It's better than no encryption.

- ✔ 40-bit WEP is almost worthless.

If you can use only WEP encryption, follow these steps to set it up on your Knoppix system:

1. **Click the Use Encryption button in the KWIFiManager dialog.**

   The Configure button next to the Use Encryption button activates.

2. **Click the Configure button.**

   The Configure Encryption – KDE Control Module dialog opens.

3. **Click the Restricted button.**

4. **Type your AP's encryption key in the Key 1 text box.**

   Encryption keys can be entered in either *hexadecimal* (which is an easier way of working with binary data) or as human-readable *text strings*.

5. **If the encryption key is a text string, click the String button.**

6. **Click OK.**

   Control returns to the Configure – KDE Control Module dialog.

7. **Click Apply.**

8. **Click the Activate button.**

9. **Click OK to exit the dialog.**

   The KWiFiManager dialog shows the connection speed, the IP address, and other wireless network information.

KWiFiManager doesn't know how to get IP addresses for any of the NIC chipsets that Knoppix automatically supports. If you have one of those NICs, follow these steps to manually obtain an IP address:

1. **Click the K-Menu and select Utilities⇨Terminal.**

   The Shell – Konsole window opens.

2. **Change to the Super User.**

   Type the following command and press Enter.

   ```
   su -
   ```

3. **Obtain your IP address.**

   Use your NIC in the following command and then press Enter:

   ```
   pump -i nic_device
   ```

For example, enter the following command for Atheros-based NICs:

```
pump -i ath0
```

Use the following command for Ralink-based NICs:

```
pump -i ra0
```

4. **Type exit and press Enter to quit the terminal window.**

The AP assigns your NIC an IP address, and the value is shown in the KWiFiManager dialog. Your computer is connected to your wireless network.

Open source jujitsu: Using Windows WiFi drivers

Many WiFi NIC manufacturers don't release their product specifications to the open source community. The lack of information makes it difficult or impossible to write Linux *kernel modules* (drivers) to work with undocumented devices, such as wireless network interfaces. Everyone loses:

- ✔ Manufacturers lose a significant market segment: *us*.
- ✔ Knoppix and other Linux systems can't use cutting-edge devices.

Using Windows drivers

You can run many undocumented devices on Knoppix if you have their *Microsoft Windows drivers*. The ndiswrapper project uses Windows drivers for WiFi NICs in Linux.

Brilliant!

Linuxant, Inc., sells Driverloader to simplify the process of using Microsoft drivers. It does a pretty good job. At $19.95, Driverloader is inexpensive. You can download a free 30-day trial version from www.linuxant.com.

Protect your wireless network with at least 128-bit WEP. WEP provides fragile protection, but it's better than nothing. With a laptop and publicly available software, you can drive down almost any street and detect many unprotected wireless APs. With so much low-hanging fruit available, someone has to *want* to break into your wireless network if you use WEP. Therefore, a little WEP is better than no WEP.

You might *freeze* your computer by using ndiswrapper. (It froze about 10 percent of the wireless NICs I've experimented with.) If ndiswrapper freezes your computer, you need a wireless NIC with a chipset that is directly supported by Knoppix. Unfortunately, there's no way to find out whether ndiswrapper works on your system without installing it and trying it.

Before trying to use `ndiswrapper` and a Windows driver, find out whether your wireless NIC can use Knoppix's built-in drivers. Table 11-2 lists Knoppix-compatible NICs. Use the instructions in the section "Knoppix-supported WiFi NICs" if your NIC is supported.

Finding Windows drivers

Using Windows WiFi NIC drivers means you need to *obtain* Windows drivers. Where are they? Your Windows computer, Windows CD-ROM, or the manufacturer's Web site.

The following sections show how to obtain the driver for your WiFi NIC.

Hard drive

If your Windows computer already uses your wireless NIC, you can get your Windows WiFi driver from your computer.

The following instructions don't care whether you boot Knoppix from the *Knoppix For Dummies* DVD or from a permanent installation.

Follow these steps to find your Windows WiFi driver and copy it to your Knoppix partition:

1. **Boot your Knoppix computer by using one of the following options:**

   • *DVD:* Boot your Knoppix computer.

   • *Permanent Knoppix installation:* Boot your Knoppix computer and log in as a regular user.

2. **Double-click the hard drive icon that corresponds to your Windows partition.**

   A Konqueror dialog opens, showing the contents of the Windows partition.

3. **Choose Tools⇨Find File.**

4. **In the Named text box, substitute the name of the WiFi NIC driver you're looking for and press Enter.**

   ```
   driver*.inf
   ```

   For instance, type `b57win32.inf` if using a Broadcom WiFi NIC.

5. **Click the Home icon on the KDE Kicker (the horizontal menu bar at the bottom of the KDE Desktop).**

   A Konqueror dialog opens, showing the contents of your home directory.

6. **Copy the `.inf` file from the Windows partition to your home directory.**

   Click the results and drag them to your home directory icon.

   A query submenu dialog opens.

7. **Select the Copy menu option.**

   The `.inf` file(s) is copied to your home directory.

8. **Click the Windows Konqueror dialog that you opened in Step 2.**

9. **Choose Tools⇨Find File.**

10. **Enter the name of the WiFi NIC driver you're looking for into the Named text box and press Enter, like this:**

```
driver*.sys
```

   For instance, type `b57xp.sys` if using a Broadcom WiFi NIC.

11. **Copy the .sys file from the Windows partition to your home directory.**

    Click on the results and drag them to your home directory icon.

    A query submenu dialog opens.

12. **Select the Copy menu option.**

    The `.sys` file is copied to your home directory.

CD-ROM

If your NIC's Windows XP drivers are on a CD-ROM, follow these steps to copy the wireless card's Windows drivers to your Knoppix system:

1. **Insert your NIC's support CD-ROM.**

2. **If you're running from a live Knoppix installation, type the following command to mount the CD-ROM:**

```
mount /mnt/auto/cdrom
```

3. **Find the Windows .inf information file and the .sys driver file on the CD-ROM.**

   Enter the following commands to locate the Windows WiFi NIC configuration files:

```
find /mnt/auto/cdrom -iname '*.sys"
find /mnt/auto/cdrom -iname '*.inf"
```

   You should see files like `oem10.inf` and `RT2500.sys`.

4. **Copy the Windows driver .inf and .sys files from the CD-ROM into your home directory.**

   Enter the following commands:

```
cp /mnt/auto/cdrom/Drivers/"Windows XP"/*sys ~
cp /mnt/auto/cdrom/Drivers/"Windows XP"/*inf ~
```

Download

You can download a Windows XP driver from the manufacturer's Web site. How you download the file depends on the resources you have:

- ✔ **Other operating systems.** If your computer can access the Internet through another installed operating system (such as Windows or another Linux version), use that access to download the wireless NIC driver.

  This chapter shows how to copy drivers from a Windows partition to a Knoppix partition.

- ✔ **Wired Linux networking.** If you can connect your Knoppix computer to a wired network with Internet access, you can use that connection to download the wireless NIC driver. Chapter 10 shows how to configure a Knoppix computer for wired network access.

  Many wireless networks have built-in connections for wired networking.

- ✔ **Dialup networking.** If you have dialup Internet access, Chapter 9 shows how to use a modem with Knoppix.

  Many built-in WinModems don't work with Knoppix.

Starting ndiswrapper modules

Follow these steps to create and install an `ndiswrapper` kernel module:

1. **Open a terminal window and change to the** `root` **user by typing** `su -`.

   Knoppix provides a graphical `ndiswrapper` interface (K-Menu⇨ KNOPPIX⇨Network⇨ndiswrapper). However, `ndiswrapper` is still learning to walk, so I recommend manually configuring your kernel module. The following manual method avoids the limitations of the nascent graphical tools.

   The Super User is synonymous with the root user.

2. **Insert the information filename into the following command:**

   ```
   ndiswrapper -I /etc/driver.inf
   ```

   For example, if the information file is called `oem10.inf`, enter the following command:

   ```
   ndiwrapper -i /etc/oem10.inf
   ```

   This command "wraps" the Windows `.inf` file so that Linux can use it.

3. **Tell Knoppix about the new `ndiswrapper` kernel module.**

   Enter the following command:

   ```
   ndiswrapper -m
   ```

4. **Remove the `ndiswrapper` module from the Linux kernel and then reload the module.**

   Enter the following commands to load (or reload) the kernel module:

   ```
   rmmod ndiswrapper
   modprobe ndiswrapper
   ```

5. **Check whether the module is loaded.**

   Enter the following command to display the newly loaded kernel module:

   ```
   lsmod | grep ndiswrapper
   ```

   If the `ndiswrapper` module is loaded, you see it listed.

   If you don't see ndiswrapper listed,

   a. *Reinsert the NIC.*

   b. *Open a terminal window.*

   c. *Change to the `root` user by typing `su -`.*

6. **Finish configuring your wireless connection:**

   - *No encryption.* If your AP doesn't use encryption, enter the following command to assign an IP address to your WiFi NIC:

     ```
     pump -i wlan0
     ```

   - *WPA encryption.* See the next section of the book ("WPA: Better Security") for configuration instructions.

   - *WEP encryption.* Use the following commands:

     First, use your encryption key in the following command:

     ```
     iwconfig wlan0 key encryption-key
     ```

     Wireless networks use binary encryption keys. The binary keys can be represented in either hexadecimal or text format. Here are a couple of examples:

     If your encryption key is 00-11-22-33-44-55-66-77-88-99:

     ```
     iwconfig wlan0 key 00-11-22-33-44-55-66-77-88-99
     ```

     If your encryption key is the text string `iamnotanumber`:

     ```
     iwconfig wlan0 key s:iamnotanumber
     ```

     Finish by entering the following command to assign an IP address to your WiFi NIC:

     ```
     pump -i wlan0
     ```

   Your computer is connected to your wireless network!

WPA: Better Security

WiFi Protected Access (WPA) is the best current protection you can use when using wireless networks. It's an option on most current 802.11g-capable APs and NICs.

You can upgrade older 802.11g equipment to use WPA by installing firmware upgrades. Consult your NIC manufacturer's Web site to obtain the upgrade and instructions to use it.

Linux WPA requires some work to configure and use. It's worth considering because

- ✔ WPA offers a high degree of security.
- ✔ WPA is easy to configure on Windows XP computers.

    After you get WPA working on your Linux computers, you can easily upgrade your home network to use WPA encryption exclusively.

The following instructions describe how to configure a consumer-level AP and 802.11g NICs to use the new-and-improved WPA encryption.

WPA pass phrases are similar to passwords. They're used to encrypt wireless communication. The pass phrase source depends on what type of wireless network you're connecting to:

- ✔ **Home or personal network:** *Create* a pass phrase (think up a phrase and then change some of the letters into numbers and other characters, like #, $, and @).

    WPA pass phrases should be at least 22 characters long.

- ✔ **Someone else's network:** *Obtain* the AP pass phrase from your friendly system administrator.

Configuring an AP to use WPA

The following instructions configure an AP to provide WPA encryption:

1. **Turn on the WPA Preshared Key security mode on your 802.11g AP.**

    If your AP is at least two years old, you probably need to update its firmware to enable WPA encryption. Follow the instructions in your AP's manual.

2. **Set the WPA encryption key type to TKIP (Temporal Key Integrity Protocol).**

3. **Enter a WPA pass phrase on your AP.**

You're ready to configure your NIC to use WPA.

Configuring Knoppix to use WPA

Configuring a WiFi NIC on your Knoppix computer requires you to perform the following tasks.

1. **Create a WPA configuration file.**

2. **Optionally load an ndiswrapper module (driver).**

3. **Start the WiFi NIC.**

4. **Start the WPA daemon.**

The following sections describe how to configure WPA encryption.

Create a WPA configuration file

Use the following steps to create a WPA daemon configuration file:

1. **Open the new WPA configuration file by typing this command:**

   ```
   kwrite /etc/wpa.conf
   ```

2. **Enter the following code in the Kwrite window to open a text editor.**

   Insert your `ssid` (the `ssid` is really your `essid`) and `psk` (pass phrase) values into the following code:

   ```
   eapol_version=1
   ap_scan=1
   fast_reauth=1
   network={
           ssid="linky"
           proto=WPA
           key_mgmt=WPA-PSK
           pairwise=CCMP TKIP
           group=CCMP TKIP WEP104 WEP40
           psk="iamnotanumber"
   }
   ```

3. **Choose File➪Quit.**

4. **Click the Save button in the dialog that opens and exit the file.**

The following section shows how to start (or restart) `ndiswrapper`.

Loading an ndiswrapper kernel module

Knoppix automatically loads supported WiFi NIC kernel modules. However, you need to use the `ndiswrapper` module (driver) for unsupported NICs.

If Knoppix automatically supports your NIC without `ndiswrapper`, skip to the next section and start your network interface.

If your NIC requires `ndiswrapper`, follow these steps to install (or restart) the `ndiswrapper` kernel module:

1. **Click the Terminal icon on the Kicker to open a terminal window.**

2. **Load (or reload) the `ndiswrapper` module into the Linux kernel:**

```
rmmod ndiswrapper
modprobe ndiswrapper
```

Starting your network interface

The WPA daemon needs the WiFi NIC to be active so it can authenticate with the AP. The following instructions activate your NIC:

1. **Click the Terminal icon on the Kicker to open a terminal window on your Knoppix computer.**

2. **Start your wireless NIC by using the `ifconfig` command:**

```
ifconfig wifi_nic up
```

Here are some examples:

- *ndiswrapper:*

```
ifconfig wlan0 up
```

- *Atheros-based NICs:*

```
ifconfig ath0 up
```

- *Ralink-based NICs:*

```
ifconfig ra0 up
```

This turns on your NIC without setting an IP. The WPA key-setting software requires the NIC to be in that state.

Starting WPA encryption

Linux uses the `wpa_supplicant` program to use WPA encryption with your 802.11g NIC.

Run the following commands to set up `wpa_supplicant` as a running program:

1. **Substitute your NIC in the following command to turn on WPA encryption:**

```
wpa_supplicant -D ndiswrapper -I wifi_nic -c /etc/wpa.conf
```

The addition of `-B` in the WPA encryption command tells `wpa_supplicant` to run in the background as a daemon. For instance, using the command `wpa_supplicant -B -D ndiswrapper -I wifi_nic -c /etc/wpa.conf` forces the utility to run as a daemon. Use this option after you've successfully tested the `wpa_supplicant` configuration.

Here are some examples:

- *ndiswrapper:*

```
wpa_supplicant -D ndiswrapper -iwlan0 -c/etc/wpa.conf
```

- *Atheros-based NICs:*

```
wpa_supplicant -D madwifi -I ath0 -c/etc/wpa.conf
```

2. **Give the WiFi NIC an IP address.**

Substitute your NIC into the following command:

```
pump -i wifi_nic
```

Here are some examples:

- *ndiswrapper:*

```
pump -i wlan0
```

- *Atheros-based NICs:*

```
pump -i ath0
```

When the pump command finishes, you have a WPA-protected WiFi connection. *Dyn-o-mite!*

Chapter 12

Browsing and E-mailing

....

....

*W*hat do people use their computers for? To browse the Web and to send e-mail, of course. The Internet is all about browsing and e-mailing.

This chapter shows how to use your Knoppix computer for Web surfing and e-mail. (Part IV shows how to connect your Knoppix computer to the Net.)

You can use the setup steps in this chapter whether running a permanent or live Knoppix instance. However, if you're running live Knoppix from the *Knoppix For Dummies* DVD (or a CD you download from www.knoppix.net), you must *repeat* the steps every time you reboot the PC unless you use a persistent home directory. (Chapter 3 shows you how to use a persistent home directory.)

Firefox Web Browser

Mozilla Firefox is the new fire-breathing monster of the Linux world. But Mozilla is a good monster. It's a friendly guy who wants to make your life easier and more fun. Mozilla Firefox (just Firefox for short) sets a standard for browsers that even the big, true monsters are watching.

Any way you look at it, Firefox is a cool system. The following sections describe how to use and configure it. Browse away!

Firefox runs away from the chase

Firefox evolved from the Mozilla version 1.7 browser. Old Mozilla was a great system, but Firefox has taken a big step forward and offers the following new qualities and functions:

- **Speed and agility:** Mozilla went on a diet and became the lithe and quick Firefox. It concentrates on the basics: browsing. Firefox divested itself of all the nonbrowsing functions that Mozilla performs. No more e-mail client, newsreader (similar to a mailing list or chat room), or unused Web page editors. Firefox is a mean, lean, browsing machine. The lost weight means Firefox loads fast and reacts quickly to your commands. Why can't real dieting be this easy?

- **Tabs:** Firefox introduces the concept of tabbed browsing. In the past, you had to open a new browser window — or have it opened for you — when selecting a new Web page. Select File⇨New Tab to open a tab; open as many as you want. Clicking a tab immediately switches to a window connected to another Web page.

- **Pop-up blocking:** Don't you hate advertisements that inexplicably pop up while you're trying to surf? Well, pop-ups are a thing of the past thanks to Firefox. It keeps those annoying nasties from cluttering your browsing experience. Now, if only Firefox could block telemarketers.

- **Spyware blocking:** Spyware are the little nasties you can get by innocently browsing the Internet. Spyware range from the annoying adware programs that provide advertisers with your surfing habits to the harmful ones that provide hackers with your system information. Firefox prevents

spyware that leverage Microsoft's ActiveX against the browser and computer. That's a Microsoft problem, not a Knoppix problem, but this is a useful fact to know!

Firefox is better than Internet Explorer when it comes to blocking spyware. However, Firefox doesn't block all spyware. Nearly every browser is vulnerable to Javascript-based spyware. You can only completely avoid spyware by using a text-based browser such as elinks. The amazing elinks provides a non-graphical interface that handles frames and tables while also accepting mouse clicks! It's a wonderful browser that can be accessed by clicking K-Menu and selecting Internet⇨ELinks (Web Browser).

- **Better plug-in handling:** In the same way that Firefox blocks pop-ups, it encourages plug-ins. Plug-ins provide browsers with extra capability to view and display content. Browsers don't have the innate capability to show the animated content you see at many Web sites. Plug-ins bridge the gap, and Firefox makes it easy to get the plug-ins you need.

Plug-ins also present potential security holes. However, Linux provides better file system and memory management than other operating systems, which minimizes potential vulnerabilities.

- **Google for all:** Firefox provides a link in its toolbar to `www.google.com`. Google is effectively Firefox's default search engine, which is appropriate because Google is the default search engine for Linux and much of the rest of the world.

Browsing the Web

Common browsing functions make Firefox a blast to use.

Exploring Firefox

On the Kicker, click the blue globe surrounded by a fiery fox icon (look closely) and Firefox fires up, as shown in Figure 12-1.

Figure 12-1:
The Firefox
browser.

Figure 12-1 shows the Firefox window with

✔ **Toolbars**

The Firefox toolbars are listed in Table 12-1.

Table 12-1	Firefox Window Toolbars	
Name	*Location*	*Functions*
Navigation	Top	Go (Forward, Back, and Home), URL text box
Bookmarks	Top (below Navigation)	Bookmarks saved in the Personal Toolbar folder
Status	Bottom	URL and progress bar for displayed page
Sidebar	Left	Bookmarks, History

Toolbars are collections of similar icons and menus aligned in a row.

✔ **The Location text box**

Typing a Web page URL in the Location text box instructs Firefox to go to that page. For example, type `www.theonion.com` in the text box if you need a laugh.

✔ **The workhorse browsing window (bracketed by the toolbars)**

The Firefox menu

The following summarizes the important Firefox menu options:

✔ **File**

- Open new windows and tabs; then close them.

- Open Internet Web pages and files (for instance, you can browse help files on your computer).

- Save Web pages on your computer, print them, and quit the browser.

✔ **Edit**

- Undo and redo changes you make to the Location text box and interactive Web pages (for instance, entries you make in forms).

- Cut, copy, paste, and delete text that you highlight with your mouse.

- Open a search dialog to find text in a Web page.

  Pressing Ctrl+F opens the Find text box and extra search option buttons in the lower-left corner of the Firefox window. Enter text to search for in the Web page.

- View and change numerous Firefox options by clicking the Preferences menu.

The Search and Preference options are covered later in this chapter.

✔ **View:** Lets you adjust and modify Firefox's toolbars (as listed in Table 12-1).

Starr Jones ain't got nothin' to say in this "view."

✔ **Go:** From this menu choice, you can go home, go back, and go forward. The Go menu also shows the history of the last ten locations you visited.

These are the same functions found in the Navigation toolbar.

✔ **Bookmarks:** Firefox offers the convenience of saving your favorite Web pages in an easy-to-access format:

- To mark a Web page so you can return to it, click Bookmarks and select Bookmark This Page. The Add Bookmark dialog opens. Select a folder in the Create In submenu and click Add. You can then go back to that Web page at any time by selecting it from the menu that opens by clicking the Bookmarks button.

- To edit your bookmarks, choose Bookmarks⇨Manage Bookmarks. A dialog opens in which you can modify, delete, and obtain information about any bookmark, and create and delete bookmark folders.

- Bookmarks placed in the Personal Toolbar Folder show up in the Bookmarks Toolbar near the top of the Firefox window.

If you run live Knoppix from the *Knoppix For Dummies* DVD (or a Knoppix CD that you download from www.knoppix.net), you lose the bookmarks every time you reboot the PC. You can save your bookmarks and other Firefox settings by using a persistent Knoppix disk image, which I describe in Chapter 3.

✔ **Tools:** This menu helps you configure Firefox actions, such as what directory to save downloads to.

✔ **Help:** Select Help⇨Help Contents to open a dialog connected to a comprehensive database of Firefox information. The dialog gives access to a glossary of Firefox terms, an index, and a search engine. Help topics are shown in a table of contents.

Configuration options

You can start using Firefox as soon as you fire up Knoppix. No configuration necessary. The default settings work very well. But, with a little bit of work, you can also customize it to your own needs and preferences. Firefox is highly configurable.

You can customize Firefox when you run a live Knoppix instance from the *Knoppix For Dummies* DVD (or from a Knoppix CD that you download from www.knoppix.net), but Firefox reverts to its default settings every time you reboot the PC. You can save your bookmarks and other Firefox settings by using a persistent Knoppix disk image, which I describe in Chapter 3.

Firefox has one primary configuration utility. Select Edit⇨Preferences, and the Preferences dialog opens.

The Preferences utility helps you modify Firefox's behavior. The following sections describe each major function. Click an icon on the left side of the Preferences dialog to access each function.

General

This window provides options that allow you to make changes that affect the general operation of Firefox. The following bullets describe the general functions.

- **Home Page:** Use this window to change your default home directory, fonts, language, and connection type. Firefox displays its own home page — www.mozilla.org/products/firefox — by default.

  You can change the home page to another location by typing the URL into the Location(s) text box and clicking OK on the bottom-right section of the dialog.

- **Fonts & Colors:** Click this button to open a dialog in which you can change such options as your font type, size, spacing, and color.

- **Language:** No mystery here. Use the dialog that opens by clicking the Language button to change — yes — your language.

  Too bad learning a language isn't this easy. *¿Tu hablas Knoppix? Sprechen Sie Knoppix?*

- **Connection:** If you need to connect to a Web proxy, the sidebar "Setting a Web proxy" guides you through the steps.

  You don't connect to a Web proxy if you connect *directly* to the Internet:

  - Dialup, DSL, and cable modems are direct Internet connections.

  - Private home networks are direct connections unless you've *added* a proxy.

You can build your own Web proxy by using the open source Squid system. See www.squid-cache.org for information about creating and using the proxy.

Many LANs require that you connect to a Web proxy in order to browse the Internet. Web proxies can control *where* and *what* users browse:

- A Web proxy can accept or reject *outgoing Internet connections* based on their destinations (and sometimes their contents).

- A Web proxy can accept or reject *incoming Internet connections* based on whether they belong to an existing outgoing connection. (Proxies act as *firewalls* in this capacity.)

Web proxies can speed up browsing by *caching* (saving) Web pages. When you return to a page, you connect to a local copy instead of to the actual site. However, be forewarned that you can be certain that you're viewing the most recent version of the Web page only by clicking the Reload button. Otherwise, the cache might provide an outdated version of the page.

Setting a Web proxy

If your Web browser requires a proxy connection, the steps to configure Firefox depend on whether you're using a *manual* or *automatic* proxy. (I always use the manual settings because the Auto-detect option doesn't work in some networking environments.)

To set up a manual proxy, you need these parameters from your network administrator:

✔ Proxy URL

✔ Proxy port number

✔ SSL proxy settings (if using encrypted proxy)

Follow these steps to set up your Web browser to use a manual proxy:

1. **Open the Preferences dialog by selecting Edit⇨Preferences.**

2. **Click the General icon.**

3. **Click the Connection Settings button.**

4. **Click the Manual Proxy Configuration.**

5. **Enter the Proxy URL in the HTTP Proxy text box.**

6. **Enter the proxy port number in the Port text box.**

7. **Enter the SSL proxy settings in the SSL Proxy text box.**

8. **Click OK to exit the Preferences dialog.**

To use an automatic proxy, follow these steps:

1. **Obtain the *automatic proxy URL* from your network administrator.**

2. **Open the Preferences dialog by selecting Edit⇨Preferences.**

3. **Click the Connection Settings button.**

4. **Click the Auto-detect Proxy Settings for This Network button.**

5. **Enter the automatic proxy URL in the text box and then click OK.**

   You return to the Preferences dialog.

6. **Exit the Preferences dialog by clicking OK.**

Saving and protecting passwords

Using the Web means visiting a lot of Web sites that ask for your information. Modern browsers help ease your browsing experience by storing information like passwords locally on your computer. That information is potentially vulnerable if your computer is ever hacked, and you must protect it from hackers and criminals as best you can. As the song goes, "One way or another, they're gonna get you," or at least try to get your information. So protecting your valuable information is very important.

When you visit a Web site that asks for a username and password, Firefox asks you if it should remember the password for you. Firefox remembers passwords you enter on Web pages if you click the Remember Passwords button. (You can save passwords even when browsing from a live Knoppix instance. However, your passwords will not survive a reboot unless you create a persistent Knoppix disk image, which I describe in chapter 3.)

Saving passwords in your browser is both a great convenience and a danger! Anyone who steals or hacks into your computer can access your passwords all in one place. Fortunately, Firefox offers a solution by encrypting your saved passwords. You can create a *master password* that's required to access your encrypted passwords when you start Firefox. Follow these steps:

1. **Click the Change Master Password button.**

2. **If you've previously created a master password, enter the old one into the Change Master Password... dialog.**

3. **Enter the new master password into the Change Master Password... dialog.**

✔ **Download Manager History:** When you download a file from the Internet, the Download Manager dialog opens. You can use the dialog to cancel the download. If you don't cancel the download, upon completion of a download, the window shows the downloaded file. Use this window to modify the Download Manager's operation.

✔ **Cookies:** Use the options in this window to modify your cookie behavior. (The following sidebar "Mmm, Firefox like cookies" explains what cookies do.)

Privacy

The Internet is a highly useful and convenient tool. It's also filled with nosy people with prying eyes trying to find information about people who use the Internet. But you don't want to miss using the Internet because of privacy concerns. The following list describes some Firefox features that you can use to protect your information:

✔ **History:** Firefox saves your browsing history, which you can use to return to pages you want to revisit. You can change the length of time that your history is saved; the default is nine days.

✔ **Saved Form Information:** Filling out forms is nearly as much of a pain on a computer as it is on paper. Firefox makes your form filling a little easier by saving information you enter into forms.

✔ **Saved Passwords:** See the sidebar "Saving and protecting passwords" for the lowdown on this option.

✔ **Cache:** Firefox speeds up your browsing by saving, for later retrieval, any Web pages you view. When you revisit a page, Firefox uses the cached page if possible before going back to the Web site.

Web features

Firefox provides several features that make browsing more fun and less stressful. You can access the following menu options by clicking Web Features in the Preferences dialog:

✔ **Block Popup Windows:** Firefox blocks pop-up windows by default! As Homer Simpson would say, "Woohoo!!!" Use these options to modify the pop-up blocker.

✔ **Allow Web Sites to Install Software:** Firefox asks whether you want to let a Web site install software or to block such actions. The default is to allow installations.

✔ **Load Images:** Firefox displays a Web site's text and graphics by default. Use this option to block images from either

- Advertisements

- Third-party sites

✔ **Enable Java:** Turned on by default. Many Web sites use Java to provide better graphics and animation. You shouldn't have to change this option.

✔ **Enable JavaScript:** JavaScript is turned on by default. However, Javascript presents a large security hole. Hackers can potentially use JavaScript to steal passwords, automatically sign and send order forms, redirect bank access information, and more. You can turn this option off as follows:

1. Click Edit and select Preferences.

The Preferences window opens.

2. Click the Web Features link.

3. Click the Enable JavaScript button to toggle it off.

4. Click OK.

Turning off JavaScript limits your ability to use Web pages that use it to provide interactive functions. I personally turn JavaScript on when I need it and then turn it off again.

You must use the `Create a persistent Knoppix disk image` utility to save any changes you make to the Firefox defaults described in this section. See Chapter 3 for details.

Mmm, Firefox like cookies

Cookies can make Web servers more convenient. A *cookie* is a small text file that saves your own information on your system when you use a Web server. For instance, some Web pages (like my.yahoo.com) can automatically log you in. If you want to log in automatically, the Web server checks your system for a cookie with your password.

Malware uses cookies in ways that cookies were never intended:

✔ *Adware* installs menu bars or displays advertisements on your computer.

✔ *Spyware* secretly monitors your actions (perhaps stealing your passwords).

Knoppix (along with other Linux distributions) is relatively free from malware for now, but malware someday may be a common problem for Knoppix systems.

Downloads

Firefox downloads all sorts of files, such as software packages and multimedia.

The following options help you manage downloads:

✔ **Download Folder:** Choose the default download directory (folder).

✔ **Download Manager:** Control whether the Download Manager opens during a download and whether it closes automatically after completion.

✔ **File Types:** Associate certain actions with the type of file you download. For example, you can tell Firefox to open the XMMS multimedia player when downloading OGG files (see Chapter 14).

✔ **Plugins:** Click this button to see plug-ins Firefox can use.

See the sidebar "Plugging in Firefox" for more information about plug-ins.

Advanced

Firefox is highly configurable and provides secure (SSL) connections when needed. You can find the SSL options in the Advanced window. You can control how Firefox's tabs work from the Tabbed Browsing menu.

You shouldn't have to modify the security functions at all.

Thunderbird E-mail Client

Mozilla Thunderbird doesn't blast off like the TV puppet series did. Thunderbird is an e-mail application (or *client*). Use it to read and write your e-mail. Engineer Brains would have given his left string to use Thunderbird.

Plugging in Firefox

Plug-ins are small pieces of software that give a browser extra capabilities. They perform specific functions, such as displaying animated graphics.

Firefox is good at automatically downloading and installing plug-ins. When Firefox needs a plug-in, it asks you if you want it to download and install the plug-in. Click OK, and Firefox does the rest. (It does the work most of the time, but there are times when you must manually install the plug-in. In such cases, check out the instructions provided with the plug-in.)

Here's how to manually install popular plug-ins from the Internet:

1. **Open Firefox and go to** `www.shockwave.com`.

   You should see a blank white box marked `Click here to download the plugin` in the upper-middle area of the window.

2. **Click the blank area.**

The Plugin Finder Service dialog opens, showing that the Macromedia Flash Player plug-in is available.

3. **Click Next.**

The next dialog shows you the Macromedia license agreement. Call in your legal team and review the document when you're having trouble sleeping.

4. **Click the I Agree button and then click Next.**

The plug-in downloads and installs.

5. **Click the Finish button.**

Firefox refreshes itself and you see the Shockwave content in the formerly blank spot.

Displaying your plug-ins:

- ✔ To see Firefox plug-ins, type `about:plugins` in the Location text box.

- ✔ To find numerous popular plug-ins, click the `plugindoc.mozdev.org` link.

Secure browsing

Encrypting and authenticating your transactions is the only way to safely conduct business over the Internet. Encryption is the act (or art) of scrambling information so it can be read only when properly unscrambled. Scrambling and unscrambling is performed by a *cipher* that uses the encryption and decryption keys. Encrypting a communication channel requires that both parties share a common encryption key. At the same time, it's essential to prevent anyone else from obtaining the key. Finding a way to share an encryption key is the "key" to practical secure Internet communications.

Public Key Encryption (PKE) allows secure communication with Web sites. PKE uses two keys:

✔ **Private key:** Only the owner of the private key can decrypt (decipher) information encrypted by the public key. Anyone with a public key can secretly communicate with the private key owner. The Web server with the private key can accept secure connections from many clients. Public key clients can't eavesdrop on each other without the private key.

✔ **Public key:** *Anyone* with the public key can decrypt information encrypted by the private key. This allows the private key server to send its public key clients an encrypted fingerprint that verifies its authenticity. Only the private key can encrypt the fingerprint so the public key client can decrypt it.

PKE lets you connect securely to Web servers. But there's a catch: How does a server securely distribute its public key? Netscape solved this problem with a key distribution system: *Secure Sockets Layer (SSL)*. SSL self-distributes public keys via certificates. When you connect to a Web server with SSL, the server sends you its *certificate.* The certificate is a file with the server's public key and fingerprint, the name of a *certificate authority* (CA), and the CA's fingerprint.

A CA is a trusted authority in the computer world. Web servers that want to provide an authenticated certificate to their clients pay a CA to sign their certificate. When you browse the site, you download the certificate and verify the CA signature. Once verified, your browser extracts the server's public key and starts an encrypted connection.

PKE is used only to start an encrypted connection that's used to exchange symmetrical encryption keys. Here's how your browser authenticates the CA:

1. When your browser connects to an SSL server, it accepts the server's SSL certificate and extracts the CA signature.

2. If your browser can decrypt the certificate with the CA's public key, then the CA is *validated.*

3. The browser extracts and verifies the server's public key.

SSL-based connections use HyperText Transport Protocol (Secure) — HTTPS. SSL URLs look like this: `https://signin.ebay.com`. Your Web browser shows a *lock icon* in the bottom-left corner of the window when an SSL connection is active.

Web servers can also "self-sign" their own certificates. When you browse a Web site and a dialog tells you that the browser can't verify a certificate, you've encountered a self-signed certificate. If you can't verify the certificate, you're vulnerable to a *man-in-the-middle attack* (someone masquerading as the Web site). However, if you can verify the certificate, then you're safe. Many companies and organizations, for instance, self-sign the certificates for their internal Web sites.

Thunderbird provides all the features you want in an e-mail client. It offers many useful capabilities, such as

- **Multiple e-mail accounts:** Set up accounts for yourself and your friends.
- **Spell checking:** Check your spelling before you send out a message.
- **Message searching:** I save all important (and many other) messages and search Thunderbird's message folder when I need to find personal information. (I also regularly back up my saved messages.)
- **IMAP capability:** IMAP (Internet Message Access Protocol) lets e-mail clients download message headers but not the messages themselves (unless you explicitly download the message). This lets you browse an e-mail account from many locations without affecting your messages.
- **SSL connections:** Thunderbird can securely connect to your mail server (usually your ISP) if you turn on SSL. You can configure IMAP to work via SSL, too.

Thunderbird is easy to use. Click the blue globe/envelope icon on the KDE Kicker, and it starts up.

You are presented with a configuration wizard the first time you use Thunderbird. The following instructions show how to configure the bird.

You can use the setup steps in this chapter whether running a permanent or live Knoppix instance. However, if running live Knoppix from the *Knoppix For Dummies* DVD (or a CD you download from `www.knoppix.net`), you must *repeat* the steps every time you reboot the PC unless you use a persistent home directory. (Chapter 3 shows you how to use a persistent home directory.)

Adding an e-mail account

Use the following instructions with Thunderbird to set up an IMAP-based e-mail account:

1. **Start Thunderbird by clicking its icon on the Kicker.**

   The Import Wizard dialog opens.

2. **Click the Next button.**

   The Thunderbird Mail and Newsgroup window opens (as shown in Figure 12-2) and the Account Wizard opens.

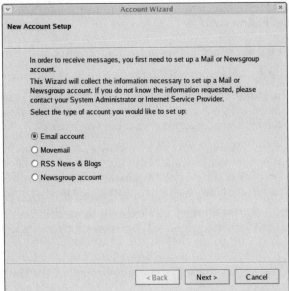

Figure 12-2:
The
Thunderbird
configura-
tion utility.

3. **You have the option of creating other types of accounts, but leave the Email Account option checked and click Next.**

   The Identity option opens in the Account Wizard.

4. **Enter your name and e-mail address in the boxes provided.**

   Your ISP supplies your e-mail address. Your mother and father supply your name.

5. **Click Next.**

   The Server Information option opens in the Account Wizard.

6. **Your ISP provides you with either a Post Office Protocol (POP) or an IMAP account — or both. Click IMAP if you have a choice.**

7. **Enter the names of your mail servers and then click Next.**

   • Enter the server name that *receives* your mail in the Incoming Server text box.

   • Enter the server that *sends* your mail in the Outgoing Server text box.

   The Account Wizard switches to the User Names option. The wizard uses your first initial and last name to construct a default e-mail account username.

8. **Change the default username to your ISP-assigned username (if they're different) and click Next.**

   Your e-mail address is displayed in the wizard.

9. **Change your e-mail address to your ISP-assigned address (if they're different) and click the Next button.**

   The Account Wizard displays the information you just entered.

10. **Click the Finish button and you exit from the wizard.**

Your new e-mail account is displayed as a folder in the upper-left corner of the Thunderbird window.

Before using your new Thunderbird e-mail account, you need to log into your ISP e-mail server.

1. **Click the Inbox subfolder of your ISP e-mail account.**

   The Mail Server Password Required dialog opens.

2. **Enter your ISP password in the text box.**

3. **Click the Use Password Manager to Save This Password button.**

4. **Click OK.**

   The Alert dialog opens, warning that you should protect your password. The following section describes how to do just that.

5. **Click OK in the Alert dialog.**

After you configure your ISP password, you should protect it by setting a Master password.

Setting and protecting your account password

When you enter an ISP e-mail account password, Thunderbird asks you if you want to save the password locally. Saving passwords locally means you don't have to manually enter them every time you access an account. This is very convenient but is a security hazard. Putting all your passwords in one place makes life very easy if a hacker finds them.

Fortunately, Thunderbird provides an option for encrypting your passwords. You set a Master password, and Thunderbird encrypts passwords whenever you enter them. All saved passwords are stored locally with strong encryption.

Protecting e-mail connections with SSL

You can increase your protection from hackers by using SSL to protect your IMAP (imaps) connections to your ISP. Depending on your ISP's sophistication, you can protect *e-mail you receive, e-mail you send,* and *your e-mail account password.*

Use the following instructions to set up imaps on your Thunderbird e-mail client:

1. **Select Tools⇨Account Settings.**

   The Account Settings dialog opens.

2. **Click Server Settings.**

   The right window switches to Server Settings.

3. **Select the Use Secure Connection (SSL) radio button.**

   This protects your *incoming* mail. The imap port number changes from 143 to 993.

4. **If your ISP offers encryption for *outgoing* messages, click the Outgoing Server (SMTP) option and then click the button for your ISP's mail server.**

   Depending on what your ISP offers, click the *TLS* (transport-layer security) button or *SSL* button. If you're not sure that your ISP offers outgoing encryption but think it might, click TLS (if available).

5. **Click OK.**

Whenever you start Thunderbird, you enter your Master password, and your individual passwords are decrypted and available for you to use. The decrypted passwords are stored in memory, not on your hard drive. When you exit Thunderbird the decrypted passwords disappear.

If your ISP lets you use *IMAP over SSL (imaps),* you can protect your incoming e-mail-reading sessions and your e-mail account password from prying eyes. The imaps protocol protects your incoming e-mail connection just like https protects your browsing sessions. The sidebar "Protecting e-mail connections with SSL" shows how to configure Thunderbird for imaps. If you want to configure for imaps before you enter your e-mail account password, follow the steps in that sidebar before setting your password.

Follow these steps to set the Master Password:

1. **Click Tools⇨Options in the Thunderbird window.**

   The Options window opens.

2. **Click the Saved Passwords option and click the Master Password button.**

   The Master Password dialog opens.

3. **Click the Use a Master Password to Encrypt Stored Passwords button.**

4. **Click the Change Password button.**

   The Change Master Password dialog opens.

5. **Enter your Master password in both of these text boxes:**

   - New Password
   - New Password (Again)

6. **Click OK.**

   Control returns to the Master Password dialog.

7. **Click OK.**

8. **Click OK one more time in the Options dialog.**

Your e-mail account password is now encrypted and protected from hackers. You must enter the Master password when you start up Thunderbird to decrypt and access your e-mail account password. You can sleep well at night again.

Part V
Working (And Playing) with Knoppix

The 5th Wave   By Rich Tennant

"We take network security very seriously here."

In this part . . .

Knoppix provides the tools you need for common computing tasks, and this part shows how to use them.

Chapter 13 introduces OpenOffice.org's desktop productivity suite. The suite provides the same functionality as Microsoft Office — word processing, spreadsheets, slides, and so on — and reads and writes to Microsoft files, too! Chapter 14 shows how to listen to MP3 and Ogg Vorbis music as well as watch TV. Chapter 15 describes how to connect your Knoppix workstation to an existing printer. Chapter 16 shows how to connect your computer to a file server.

Chapter 13

Using OpenOffice.org

*O*penOffice.org is an open source project to develop a Linux office-software suite (like Microsoft Office). OpenOffice.org's office suite provides all the functions you need on a desktop computer, such as word processing, spreadsheet creation, slide presentation, and drawing utilities.

The OpenOffice.org office suite is compatible with Microsoft Office. I wrote this book on OpenOffice.org Writer, and I had no problem interacting with my editors, who use Microsoft Word. Writing and editing books pushes word processors to their limits with macros, style sheets, and multiple layers of change tracking. This book shows OpenOffice.org's capability and reliability.

OpenOffice.org office suite consists of a word processor, spreadsheet application, presentation creator, and drawing applications. This chapter describes how to use these functions.

Working in the OpenOffice.org Window

To open an OpenOffice.org window, click the icon of a seagull on a background of blue water on the KDE Kicker. OpenOffice.org Writer opens, as shown in Figure 13-1.

Word processing is the most popular office application, so Knoppix opens it by default.

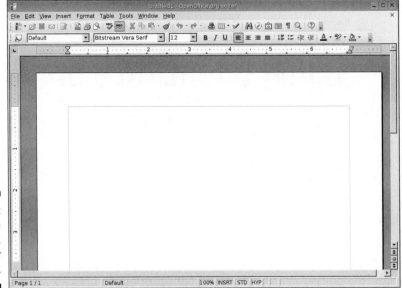

Figure 13-1:
The
OpenOffice.
org Writer
window.

The Writer window is virtually identical to any other OpenOffice.org window (Calc, Impress, and so on). The only differences are the functions each window performs.

You start the other OpenOffice.org applications from Writer by either

- Choosing File➪New and selecting the file type.
- Choosing K-Menu➪OpenOffice.org and selecting the application from the pull-down menu.

Starting any OpenOffice.org application opens a window that shows the same functional layout. Each application uses the same menu and toolbar layout and configuration. This makes using OpenOffice.org very easy and intuitive.

You can insert OpenOffice components within OpenOffice components. For instance, you can put a spreadsheet inside a drawing, which you can place inside a text document.

Toolbars

Open any OpenOffice.org application and you see several toolbars at the top, sides, and bottom of the window. The window layout includes the following objects:

- ✔ **Menu:** Houses the primary functions for the application at the top of the window.

- ✔ **Function bar:** Provides shortcuts to the most common functions in the Menu.

  For instance, click the floppy diskette icon to quickly save your document or spreadsheet.

- ✔ **Object bar:** Provides shortcuts to common object-oriented menu functions.

  You can simply click the Underline icon on the Object bar to underline a character instead of choosing Format⇨Character and selecting Underline.

- ✔ **Main Menu toolbar**

- ✔ **Status bar**

- ✔ **Ruler**

The Function and Object toolbars are positioned horizontally along the top of window and contain icons representing major functions like formatting and file operations. Position the mouse cursor over an icon and you see its name or a short description of its function.

I describe some of the primary OpenOffice.org functions in the following section.

Menus

Every OpenOffice.org application uses the same menu system. The common functions and actions are

- ✔ **File operations:** Gives you access to many file-oriented operations. The most useful options are described in the section "File Management" later in this chapter.

- ✔ **Edit:** Performs standard editing tasks such as cut, copy, and paste; accesses such useful functions as search options and change tracking.

  Change tracking reveals all of the author's blemishes and mistakes. It's the editor's communication channel of choice. It's also the bane of the poor author's existence. (I blame my mistakes on my high school for making it so easy to consistently cut English class.) Change tracking is useful for

  - • Collaborating with other people on a project.

  - • Keeping a log of your own changes.

✔ **View:** Change how you see on-screen elements such as magnification, toolbars, ruler bar, and text boundaries.

Zooming doesn't change the font size; it's like using a magnifying glass to look at a document.

✔ **Insert:** Places objects such as special characters, macros, tables, figures, and other documents into your OpenOffice.org document.

Click Insert⇨Special Character and a dialog full of character symbols opens. If you want to list the price of Knoppix in euros, find (toward the bottom of the menu) and click the € symbol and add a zero. Even given the U.S. dollar's fall against the euro, Knoppix is still a deal at € 0.0.

✔ **Format:** Changes your formatting. Highlighting text and choosing Format⇨Default changes the text to a default of a 10-point Times New Roman font. You can change the format of a character, a paragraph, or an entire page at once, depending on what you select.

✔ **Tools:** Accesses a spell checker, a thesaurus, and such helpful functions as a general-purpose OpenOffice.org configuration utility. If you're a terrible speller (like me) or a terrible word-comer-upper-with (also like me), these functions help.

✔ **Help:** "Help! I need some help!" Well, go get some. Click Help⇨Contents, and the OpenOffice.org Help window opens. Use its Table of Contents tab, Index tab, Find fields (to search on keywords), and Bookmarks to find the help you need.

File Management

This section describes how to open and save files with OpenOffice.org.

Opening files

Use the File menu to access OpenOffice.org files. These are the most useful file-oriented functions:

✔ **New:** Select File⇨New, and a menu appears.

You select the file type of the new file that you want to create. File types include

• Text documents

• Spreadsheets

- Presentations (slide shows)
- Drawings

✓ **Open:** Select File➪Open and the File Selection dialog appears.

The dialog is a mini file manager that you use to select a file to open.

If you have trouble opening existing files, use the sidebar, "Opening existing files."

✓ **Save:** Choose File➪Save to save the file you're working on. You can continue using the file after saving. Alternatively, press Ctrl+S or click the floppy diskette icon in the Object bar to save the file.

✓ **Save As:** This menu opens a dialog that lets you select the name, location, and type of the file you want to save. See the section "Saving files" for more information.

✓ **Close:** Select File➪Close to close your current file without exiting from the OpenOffice.org window.

✓ **Exit:** Choose File➪Exit to close your current file and exit from OpenOffice.org.

Opening existing files

In some cases, OpenOffice.org Writer *freezes* in Knoppix when you try to reopen a file. If it freezes on your Knoppix system, you can easily fix the problem. Follow these steps:

1. **Click the Konsole (Terminal Program) icon in the KDE Kicker.**

2. **Enter the following commands:**

```
sed @@hye 's/export OPENOFFICE_MOZILLA_FIVE_HOME\
/#export OPENOFFICE_MOZILLA_FIVE_HOME/' \
/opt/openoffice/program/soffice > temp
```

This finds and inactivates the offending environmental variable from the script that starts OpenOffice.org Writer.

3. **Type this command to save the changes to the OpenOffice.org Writer startup script:**

```
sudo mv @@hyf temp /opt/openoffice/program/soffice
```

4. **Type this command to make the new script executable:**

```
sudo chmod 755 /opt/openoffice/program/soffice
```

After you apply this fix once, it's *automatically* applied every time you start Knoppix if you either

✓ Run Knoppix from a permanent installation.

✓ Use the Persistent Knoppix Image option when you boot Knoppix directly from the DVD.

You can also do other interesting and useful operations, like exporting a file as a PDF (Portable Document Format) document. Just select File⇨Export as PDF. PDF documents are used extensively to distribute documents.

Saving files

Choose File⇨Save As to open the Save As dialog. This dialog lets you select the name of the file, the directory (folder) and device to save the file to, and the file type. The following list describes your options:

- ✔ **Filename:** If you're saving a new file for the first time, enter the name to save the file as in the Name text box. Otherwise, the text box displays the original filename, which you can change or not as desired.

- ✔ **Save in folder:** This pull-down menu lets you select other common locations and devices in which to save your file. For instance, select Home to save to your home directory.

- ✔ **Browse for other folders:** Clicking this pull-down menu opens a mini file manager that defaults to your current directory. Use it to select another folder in which to save your file if you want to change locations.

- ✔ **File type pull-down menu:** OpenOffice.org lets you save to other file formats. The default is always the native OpenOffice.org format, but OpenOffice knows about common formats, such as word processing and spreadsheet file types.

Configuration

OpenOffice.org has many configuration options. You can control most of them through the Configuration and Options utilities. Choose Tools⇨ Configuration to open the configuration utility.

The configuration utility modifies the following OpenOffice.org functions:

- ✔ **Menu:** Reprograms the menu functions and creates new menus.

- ✔ **Keyboard:** Reprograms the keyboard to fit your preferences.

- ✔ **Status bar:** Shows what's going on with your OpenOffice.org window. You can toggle display options such as date and time through this tab.

- ✔ **Toolbars:** Creates, deletes, customizes, shows, and hides toolbars.

- ✔ **Events:** Assigns macros to actions like opening or closing OpenOffice.org.

Writing with Writer

OpenOffice.org Writer can read and write several common file formats. To save a file in another format, click File⇨Save As. The File Selection dialog opens. You can save Writer files in these formats:

✔ **Microsoft Word 97/2000/XP:** These files use the .doc suffix and are compatible — as you might expect — with Word 97, Word 2000, and Word XP documents; Word 2003 formatting is not yet available.

✔ **Microsoft Word 95:** These files use the .doc suffix and are compatible with Word 95 documents.

✔ **Microsoft Word 6.0:** These files use the .doc suffix and are compatible with the very old Word 6.0 documents.

✔ **Rich Text Format:** Rich Text Format (RTF) is a universal document format that all popular word processors understand.

✔ **Starwriter:** Sun Microsystems sells the Starwriter word processor. OpenOffice.org's

Writer is derived from Starwriter. Save files in these formats to exchange with Starwriter.

✔ **Text:** You can save files as simple text with no formatting.

✔ **HTML:** OpenOffice.org provides an HTML (HyperText Markup Language) editor to create Web pages. Click File⇨New⇨HTML Document to access the editor.

When you first open Writer, you see the main window plus the Paragraph Styles dialog (refer to Figure 13-1). Writer gives you many formatting styles to select from in this window. For instance, I used the Heading 1 style to format the heading of this section.

You can open the Paragraph Styles dialog at any time by pressing F11. Formatting text with a style inserts the style into the Apply Style submenu near the upper-left corner of OpenOffice.org Writer window.

The configuration utility is *context-driven.* It gives specific options for the OpenOffice.org application you configure with it. For instance, the Keyboard options are different for Writer and Calc.

Reprogramming the keyboard can save time and effort. OpenOffice.org Writer comes with built-in function shortcuts. For instance, pressing F1 opens the Help window. You can reprogram the keys to meet your preferences. Use the following instructions to change the F4 key to reformat the selected word or words to boldface:

1. **Click Tools⇨Customize.**

    The Customize dialog opens.

2. **Scroll down and click the Format option in the Functions/Category menu.**

3. **Scroll down and click Bold in the Functions/Function menu.**

4. **Click F4 in the Shortcut keys menu and click the Modify button.**

The F4 key (along with the default Ctrl+B combination) appears in the Keys submenu.

5. Click OK.

The dialog closes and the F4 key is set to format text with bold font.

The Configuration dialog provides radio buttons that set the context for any changes you make for either

✔ **OpenOffice.org:** This gives you the universal configuration context.

✔ **Individual OpenOffice.org applications (such as Writer):** This option (the default) makes the utility context-specific to the application in use (in this case, Writer).

Chapter 14

Using Multimedia

Knoppix is a great multimedia platform. It provides audio and video applications that make it your portal into the world of entertainment.

This chapter describes how to use the Knoppix multimedia applications, such as XMMS, Xine, and xawtv.

Multimedia applications are best run from a permanent Knoppix installation. Running off a hard drive is faster and provides more space for saving and working with media; you can also more easily use your DVD or CD-ROM drives. However, you can use the instructions in this chapter when you run a live Knoppix instance from the companion DVD (or a CD you download from www.knoppix.net or www.knoppix.org). When necessary, I point out what you have to do when running from a live Knoppix instance.

Using Knoppix to Play Audio Media

The following sections describe how to use Knoppix to play audio files. Your audio source can be traditional music CDs or newer MP3 files. I also describe how to connect to open source radio streams.

Playing CDs

No computer worth its salt gets out of bed without working as a CD player. Knoppix gets out of bed early *every* morning.

Working from live Knoppix

If you're running a live Knoppix instance, you first have to eject the Knoppix DVD or CD. How is that possible if you're running Knoppix from the disc? The following instructions describe the process:

1. **Click the Konsole (Terminal Program) icon on the Kicker.**

   You're about to remove the Knoppix DVD that stores all Knoppix programs and utilities. Much of the software that live Knoppix uses is already stored on ram disk and isn't affected by removing the Knoppix disc. However, Knoppix might not be able to access some programs while you're playing audio CDs. In that case, you have to wait until you return the Knoppix disc to access the software. There's also a chance that Knoppix might freeze up, in which case you have to reboot.

2. **Enter the following commands in the Konsole window.**

   ```
   sudo umount -l /cdrom
   sudo eject
   ```

   Your CD/DVD drive opens.

3. **Remove the Knoppix DVD and insert the music CD.**

4. **Click the K-Menu and select Multimedia⇨xine.**

   Xine opens two windows: a control GUI and a display GUI. The control GUI controls the operation of the media, while the display GUI shows videos or graphical representations of the music. Figure 14-1 shows the control window.

Figure 14-1:
The Xine
control
window.

5. **Click the CD button toward the right side of the control window.**

   The CD starts playing. Can you dig it?

6. **Eject the CD when you're done listening and replace it with the Knoppix DVD.**

7. **Type the following command in the Konsole window.**

```
sudo mount /dev/cdrom /cdrom
```

The Knoppix DVD is mounted and ready to go.

Working from a permanent Knoppix installation

Here's how to play an audio CD from a permanent Knoppix instance:

1. **Put your CD in the drive.**

   An icon for the CD eventually appears on the Desktop.

2. **Start the player.**

   You can either

   • Right-click the icon and select the Play option.

   • Click the K-Menu and select Multimedia⇨xine.

   Your CD starts playing. Can you dig it?

3. **Eject the CD when you're done listening.**

Listening to MP3s

MP3 is a commercial, proprietary audio format that compresses analog audio signals into a digital form, so you can store a lot of tunes on a small player or CD.

If you own an iPod or similar player, or if you download music to your computer, the files probably are encoded in the MP3 format.

The X Multimedia System (XMMS) comes ready to play MP3s. Rock on:

1. **Download (legally) an MP3 file to your computer.**

2. **Open XMMS (K-Menu⇨Multimedia⇨XMMS).**

3. **Right-click anywhere on the right half of the XMMS dialog and select Play File.**

   The Play Files dialog opens.

4. **Select the MP3 file and click Play.**

   You groove to your music.

Klaus likes the XMMS visualization plug-ins, especially "What a goom." They provide colorful and fun-to-watch visual metaphors to enhance your listening experience.

Tune in with Ogg Vorbis

Ogg Vorbis is an open source audio format that provides an alternative to the proprietary MP3. It also provides better fidelity and compression than MP3, plus it contains no patented algorithms or restrictively licensed software.

Knoppix packs several Ogg Vorbis–capable multimedia players. XMMS is a nice tight package for playing Ogg and MP3 encoded music files. The following section describes how to use XMMS.

XMMS playback

You can use XMMS to listen to the radio online by following these instructions:

1. **Make your Internet connection, if necessary.**

   Part IV has information and instructions about making Internet connections.

2. **Open Firefox.**

   Virgin Radio — `www.virginradio.co.uk` — is just one Web site that provides great Ogg streams.

3. **Type the URL of the streaming Ogg source into your Firefox browser.**

   For instance, type Virgin's URL — `www.virginradio.co.uk` — in the Firefox text box in the upper-middle of the window and press Enter.

   You go to Virgin Radio's home page. (I like Virgin Radio, especially because the eight-hour Albuquerque-to-U.K. time difference makes it easy to pick up their late-night/early-morning rotations.)

Navigating XMMS

You can manually start XMMS playing an Internet stream if you know the URL. You can find the URL from either looking at the Web site or at XMMS itself.

XMMS gives you two methods to figure out the URL for an audio stream:

✔ Open the File Info dialog and click the "I" button on the left side of the window.

The dialog shows the URL.

✔ Check your `/tmp` directory for the `/tmp/live.pls` (live playlist). It contains the URL for the Internet audio stream.

For example, you can play the URL for Virgin Radio as follows:

1. Click the Konsole (Terminal Program) icon on the Kicker.

2. Type the following command in the window:

   `xmms http://ogg.smgradio.com/vr160.ogg`

4. **Click the Click Here link.**

5. **Click the LISTEN NOW link on the Virgin Radio home page.**

   The LISTEN TO US ONLINE window opens.

6. **Click the button for your connection type:**

   - Ogg Vorbis Modem

   - Ogg Vorbis Broadband

   The Opening Live.pls dialog opens. It defaults to using Rhythmbox to play Ogg Vorbis and MP3–formatted streams.

7. **Click OK.**

   The Rhythmbox configuration dialog opens.

8. **Click Next.**

9. **Click Skip and then click Finish.**

   The Rhythmbox window, like the one shown in Figure 14-2, opens.

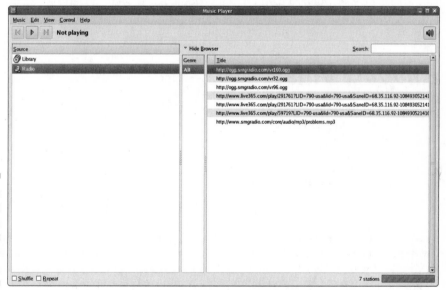

Figure 14-2:
Rhythmbox playing an Internet radio station.

10. **Click the Play button at the top of the Rhythmbox window.**

Rhythmbox works like a typical physical or software-based player. Click the standard buttons to play, pause, stop, and so on.

XMMS shortcuts

XMMS provides *shortcut buttons* on the left side of its window. The buttons are labeled *O, A, I, D,* and *V.*

The shortcut buttons are difficult to see. Click D to double the window size.

The shortcut buttons correspond to the following options.

- ✔ **O:** Opens the Options menu.

  You can access every XMMS configuration and feature from this menu.

- ✔ **A:** Toggles the Always on Top feature.

  When toggled on, the XMMS window remains on top of other windows.

- ✔ **I:** Opens the File Info dialog. It displays information about the filename, directory (for instance, the CD-ROM), or Internet stream.

- ✔ **D:** Doubles the size of the XMMS window. Clicking a second time returns it to the normal size.

- ✔ **V:** Opens a menu that lets you change what the left — visualization — side of the window displays.

Knoppix Video

Knoppix also acts as a mini movie theater. You can watch DVDs by using utilities supplied by Knoppix.

DVDs with Xine

This section shows how to play older, unencrypted DVDs.

The content gatekeepers of the world like their comfy, cloistered environment. They ensure it stays that way by *encrypting* their DVDs to prevent viewing by both pirates and honest individuals. That's right, you might not be able to watch the DVD you legitimately purchased. The DVD gatekeepers even sue open source developers who figure out their encryption schemes, so playing commercial DVDs on Linux is limited. It's no different than if a book publisher encrypted its text and allowed you to decrypt it only if you purchased a commercial product. It's a terrible situation.

Knoppix includes the Xine DVD player. So get your DVD, some popcorn, a couch, and a potato. Here's how to watch:

1. **Pop that DVD into your DVD-ROM drive.**

   Unfortunately, you need a DVD-capable drive to use these instructions.

2. **Right-click the CD-ROM icon on the KDE Desktop (upper left).**

   A pop-up (video) menu appears. (Don't let your popcorn burn.)

3. **Click Actions and select DVD/VCD-Player.**

   The fabulous Xine window opens dramatically.

4. **Right-click anywhere in the Xine window and select GUI Visibility.**

   The Xine control panel dialog opens.

5. **Click the DVD button on the player window.**

   If you're trying to play an *encrypted* DVD, an error dialog appears. Click the Done button to finish your frustration.

   The FBI doesn't encrypt the warning message it puts at the beginning of DVDs. You can always watch it. Mulder would be proud.

I want my Knoppix TV

You can't get away from TV when you're on your computer. Ironic, huh?

To watch TV through your Knoppix computer, you need a PCI TV tuner card. Knoppix works with PCI- and USB-based tuners based on the bttv-compatible chipset. You can find more information about compatible TV tuner cards in the file /usr/src/linux/Documentation/video4linux/CARDLIST.bttv.

Follow these steps to install and configure your tuner:

1. **Connect your TV tuner card and record its chip and tuner type.**

   • If you're using a PCI TV device, insert it into your computer's motherboard.

   Consult the owner's manual before installing the tuner into your computer.

   • If you're using a USB TV device, plug it into your USB port.

   You need the chipset and tuner information in the following steps.

2. **Click the K-Menu and select KNOPPIX⇨Configure⇨TV card⇨ Configure TV card (bttv-chipset).**

The Run as Root – KDE su dialog opens.

3. **Type the** `root` **password and optionally click the Keep Password button.**

   The Initial Setup of TV-card (Step 1/3) dialog opens.

4. **Select your TV Card type from the menu and click OK.**

   The Initial Setup of TV-card (Step 2/3) dialog opens.

5. **Select your tuner from the menu and click OK.**

   The Initial setup of TV-card (Step 3/3) dialog opens.

6. **Click OK.**

   The Initial Setup of xawtv (Step 1/4) dialog opens.

7. **Select the TV norm for the type used where you live and click OK.**

   The United States uses NTSC; Japan uses NTSC-JP; and Europe mostly uses PAL, although France and Eastern Europe use SECAM. You can find the standard for your geographical location at `www.alkenmrs.com/video/wwstandards1.html`.

8. **Select your geographically dependent broadcast frequency table and click OK.**

   The Initial Setup of xawtv (Step 3/4) dialog opens, asking whether you accept the configuration.

9. **Click Yes.**

The xawtv software opens a window that displays its progress as it searches each channel (frequency) for an active signal. When it finishes, the xawtv TV window opens. *Happy Days* for all — you'll be in *7th Heaven!*

Chapter 15

Printing with Knoppix

. . . .

In This Chapter

▶ Connecting to a local printer

▶ Connecting to a networked printer

. . . .

*P*rinting is a messy and sometimes difficult process. Bits of ink or toner must be precisely placed on paper to create legible text and images. The job of configuring your computer to print can make you crazy.

Knoppix, however, makes printing a breeze. It provides an easy-to-use and comprehensive printer configuration utility. This chapter describes how to connect and configure a printer to your Knoppix computer. It also shows how to connect to a networked printer.

Johannes Gutenberg would be proud.

 The instructions in this chapter are oriented toward a permanent Knoppix installation. You can also use the steps in this chapter when running a live Knoppix instance from the *Knoppix For Dummies* DVD (or a CD that you download from www.knoppix.net or www.knoppix.org). However, in that case, you must *repeat* the steps every time you reboot the PC unless you use a persistent home directory. (Chapter 3 shows you how to use a persistent home directory.)

Locally Connected Printers

This section describes how to — ta-da! — print from a Knoppix computer to a locally connected printer.

Connection

Connecting your printer to your Knoppix computer requires that the printer be close enough to connect to your computer:

- *Parallel* cables are reliable to roughly 20 feet (or, more roughly, 6 meters).
- *USB* cables are reliable to 16.5 feet.

Configuration

When your printer is connected to your Knoppix computer, follow these instructions to make it work:

1. **Select K-Menu⇨KNOPPIX⇨Configure⇨Configure Printer(s).**

    If running from a permanent Knoppix installation, the Run as Root – KDE su dialog opens.

2. **If prompted, type the `root` password in the dialog and click OK.**

    Click the Keep Password button if you don't want to re-enter the `root` password the next time you run the printer configuration utility.

    The Configure – KDE Control Module dialog opens, as shown in Figure 15-1.

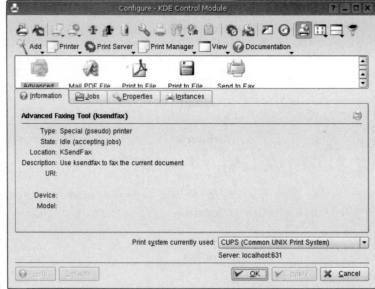

Figure 15-1:
The
Configure –
KDE Control
Module
helps you
configure
your printer.

Meta-view: Printing locally

Setting up a local printer is as simple as *one-two-three:*

1. Connect the printer.

2. Configure your computer for the printer.

3. Print to the printer.

---

3. **Choose Add⇨Add Printer/Class.**

   The Add Printer Wizard opens.

4. **Click Next.**

   The dialog shows a menu of printer queue types.

5. **Click the Local Printer (Parallel, Serial, USB) button and then click Next.**

   The dialog shows the Local Port Selection menu. Knoppix is good at detecting printers, so your printer should show up in this menu.

   Knoppix supports serial printers, but good luck finding one. Serial printers have gone the way of the eight-track player. I don't discuss configuring serial printers because they're so rare.

6. **Perform the following step, depending on whether your printer is detected:**

   • If your printer is detected, select your printer (which shows up in the URI text box).

   • If your printer isn't detected, click the port type *(USB* or *Parallel).*

7. **Click Next.**

   The dialog shows the Printer Model Selection window.

   The printer manufacturer and model are shown if they were detected in Step 6.

8. **Find and select your printer's manufacturer and model and then click Next.**

   The Driver Select dialog opens. You're given a choice of several printer drivers, including one that is recommended.

9. **Select the recommended driver type by clicking the driver.**

10. **Click Next.**

    The Printer Test dialog opens.

11. **Start or skip printer testing.**

- • If you want to test the printer, click Test and then follow the instructions in the sidebar "Testing your local printer."

   I recommend testing.

- • If you want to skip testing, click Next.

12. **Skip the banner selection and click Next.**

   The Printer Quota Settings dialog opens.

   The banner section is important only when many people print to the same printer.

13. **You can skip setting quotas and click Next.**

   The Users Access Settings dialog opens. It allows you to deny certain users printer access.

14. **You can skip setting any user access limitations and click Next.**

15. **Assign your printer a name and click Next.**

   The Confirmation dialog shows the results of your configuration labor.

   Traditionally, Linux uses the default printer name of lp. Many applications print using the default. Using the name lp increases the chances that Linux applications will work without modifying their default printer configuration.

16. **Click Finish.**

   Control returns to the Configure – Printer window.

17. **Click Close.**

You can now print to your printer. For instance, to print from Firefox, Thunderbird, or OpenOffice.org Writer, choose File⇨Print. A dialog opens from which you can select the printer to use (if necessary) and then print by clicking OK.

Testing your local printer

If you use the Test option when you configure a local printer, the Information – KDE Control Module dialog opens. You can then send a print job to your printer. If it prints, your printer configuration is good. If not, you should repeat the configuration steps and use a different driver.

Check your printer's output:

✔ If the output text looks crisp and readable, click OK.

Knoppix automatically returns to the Add Printer Wizard so you can finish the configuration.

✔ If the output doesn't look crisp or if it looks like random characters, then revisit the printer configuration instructions in this section but select and test a different driver.

Networked Printers

The Knoppix printer configuration utility makes it easy to connect to a networked printer. The rest of this chapter guides you through the process.

For you to connect to a networked printer, your Knoppix computer must be able to access a networked print server.

Essential information

When you connect to a network printer, you may need the following information about the print server:

- ✔ Network share name or IP address
- ✔ Username and, if necessary, password
- ✔ Queue type

These queue types are often used:

- ✔ **CUPS:** The *Common UNIX Printer System* is the standard Linux printer system.

- ✔ **LPD:** The *Linux Printer Daemon* (LPD) is the traditional printing service that is quickly being replaced by CUPS.

  LPD Must Die! That isn't a Quentin Tarantino movie; it's the opinion of the Linux printing community.

- ✔ **Network printer with built-in print server:** Many consumer and most commercial printers provide network connections and built-in print servers.

  The most common built-in network print server is Hewlett Packard's JetDirect system.

- ✔ **SMB:** *Service Message Block* is the basis for much file sharing today. Clients transfer files to be printed to the print server via SMB. Linux computers can "speak" the SMB language (protocol) by using the Samba system.

  Samba lets Linux computers provide print services to Windows computers.

Meta-view: Networked printing

Configuring your Knoppix computer for a network printer is straightforward. The following list describes the process:

1. Connect your computer to a network.

2. Select the type of network printing service to use.

3. Configure your computer for the printer.

4. Print a test job to the printer.

Connecting to a networked printer

You need to tell your Knoppix computer where to find the remote, networked printer. After it's located, you configure Knoppix to work with the printer.

Before using the following instructions, you must

✔ Connect your computer to a private network that has a remote printer.

✔ Know the remote printer's *print queue* type.

   If you don't know what type of print queue serves the printer, either

   • Consult your system administrator or help desk (if you're working on a corporate network).

   • Log into your print server and observe the print queue type (on a home network).

You can click the Scan button to browse for network printers.

Starting the configuration

The following steps describe how to start configuring your network printer:

1. **Select K-Menu⇨KNOPPIX⇨Configure⇨Configure Printer(s).**

   If you're running from a permanent Knoppix installation, the Run as Root – KDE su dialog opens.

2. **If prompted, type the** `root` **password and click OK.**

   The Configure – Printers dialog opens.

3. **Choose Add⇨Add Printer/Class.**

   The Add Printer Wizard opens.

4. **Click Next.**

   The Backend Selection dialog shows a menu of printer queue types.

The following section shows how to select your printer's queue.

Selecting printer queue

The Backend Selection dialog lets you choose from several types of print server queues. The following sections show how to use your printer's print queue type.

CUPS print servers

If your network has a CUPS network print server, follow these steps to use it:

1. **In the Backend Selection dialog, click the Remote CUPS Server (IPP/HTTP) button and then click Next.**

   The User Identification dialog opens.

2. **If the print server requires *authentication,* click the Normal Account button and enter a username and password.**

   The Remote IPP Server dialog opens.

3. **Enter the printer server name in the Host text box.**

   The Remote IPP Printer Selection dialog opens.

4. **Select your printer from the window and click Next.**

SMB print servers

If your network has an SMB network print server (either Windows or Linux with Samba), follow these steps to use it:

1. **In the Backend Selection dialog, click the SMB Shared Printer (Windows) button and then click Next.**

   The User Identification dialog opens.

2. **If the print server requires *authentication,* either**

   • Click the Normal Account button and enter a username and password.

     Use a Normal Account if you have a user account on the print server.

- Select the Guest account option.

  Use the Guest account option if you don't have a user account on the print server.

3. **Click Next.**

   The SMB Printer Settings dialog opens.

4. **Enter the Workgroup, server name, and printer name as appropriate.**

5. **Click Next.**

Network printers with built-in servers

If your network printer has an embedded print server (such as JetDirect), follow these steps to use it:

1. **Click Network Printer (TCP) and then click Next.**

   The Network Printer Identification dialog opens.

2. **Enter the printer network share name or IP address.**

   If you don't know the network name or IP address, click the Scan button and let Knoppix find them.

3. **Press Enter to select the prefilled value of** 9100 **in the Port text box.**

   9100 is the default JetDirect port.

4. **Click Next.**

LPD print servers

If your network has an LPD-based network print server, follow these steps to use it:

1. **Click the Remote LPD Queue button and then click Next.**

   The LPD Queue Information dialog opens.

2. **Enter the printer's hostname (or numerical IP address) and the queue name in the respective text boxes.**

3. **Click Next.**

Finishing the configuration

After you select and configure your printer server type, the Printer Model Selection dialog opens.

Use the following instructions to finish your network printer configuration:

1. **If the dialog doesn't recognize your printer, identify the printer:**

   a. Scroll down the Manufacturer submenu and click your printer's manufacturer.

   b. Scroll down the Model submenu and click your printer model.

2. **Click Next.**

   You're given a choice of several printer drivers, including a recommended or default type.

3. **Select the recommended driver type by clicking Next.**

4. **Click the Test button.**

   The Information – KDE Control Module dialog opens.

5. **Check your printer's output and click OK.**

   Control returns to the Add Printer Wizard.

6. **Click Next to *skip* the banner selection.**

   The banner is important only when many people use the same printer.

7. **Click Next to *skip* the quota settings.**

   The Users Access Settings dialog opens. It lets you deny a user printer access.

8. **Click Next.**

9. **Assign your printer a name and click Next.**

   The Confirmation dialog shows the results of your configuration labor.

10. **Click the Finish button.**

    Control returns to the Configure – Printer window.

11. **Click Close.**

Good deal — you can print across your private network. Your computer no longer needs to be in proximity to that mechanical beast.

You can check the status of your print jobs by clicking the Jobs tab in the Configure – KDE Control Module dialog. You'll see all the queued jobs — if there are any — in the subwindow at the bottom of the dialog. You can pause, cancel, and change the order of the jobs by clicking the appropriate buttons above the queue subwindow; move the mouse cursor over the buttons to find out their names.

Chapter 16

Sharing Files on Your Network

*K*noppix has the great advantage of booting directly from DVD or CD-ROM, so you don't have to install Knoppix on your computer. Insert the DVD and go to town. But sunny days are followed by rain. The down side of this arrangement is the lack of a place to hang your hat. Booting Knoppix live from DVD doesn't automatically give you a permanent home directory.

Actually, the weather forecast is for a very short period of light rain followed by sunshine: The lack of a permanent home directory isn't that much of a problem. Knoppix provides several methods to save your work. This chapter shows how to use network-based storage (if available) for your home directory.

File-Sharing Basics

Knoppix file sharing lets its users have their cake and eat it, too:

- ✔ **Lower administration costs** come from building and managing one central file server, not many individual disks.

- ✔ **User convenience** comes from using one home directory, not many.

This chapter shows how to use both major types of network-based storage:

- ✔ **Network File System (NFS):** This system is found primarily on Linux and UNIX systems.

  Knoppix provides NFS by default.

- ✔ **Windows file shares:** Microsoft Windows file servers share their files with other Windows computers. Knoppix provides the *Samba file share system* that's compatible with Windows and allows you to use Windows file shares.

The NFS and Samba file-sharing systems

- ✔ Let you use remote directories (*folders* in Windows-speak) as if they were located on your local computer.
- ✔ Are based on the client-server model. The server provides services to the client; multiple clients can connect to a server.

In this chapter, I assume that you have access to a network that provides either NFS, Samba, or both.

This chapter is geared toward helping you configure a Knoppix DVD or CD to use NFS and Samba file shares. However, you can use remote file systems on a permanent Knoppix installation.

Configuring an NFS Client

NFS is found primarily on Linux and UNIX systems.

NFS isn't the government agency that funded the early development of the Internet — that's the National Science Foundation (NSF). NFS is a network-based file-sharing system that's quite easy to use. This section assumes that your Knoppix computer is connected to a local area network (LAN) that provides NFS service. You find NFS servers in many professional network environments, such as businesses and universities.

Chapter 23 shows how you can build your own NFS or Samba file server for your private network.

The sidebar, "Meta-view: Connecting to an NFS server," provides an overview of the process of connecting to an existing NFS server.

NFS is commonly used to provide centralized home directories:

- ✔ The server exports the /home directory, and the clients mount it.
- ✔ User accounts on the client use the mounted /home directory to provide local users with a home directory.

The following section shows how to mount an NFS file system from an NFS file server. Connect your computer to the LAN and then use the following sections to access NFS shares from your Knoppix computer.

Chapters 10 and 11 show how to connect your Knoppix computer to a private network — either wired or wireless. NFS works on both, although a wireless network is generally slower than a wired one.

Meta-view: Connecting to an NFS server

Connecting to an NFS server is straightforward. You configure the server to allow your client access to its directories and then connect the client to the server.

This chapter concentrates on mounting a user account home directory. The key to this type of NFS configuration is ensuring that the user and group identifiers (uid and gid) match on both the NFS server and the client. You need to work closely with your friendly system administrator (sysadmin). If you manage your own system, consult yourself. (And charge yourself a hefty consulting fee.)

These are the basic steps to set up your NFS server:

1. Export a directory from the NFS server.

   Ask your local administrator to do this, if necessary.

You must ensure that the client and server user accounts match up. By default, NFS uses user IDs (uid) to permit or deny access. The client user account must have the same uid as the share on the server in order to fully access that resource. NFS is often used to permit a user on one machine to access the equivalent server account directories.

2. Connect your Knoppix client computer to a network with an NFS server.

3. Configure Knoppix to mount the NFS server home directory.

4. Mount the home directory from the NFS server onto your computer.

5. Save your NFS client settings to a USB drive or floppy diskette.

Create and export a user account on the NFS server

This section describes how to obtain information about your local (client) user account to be used by the NFS server. Your local user account must match the account on the NFS server.

The following instructions find the information that the NFS server sysadmin needs to export your Knoppix user account:

1. **Log in to your** knoppix **user account.**

2. **Open a terminal window.**

3. **Enter the following command to obtain your local (client) user account ID (**uid**) and group ID (**gid**).**

```
id
```

When running from the live Knoppix DVD, you're automatically logged in to the knoppix user account with a uid and gid of 1000. However, these instructions are intended to be used only from a permanent installation.

4. **Type the following command to obtain your Knoppix computer's hostname.**

```
hostname
```

The default hostname of the live Knoppix instance is box.

When you have the uid and gid for your local user account, give them to the NFS server system administrator and ask the administrator to

- ✔ Create a *user account* with the same uid and gid.

- ✔ Export your *home directory* to your Knoppix computer.

  Linux computers typically use the /home directory to house user directories. (Knoppix uses this convention.) Linux NFS servers typically export the /home directory to NFS clients.

After the NFS server is configured, you can mount it from the Knoppix NFS client.

Configure Knoppix as an NFS client

Follow these steps to export an NFS server file share to your NFS client:

1. **Open a Terminal Emulator (shell) window by clicking the Terminal icon on the Kicker.**

2. **Change to the root user by typing the following command.**

```
su -
```

3. **Enter the root password when prompted.**

4. **Start the portmap daemon.**

   This lets your computer work as an NFS client.

```
/etc/init.d/portmap restart
```

5. **Configure the portmap daemon to start automatically:**

```
update-rc.d portmap defaults
```

6. **Create a mount point (it's a home for your home) like this:**

```
mkdir /dirname
```

   For example, type mkdir /nfs to create a mount point.

7. **Modify the /etc/fstab configuration file to automatically mount the NFS file share by typing the following.**

```
nfsserver:/home  /dirname  nfs  defaults  0 0
```

Replace *nfsserver:* and */dirname* with the actual NFS server name and exported NFS share path (mount point). For instance, the following example uses the IP address of 192.168.1.1 and share path /nfs:

```
192.168.1.1:/home  /nfs  nfs  defaults  0 0
```

You can use the command `showmount -e *NFS-server-IP-address*` to find which NFS directories are exported and to whom.

Mount the remote file share

You can mount the NFS file share from the NFS server.

Type the following command to mount the NFS share:

```
mount -a -t nfs
```

The `-a` option mounts all the partitions found in /etc/fstab (including the NFS partition).

You can *test* your new configuration by entering this command:

```
ls -l /nfs-mount-dir
```

For example, if your NFS mount point is */nfs*, type `ls -l /nfs`.

You should see the contents of your remote user account home directory.

If you don't see the remote file share when you test the configuration, follow these steps:

1. **Try manually mounting the NFS share by inserting either the *actual name of the server* or the *numeric IP address* into the following command:**

   ```
   mount -t nfs *nfsserver*:/home /nfs
   ```

   For instance, if the server IP address is 192.168.1.200, enter

   ```
   mount -t nfs 192.168.1.200:/home /nfs
   ```

2. **If you can't access the NFS share after you try manually mounting the share, ask your system administrator to check the NFS server configuration.**

Saving your settings

If you run Knoppix from DVD or CD, you need to save the NFS settings on a USB memory stick or floppy diskette so you don't have to repeat these steps manually every time you boot your computer.

If you run a *permanent* Knoppix installation, your NFS configuration is saved automatically and reused every time you reboot. You don't need to save anything manually.

If you run Knoppix from a DVD or CD, the `Create a persistent disk image` utility can save your NFS client settings to a removable device. (This can be the same storage device that saves your home directory, as shown in Chapter 3.)

I use a USB drive to save my persistent settings because it's cheap, reliable, and easy to use.

Follow these steps to save your settings:

1. **Insert permanent media into your Knoppix computer.**

   You can use a USB memory stick or a floppy diskette.

2. **If you're not already running from a persistent Knoppix image, click the K-Menu and select KNOPPIX➪Configure➪Create a Persistent KNOPPIX Image.**

   The Create KNOPPIX Configuration Archive dialog opens.

3. **Click OK.**

   The dialog shows a menu of available storage devices.

4. **Click the /mnt/sda: [Disk/Partition] button and then click OK.**

   The dialog shows a progress meter as it saves your computer's configuration.

5. **Click OK.**

6. **Click the K-Menu and select Logout.**

7. **Click the Restart button to reboot your computer.**

   Enter either of the following commands at the `boot:` prompt to retrieve the settings (the first example mounts a USB stick):

   ```
   knoppix myconfig=/mnt/sda1
   ```

   ```
   knoppix myconfig=scan
   ```

8. **When the computer finishes booting, open a terminal.**

9. **Restart** `portmap` **and recreate the** `/nfs` **mount point with this command:**

```
sudo /etc/init.d/portmap restart
sudo mkdir /nfs
```

10. **Mount the remote directory with this command:**

```
sudo mount -a -t nfs
```

You can now use the `/nfs` directory to store files. Your home directory is still `/home/knoppix`, which lives in ram disk. However, everything you save to `/nfs/knoppix` is actually saved. You see it even after you reboot.

Using Samba and Windows File Shares

This section shows how to browse and mount an existing Windows file share.

The following sections show exactly how to make Samba mounts.

The instructions assume you have access to a network that exports a Windows file share. It doesn't matter whether the file share emerges from a Microsoft Windows file server or a Linux- (or UNIX-) based one; Linux-/UNIX-based servers use Samba to mimic the Windows facility.

Meta-view: Using a Windows file share

Samba was designed by Andrew Tridgell in the mid-1990s. He reverse-engineered the SMB protocol and created the Linux client-server software. His invention helped Linux find a handhold as a popular operating system because it was able to serve files to Windows computers. Before Linux and Samba, you had to go through expensive contortions to service Windows networks. I remember fighting management to purchase Sun's PC-NFS and then struggling to keep it running. Thank goodness for Samba. You can find more Samba information at: `http://samba.org`.

The overall process of using Windows file shares is straightforward. First, you must have

a server-exporting file system(s) (Windows or Linux) on a network. Second, you find and mount the share. Knoppix uses Samba to browse, access, and mount Windows file shares; Samba also works with Samba-based file exports on other Linux/UNIX file servers.

The Samba process for exporting shares has three steps:

1. Connect your Knoppix computer to a network with a Windows file server.

2. Find an exported file share directory.

3. Configure Knoppix to mount the remote file share.

TECHNICAL STUFF

Sharing Windows XP folders

If you want to use a Windows XP computer as a platform to experiment with using Knoppix and Samba, follow these steps to configure Windows XP to export a folder:

1. **Right-click the folder you want to export.**

   For instance, select your My Documents folder.

2. **Select Sharing and Security from the folder's Sharing menu.**

   The folder's Properties dialog opens.

3. **Select the Share This Folder on the Network option.**

4. **Click Apply.**

5. **Click OK.**

   You can browse and use the folder from Knoppix.

When you finish experimenting with exporting the folder, "unshare" the folder. Use the following instructions to unshare a folder.

1. **Right-click the folder you no longer want to export and select Sharing and Security.**

2. **Click the Share this Folder on the Network button.**

3. **Click Apply.**

4. **Click OK.**

The following sections show how to prep, configure, and use Windows files shares from your Knoppix computer. (You must first be connected to a network. Chapters 10 and 11 show how to connect to wired and wireless networks.) The network must provide Windows file shares that you can browse and interact with.

Browse and use a file share

KDE's Konqueror can function as a network file share browser.

Use the following steps to browse and use file shares on your Knoppix computer:

1. **Click the K-Menu and select KNOPPIX⇨Utilities⇨Samba Network Neighborhood.**

   If you're running from a permanent Knoppix installation, the Run as Root – KDE su dialog opens.

2. **Enter the** `root` **password if prompted.**

The smb:/ – Konqueror dialog opens, showing all the workgroups that it can access.

Windows file shares use the concept of *workgroups.* Computers and servers that need to work together and share common resources such as files, folders, and printers belong to the same workgroup. Workgroups organize "like-minded" resources.

3. Click the workgroup that you want to browse.

The dialog shows all the computers that belong to the workgroup.

4. Click the computer that you want to browse.

The dialog shows all the shares the computer exports. *Shares* are folders (*directories,* in Linux-speak) that the computer "shares" with the network.

Remember what your mother always said: Sharing is good.

5. Click the share you want to browse.

The dialog shows the contents of the share. (Figure 16-1 shows an example window.)

- If the file share is set for reading and writing, you can (surprise, surprise) read and write to the files and the folder.

- If the file share is set to read-only, you can read but not write to the files.

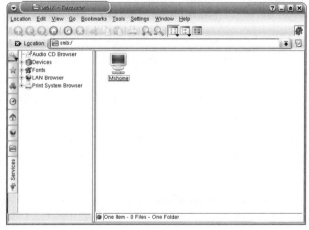

Figure 16-1:
Samba
Network
Neighbor-
hood shows
a typical
Windows
file share.

The dialog shows the contents of the file share. Take note of the file share's URL, displayed in the Location text box. The URL takes the form `//server/share`.

Automatically mounting Samba shares

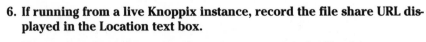

If a file share isn't password protected, you can make the file share mount permanent. Just add a line to the `/etc/fstab` file with your own configuration. Use the following format for the line:

```
//server/share /mount-point
    smbfs defaults 0 0
```

For example, use the following configuration to mount the CD-ROM drive from `192.168.1.`

```
//192.168.1.1/cdrom /samba
    smbfs defaults 0 0
```

When you reboot, the command mounts the share.

If a file share is password protected, you should manually run the `mount -a` command after reboot. (You can automatically feed the password to the mount process, but that requires saving the password in *clear text* in a file. That isn't a generally a good idea.)

6. **If running from a live Knoppix instance, record the file share URL displayed in the Location text box.**

   You can use this information if you want to mount the file share as a virtual local file system. The section "Mount the share," later in this chapter, has instructions.

7. **If you're running a permanent Knoppix installation, you can create an icon that points to the Samba share. Follow these steps:**

   a. Click and drag the file share icon onto the KDE desktop.

   b. Select the Link option when prompted to move, copy, or link the new icon.

   Now you can work with the file share folder as if it were on your own computer.

The KDE desktop file share icon is saved if you're working from a permanent Knoppix installation. You can reboot, click the file share icon, and access the files.

The following section shows how to permanently mount a Windows file share. The process works the same whether you're working from a live or permanent Knoppix instance.

Mount the share

The Samba Network Neighborhood utility lets you interactively use a remote share. The utility runs another utility (`kio_smb`), which connects to the server and shuttles data back and forth between the client and the server. When you log out or reboot, the connection disappears.

You can automate mounting the remote file share by using the `smbmount` utility. `smbmount` mounts shares as virtual file systems.

To use `smbmount`, you must know the Windows file share URL. This is the same file share URL that you use in the preceding section, "Browse and use a file share."

Follow these steps to use `smbmount`:

1. **Click the Terminal icon on the Kicker to open a shell.**

   The Shell Konsole window opens.

2. **Create a directory to mount your Samba partition on.**

   ```
   sudo mkdir /samba-mount-dir
   ```

   For example, create a directory called /samba.

   ```
   sudo mkdir /samba
   ```

3. **Type the following command to mount a Samba share:**

   ```
   smbmount //server/share /mount-point
   ```

   For example, the following command connects to the /cdrom share on the 192.168.1.1 server.

   ```
   smbmount //192.168.1.1/cdrom /samba
   ```

   The /mnt mount point is a generic location; you can create your own mount point, such as /smbmount.

4. **Enter the file share password if prompted.**

The remote file share mounts as if it were a local file system. You can use it just like any other file system.

Part VI

System Administration

In this part . . .

All work and no play, as the old bromide goes. Well, we started with the play, and now it's time to get down to work. This part shows how to perform numerous system administration functions from the simple to the complex.

Chapter 17 shows how to repair common Linux and Windows problems, such as nonbooting and otherwise misbehaving hard drives. Chapter 18 gets a little more complex, showing you how to fight malware, such as viruses and worms. Chapter 19 describes how to keep your computer software up to date, and Chapter 20 introduces system logging. Finally, Chapter 21 describes how to create your own customized Knoppix discs.

Chapter 17

Rescue Me: Repairing Linux and Windows Computers

. . . .

In This Chapter

▶ Booting with Knoppix

▶ Resetting root passwords

▶ Fixing Linux hard drives

▶ Cloning hard drives

. . . .

*D*o what I want, not what I say! If you could invent a computer that does that, you'd be a billionaire. Unfortunately, computers do exactly what they're told; that's the problem. Computers don't have minds of their own and (Hollywood portrayals aside) don't know when you or some programmer gives them the wrong instructions.

Many people (myself included) make a living fixing computers that do what they're told but not what was meant. Humans still fix computers. Knoppix plays into the equation by serving as a great platform for fixing computers and getting them to work for you instead of against you.

This chapter shows how to use Knoppix as a platform to fix some common computer problems, such as nonbooting disks. But the fix is in! Knoppix is it, so let's get on with it.

This chapter concentrates on using the *Knoppix For Dummies* DVD to fix misbehaving computers. Booting Knoppix "live" allows you to work on computers that won't otherwise boot. You can use many Knoppix utilities and programs to play doctor. (This chapter doesn't make use of a permanent Knoppix installation.)

Booting an Operating System

Like any human, computers have their good days and their bad days. Sometimes it's hard for them to get out of bed and start the day. Everyone occasionally needs a kick in the virtual pants or to pull themselves up by their own bootstraps. Knoppix helps you fix computers that have a hard time getting started.

So before using Knoppix to help overcome or fix computer problems, you should understand how computers start themselves up.

When they power up, computers (and by that I mean the computers' micro-processors) automatically start fetching information from a specific memory location. The contents of the memory location redirect the microprocessor to another location on either the hard drive, DVD/CD-ROM, floppy, USB flash drive, or network; the redirection is controlled by the BIOS (Basic Input/Output System). The microprocessor loads the contents of the first few hundred bytes of memory. Those bytes contain a small program called the *boot loader* that the microprocessor executes. The boot loader loads and starts running the operating system.

The name *boot loader* comes from the expression "pull yourself up from the bootstraps" and is where the phrase "boot the computer" comes from.

Here's a step-by-step description of the boot process:

1. The computer turns on (or reboots).

   Turning a computer on supplies power to the microprocessor (for instance, an Intel Pentium). The microprocessor immediately looks to a predetermined memory location. A microprocessor is also referred to as a *CPU* (central processing unit).

   Rebooting a computer mimics turning the power off and on again.

   CPUs "see" a contiguous sequence of memory locations or addresses. That sequence of addresses is called the *address space.* The address space of modern 32-bit and 64-bit CPUs measures in the trillions of bytes (gigabytes).

2. BIOS redirects the microprocessor to the MBR (master boot record).

   BIOS (Basic Input/Output System) is designed to map out the computer's hardware so the microprocessor knows where each element is located. One of the map functions defines where the microprocessor is redirected immediately after power-on. The redirection points (or should point) to the MBR.

The MBR is usually located on the first sector (the first 512 bytes) of a hard drive, DVD, CD-ROM, USB flash drive, or floppy diskette. (It can be loaded from a network and through other devices, too.)

3. The CPU loads and executes the contents of the MBR.

   No program or operating system controls the CPU when it's first powered on. All the microprocessor can do is sequentially step through each memory location it's pointed to.

4. The program contained in the MBR (the boot loader) loads the Linux kernel into memory.

5. The boot loader tells the processor to start executing the Linux kernel, which then mounts file partitions, services, and so on.

   The MBR contains some data and the small boot loader program. The data contains information about the computer's disk partitions. The boot loader mounts the file systems contained in the disk partition and then loads and starts running the operating system contained in the root file system.

That's a very simple overview of the boot process. Knowing how computers get started helps when you try to fix them when they won't start.

You can use Knoppix to help fix and/or rescue a computer. The following sections show how you can recover from problems such as a nonbooting disk.

Knoppix rescue DVD advantages

Being able to boot from the *Knoppix For Dummies* DVD provides you with the following advantages:

✓ **Baseline environment:** The *Knoppix For Dummies* DVD is read-only, and you're assured that the disc is exactly the same today as when it was manufactured. The DVD provides a consistent and known-good environment.

✓ **Boot options:** You can boot the Knoppix DVD into single-user, text-only, or graphical mode. You also have the opportunity to supply optional parameters during the boot.

This capability helps overcome a computer that doesn't want to boot from the operating system on its hard drive.

✓ **Many utilities and programs:** Knoppix packs a big punch. The *Knoppix For Dummies* DVD contains the entire Knoppix distribution, including all the tools (and more!) discussed in this book.

Knoppix is indeed a powerful and useful debugging and recovery tool. It should be basic equipment for any computer troubleshooter.

Knoppix DVD Rescue Basics

When you can't boot a Windows or Linux computer normally, you must boot from DVD or CD-ROM. This section shows how to use this book's Knoppix DVD as a rescue disc for either operating system.

The following instructions for booting from a Knoppix disc are the basis for many of the fixes in this chapter.

Follow these steps to boot into Knoppix single-user mode and view your hard drive's partitions:

1. **Turn your computer on.**

2. **Insert the *Knoppix For Dummies* DVD into the sick computer's disc drive and turn on the power or reboot.**

3. **Change the BIOS settings, if necessary, to boot from the DVD.**

   See Chapter 2 for information about changing BIOS settings.

4. **Type the following command at the** `boot:` **prompt.**

   ```
   knoppix 1
   ```

   This tells Knoppix to boot into *single-user* mode.

   In single-user mode, your computer runs a minimum number of processes and is useful for debugging problems. Booting into single-user mode is also faster than going into graphics mode (by default, live Knoppix boots into graphics mode — described in Chapter 2).

5. **Type the command to have the** `fdisk` **partitioning utility display your disk partitions:**

   • If you're using an average PC, Knoppix should see the hard drive as `/dev/hda`, and you should enter `fdisk -l /dev/hda`.

   • If you're using the second hard drive on a PC, enter `fdisk -l /dev/hdb`.

   • If you're using a computer with a USB hard drive, enter `fdisk -l /dev/uba`.

   • If you're using a computer with SCSI (small computer system interface) disks, enter `fdisk -l /dev/sda`.

Windows computers typically have only one or two partitions. A typical `fdisk` output looks similar to the following listing:

```
Device      Boot    Start   End     Blocks      Id  System
/dev/hda1    *      1       9012    78147889    7   HPFS/NTFS
```

Linux partitions look more or less like the following:

```
Device      Boot    Start   End     Blocks      Id  System
/dev/hda1   *       1       1274    10241406    83  Linux
/dev/hda2           1275    1529    2048256     82  Linux
```

The following sections show how to use this information.

Resetting Linux Passwords

One of the most common and simple booting problems arises when you can't remember or don't have a password. This isn't technically a boot problem because you can, well, boot your computer. But if you boot your computer from the Knoppix DVD, you can reset your password.

For example, if you forget your Linux Super User password, you might not be able to manage or effectively use your computer.

Use the following instructions to reset the password:

1. **Boot your Linux computer into single-user mode.**

   The steps are in the previous section, "Knoppix DVD Rescue Basics."

2. **Mount the root file system.**

   ```
   mount /dev/hda1 /mnt/test
   ```

   If you don't know which file partition contains your root file system, you might have to find it by trial and error. Mount the first partition and check for directories with names like usr, sbin, var, etc, and proc. If you don't see those directories, unmount the partition (umount /mnt) and mount the next one.

   Your computer is now running Knoppix from the DVD and using a file system that exists in RAM but not on your computer's hard drive. The Knoppix instance you're using knows nothing about the passwords or any other information on your computer's normal operating system. You can use this fact to modify your computer because the root password is no longer standing in your way.

3. **Type the following command:**

   ```
   chroot /mnt/test
   ```

   The root file system exists in RAM when you boot from DVD. chroot changes the effective root directory from ram disk to the file system you just mounted.

4. **Type the following command:**

```
passwd
```

5. **Type a new** `root` **password at the prompt and then retype it when prompted.**

6. **Unmount the partition.**

```
umount /mnt/test
```

You have just changed the `root` password on the mounted Linux partition but not on your Knoppix system (a live Knoppix instance doesn't use a `root` password by default).

You can use these instructions to reset passwords on any Linux distribution (and many UNIX computers).

Fixing Linux Disks

Sometimes your MBR (master boot record) gets damaged or overwritten. For instance, installing any version of Microsoft Windows overwrites the MBR, and you won't be able to boot Knoppix. In that case, you need to reinstall the MBR.

All major Linux distributions use one of two MBR configuration systems:

- **LILO (*LInux LOader*):** Knoppix uses LILO by default. LILO configures and installs the MBR that's used to load and start Linux. Figure 17-1 shows a typical LILO boot screen.

  LILO's configuration is stored in `/etc/lilo.conf`.

```
        GNU GRUB  version 0.95  (638K lower / 337856K upper memory)

    Debian GNU/Linux, kernel 2.6.11 Default
    Debian GNU/Linux, kernel 2.6.11
    Debian GNU/Linux, kernel memtest86
    Debian GNU/Linux, kernel memtest86+




    Use the ↑ and ↓ keys to select which entry is highlighted.
    Press enter to boot the selected OS, 'e' to edit the
    commands before booting, or 'c' for a command-line.
```

Figure 17-1:
The LILO
boot screen.

> ✔ **GRUB (*GRand Unified Bootloader*):** GRUB is more advanced than LILO but more difficult to administer. Funny how things work out that way.
>
> GRUB uses a configuration file typically stored in `/boot/grub/grub.conf`.

The following two sections show how to reinstall damaged LILO and GRUB systems.

Fixing LILO

Fixing LILO/MBR is simple. Follow these steps:

1. **Boot into single-user mode from the Knoppix DVD.**

   Follow the instructions in the earlier section "Knoppix DVD Rescue Basics."

2. **Mount the root file system.**

   ```
   mount /dev/hda1 /mnt/hda1
   ```

3. `chroot` **to the root file system.**

   Use the following command to make Knoppix treat a hard drive partition as the root file system:

   ```
   chroot /mnt/dev
   ```

   For instance, type the following command to make the `/dev/hda1` partition the root file system.

   ```
   chroot /mnt/hda1
   ```

4. **Run the following program:**

   ```
   lilo
   ```

   You should see output similar to the following excerpt:

   ```
   Added Linux *
   Added Linux(2.4)-1
   Added Linux(2.6)-2
   ```

5. **Reboot your computer.**

   You're greeted by the LILO prompt.

6. **Select your operating system and compute.**

Fixing GRUB

Use the following instructions to fix GRUB:

1. **Boot into single-user mode by using the Knoppix DVD.**

   Follow the instructions in the earlier section "Knoppix DVD Rescue Basics."

2. **Mount the root file system.**

   Use the following command, replacing `hda` with your computer's hard drive:

   ```
   mount  -o suid,dev  /dev/hda /mnt/hda
   ```

3. `chroot` **to the root file system.**

   Use the following command to force Knoppix to mount the hard drive as the root file system:

   ```
   chroot /mnt/hda
   ```

4. **Run the following program to reinstall GRUB onto your hard drive.**

   ```
   grub-install /dev/hda
   ```

5. **Reboot your computer by entering the following command.**

   ```
   reboot
   ```

   Your computer will display the GRUB prompt as it reboots.

Cloning Hard Drives

Hard drives occasionally wear out. You can generally tell that a hard drive is on its last leg when it starts making strange croaking sounds. Not all failing disks give you warning, but more give warnings than don't.

Before your hard drive wears out, you might have a chance to save your data. You can

- *Backup* your important files to another location. (Chapter 4 shows you how to back up your computer.)
- *Clone* the hard drive (copying from the original to a target drive bit by bit, byte by byte).

The Linux `dd-rescue` program lets you make bit-by-bit copies of either files or entire devices (such as a disk). It makes an exact copy of a disk's contents, thus rescuing a failing drive entirely.

After you start this cloning process, your computer may take a long time to finish (maybe *hours* to copy a huge hard drive).

You need a second *(target)* drive to make this work. You will be erasing everything on the target disk!

I prefer to use stand-alone (external) USB hard drives for making backups. They're exceedingly easy to use. (The disadvantage of using USB drives is that they're slower than internal IDE drives.)

The following instructions copy the entire contents from one disk to another.

The following steps *erase* the existing contents of the target disk!

This example assumes you're using a USB target disk:

1. **Power down your computer.**

2. **Set up the target drive on which to make the copy:**

   - If you have a *USB drive,* plug it in and you're ready to go.

   - If you're using a second (or third) *IDE hard drive,* install the drive, turn the computer back on, and make sure the BIOS recognizes the new drive.

   When you install an IDE drive, make sure the master/slave switches are set so only one drive is the master and one the slave.

3. **Boot from your Knoppix DVD.**

4. **Click the icon for the hard drive you want to clone (such as the one shown in Figure 17-2) on the KDE desktop.**

   This mounts the drive and opens a Konqueror file manager window showing the disk contents.

5. **Click the Terminal icon on the Kicker.**

6. **Find the source drive (or partition) to clone by typing** `df`.

   You see the mounted drives and partitions in a list similar to the following:

Filesystem	1K-blocks	Used	Available	Use%	Mounted on
/dev/root	3471	12	3459	1%	/
/dev/hdc	711574	711574	0	100%	/cdrom
/dev/cloop	1907730	1907730	0	100%	/KNOPPIX
/ramdisk	1907730	4212	284952	98%	/UNIONFS
/ntfs	11341234	44421	23234	4%	/mnt/hda1

Figure 17-2:
A hard drive
icon on
the KDE
desktop.

For the following steps, imagine that the Windows NTFS file system mounted on /mnt/hda1 is failing.

7. Copy the Windows NTFS partition to the USB disk:

```
sudo dd-rescue if=/dev/hda1 of=/dev/dev bs=512
```

For instance, if your source drive is /dev/hda1 and the target drive is /dev/sda1, then type the following:

```
sudo dd-rescue if=/dev/hda1 of=/dev/sda1 bs=512
```

You can copy the entire hard drive as follows:

```
sudo dd-rescue if=/dev/hda1 of=/dev/sda1 bs=512
```

8. The contents of the source disk partition (or the entire disk) are copied to the target drive.

The process takes a long time (even *hours* if you're cloning a large drive).

After the computer is finished with the copy, you can either

✔ Work from the target drive directly.

✔ Use the copy to create another working drive.

If you clone a failing drive, replace it with a new one and reverse the process described in the previous instructions.

CSI Knoppix: Investigating the crime scene

If (heaven forbid) you ever get hacked, you may need to perform a forensic analysis of your computer. Most home- or small-business computer owners choose merely to rebuild their computer and change passwords. However, if you own the computer, you can choose to perform an analysis, if only to satisfy your own curiosity.

However, the matter may be out of your hands if your computer belongs to someone else or if you run computers for someone else. If you're hacked and money is lost, then a crime has been committed. Management then decides the course to take.

You may need to start a computer forensics investigation, depending on management's decision. If that's the case, you must take some immediate steps to prepare for that investigation, such as disconnecting the computer's network connection and contacting the FBI.

Conducting computer forensics is beyond the scope of this book, and only superbly trained professionals who are legally entitled should do such work. In such cases, doing less is generally better. Think of every crime scene you've ever

seen on TV; you don't just walk in and start your own investigation. Computers are no different.

What happens if a serious intrusion occurs and a computer forensics professional is called in? The standard procedure defined by the SANS Institute *(SysAdmin, Audit, Network, Security)* is to ask the computer owner to pull the network plug and then occupy him or her with other tasks. Those tasks are designed to keep the computer running but without network connectivity (hopefully blocking the hacker from continued disservice) and also to keep the computer user from interfering with the investigation.

One of the first steps that a forensics investigator takes is to clone the computer's hard drive. The investigator has the overriding need to maintain a chain of evidence. That chain includes keeping the evidence on the hard drive undisturbed. The investigator also needs to find out what happened on the computer, so the disk must be cloned. The professional places the source disk and a virgin target disk in a device that copies the source to the target bit by bit. (dd performs the same function as the professional device.)

Chapter 18

Curing the Common Cold: Fighting Viruses and Other Malware

In This Chapter

▶ Detecting and eliminating Windows viruses

▶ Fixing Linux malware

▶ Patching Knoppix

*C*omputer viruses infect and spread among computers and cause them to get sick. Windows computers are especially susceptible to viruses because of design flaws and the widespread popularity of the Windows operating system, which makes it a popular target. Linux computers and Macs are theoretically vulnerable to viruses, but very few such viruses actually exist "in the wild."

In humans and animals, viruses are microscopic bits of DNA (deoxyribonucleic acid) or RNA (ribonucleic acid) wrapped in protein sheaths. DNA and RNA make our cells tick. Viruses infect cells, reproduce rapidly, and then spread from individual to individual. They wreak havoc with living beings, making us sick.

And what real viruses do to a person's bodily systems, computer viruses do to computer systems.

Viruses aren't the only form of malicious software (otherwise known as *malware*). *Trojans, spyware, worms,* and other little nasties infect all types of computers the world over.

This chapter shows how to detect and remove most common types of malware from Windows and Linux systems. No latex gloves required.

The steps in this chapter are based on running a live Knoppix instance from the *Knoppix For Dummies* DVD (or a CD that you download from `www.knoppix.net` or `www.knoppix.org`).

Calling Doctor Knoppix: Finding and Removing Windows Viruses

Microsoft Windows is vulnerable to many types of malware. One of the most common types of Windows malware is the computer virus. Viruses have been around the longest. This section shows how to use Knoppix with ClamAV (an open source anti-virus Linux tool that can detect viruses on Windows systems).

A number of good commercial tools detect and remove Windows viruses. I don't propose usurping those utilities with Knoppix. Instead, I recommend using Knoppix as an auxiliary tool in certain situations. Even in an auxiliary role, Knoppix is a powerful security tool. You might need to detect and remove viruses without using the Windows operating system in these situations:

- ✔ **Your current anti-virus system is ineffective.** Sometimes a computer is so thoroughly infected that you can't run the anti-virus software. In that case, Knoppix is your solution because you boot it instead of Windows.

- ✔ **You want a second opinion.** Anti-virus software is only as good as its database of known virus signatures. Anti-virus software can't detect and kill a new virus until vendors identify and distribute its signature. One anti-virus program may detect a problem that another program misses.

- ✔ **You're cheap, like me.** Maybe your anti-virus software has expired and you don't want to stay on the treadmill of constantly renewing your subscription. Maybe you used (like me) a trial subscription, liked it, but just don't want to pay for the real thing. All those subscriptions add up quickly. (I've got subscriptions coming out my ears.)

You can also find a commercial, anti-virus product called F-Prot. The fine people at Frisk Software International (www.f-prot.com) produce the F-Prot anti-virus system. Frisk offers a free Linux version for personal home use, and the commercial Linux workstation license costs only $29, or €21.73. You can download the personal version from this address:

```
www.f-prot.com/download/home_user/download_fplinux.html
```

The following sections provide detailed instructions for using ClamAV. Put your stethoscope on and get ready to cure your Windows computer.

Anti-virus system startup and update

Follow these steps to restart a troubled Windows PC and download the anti-virus software:

1. **Boot your Windows computer from the *Knoppix For Dummies* DVD (or the Knoppix "lite" CD that you download from** www.knoppix.org **or** www.knoppix.net**).**

   Chapter 2 shows how to start a PC with a Knoppix DVD or CD.

2. **Establish an Internet connection with Knoppix.**

   This happens automatically if your Knoppix computer is connected to a network that provides the DHCP server.

   Part IV shows you how to connect to the Internet with a dialup modem or a private network.

3. **Click the Konsole icon on the KDE Kicker.**

   The Konsole terminal window opens.

4. **Enter the following command.**

   ```
   sudo /etc/init.d/clamav-freshclam restart
   ```

   The antivirus daemon starts.

5. **Update the anti-virus signature database by entering the following command.**

   ```
   sudo freshclam
   ```

   The anti-virus database gets updated.

You can obtain the Linux version of the commercial F-Prot anti-virus system for no charge. Frisk Software International kindly provides a free version for home users. Download the free home Linux version from www.f-prot.com/download/home_user/download_fplinux.html www.fprot.org/#download.

Meta-view: Detecting Windows viruses

Here's the overview of how to find and eliminate Windows viruses:

1. Boot your Windows computer from the live Knoppix DVD.

2. Connect to the Internet.

3. Update the anti-virus signature database.

4. Mount the Windows partition.

5. Detect viruses on the Windows partition.

6. Remove or quarantine viruses.

Partition cleanup

Before you run ClamAV to detect Windows viruses, you must mount the Windows partition on your live Knoppix computer. Knoppix can mount both *FAT* and *NTFS* as read-only file systems. This section describes how to mount your Windows partition.

Mounting FAT and NTFS partitions

To mount your Windows FAT or NTFS partition in Knoppix, click the partition's icon on the Knoppix desktop. This mounts the partition and opens a Konqueror window, which you can ignore.

For instance, if `hda1` is your Windows partition, click the Hard Disk Partition [hda1] button. This mounts the partition on the */mnt/hda1* directory.

Eliminating viruses

After you update the ClamAV virus signature database, you can start *detecting* viruses. With a separate process, you can *remove* them.

Detecting viruses

The detection process uses ClamAV with a Windows FAT or NTFS file partition as its target:

1. **Click the Konsole terminal icon on the KDE Kicker.**

2. **Type the following command to scan the Windows partition** (/mnt/*mount_dir*).

   ```
   sudo clamscan /mnt/mount_dir
   ```

   For instance, if your Windows partition is /mnt/hda1, type the following command:

   ```
   sudo clamscan /mnt/hda1
   ```

   This searches the entire Windows partition and outputs all results — positive and negative — to your terminal window.

3. **You can filter the output to display only detected viruses.**

   ```
   sudo clamscan /mnt/mount_dir| grep FOUND
   ```

   For example, if your Windows partition is /mnt/hda1, type the following command:

   ```
   sudo clamscan /mnt/hda1 | grep FOUND
   ```

   This searches the entire Windows partition and outputs only positive results in the terminal window.

4. **Send the virus detection results to a file.**

```
sudo clamscan /mnt/mount_dir> file
```

If your Windows partition is `/mnt/hda1`, type the following command:

```
sudo clamscan /mnt/hda1 > virus.report
```

This searches the entire Windows partition and sends the results to the `virus.report` file.

The `clamscan` utility can search files and directories, in addition to entire partitions, for viruses. For example, the following commands search one file, many similar files, and whole directories:

- Have `clamscan` search a single file for viruses:

```
sudo clamscan file
```

- Adding the asterisk (*) metacharacter to the filename tells `clamscan` to search all files beginning with the string "file."

```
sudo clamscan file*
```

For instance, specify *xyz**** to search all files beginning with the string "xyz."

- If you specify a directory, `clamscan` searches the files in that directory. Adding the -r option forces `clamscan` to recursively search that directory; the recursive options tell `clamscan` to search the directory and all, if any, subdirectories.

```
sudo clamscan -r dir
```

The following list shows a quick way to review your virus scan results:

1. **Run the following command to extract the location of any infected files:**

```
grep FOUND virus.report
```

2. **Take note of any infected files.**

How you record the detected files depends on your preference:

- If the number of files is small, you may simply write them down.

- If the number of files is large, print the listing. (Chapter 15 shows how to configure a PC printer with Knoppix.)

You can directly print the result. Use this command:

```
grep FOUND virus.report | lp
```

You can find harmless example "viruses" to use for experimentation. (Actually, these probably shouldn't be called "viruses" because they only simulate a virus signature but don't reproduce or spread like real viruses.) You can find a virus simulator at www.rexswain.com/eicar.html, where you can download eicar.com or eicar.zip (which contains eicar.com) and test ClamAV. eicar.com presents no danger at all. The executable file only contains a string that sends a false-positive signature to your anti-virus detector.

Removing viruses

When you have a list of infected files on an NTFS Windows partition, use the following instructions to manually remove the viruses from the partition:

1. **Reboot your computer.**

2. **Immediately after the BIOS configuration prompt finishes, press F8.**

   You're prompted to start Windows in several modes.

3. **Select the Windows Safe Mode with Command Prompt and press Enter.**

4. **Click the Administrator user.**

   You're logged into a command line interface (CLI) as the administrator.

5. **Delete each offending file by using the Windows `del` command.**

   ```
   del virus-file
   ```

   For example, if C:\WINDOWS\SYSTEM32\badboy.com is a virus, type this command:

   ```
   del c:\windows\system32\badboy.com
   ```

6. **Reboot your computer.**

   Your computer should be infection-free!

If you use Knoppix to recover from an ineffective or nonresponsive Windows anti-virus program, you should

✔ Update the anti-virus program and rerun it.

✔ Consider another anti-virus vendor, such as Frisk Software International.

Calling Nurse Knoppix: Finding and Removing Linux Malware

Linux users can't relax after hearing about another round of Windows viruses. When properly configured, Linux is generally more secure than

Windows. However, Linux is vulnerable to malicious software that attacks and exploits vulnerabilities. This so-called *malware* consists of:

✔ **Viruses:** Self-executing programs that generally perform malicious actions.

   Linux isn't generally vulnerable to viruses (yet). There are Linux viruses, but most viruses are designed to work in the Windows world.

✔ **Trojans:** Software that leaves a door open for hackers.

   You have to "invite" Trojans in, just like the city of Troy mistakenly did. Fortunately, Linux protects users from Trojans more robustly than Windows does.

✔ **Root kits:** A particularly nasty form of Trojan designed to insert software into the Linux kernel and hide the software from discovery.

✔ **Worms:** Programs that send themselves out to attack other computers.

   Worms seek and attack vulnerable network services. After they gain a foothold on a vulnerable computer, worms look for other vulnerable computers and spread by hopping from machine to machine.

This section describes how to install, detect, and remove common Linux root kits. The `chkrootkit` utility helps you look for and detect the latest root kits that `chkrootkit` knows of. After you find and remove all detected root kits, you can be reasonably sure that you're root-kit-free at that point.

A live Knoppix instance can get infected when running on a network, but the infection is cured instantly by turning the power off (nothing can worm its way onto the read-only media). Therefore, this section shows how to clean a permanent Knoppix installation.

Meta-view: Scanning and removing malware

Here is a quick rundown of how to look for and eliminate malicious software on your Linux computer.

1. Reboot your computer without network connectivity.

2. Scan your computer.

3. Remove the malware.

4. Reboot your computer with network connectivity.

5. Download the newest scanning tool version.

6. Rescan your computer and remove any additional malware.

If your computer becomes infected, you can reinstall Knoppix from the *Knoppix For Dummies* DVD. A small probability exists that the scanning tool will miss malware. Any scanning tool is only as good as its database of known signatures. New malware or old ones that "fly under the radar" can get past the utility. Therefore, the only sure way of eradicating malware is to reinstall the operating system from pristine media.

To fix a permanent Knoppix or other Linux distribution, boot from the live Knoppix DVD and run `chkrootkit` on the Linux hard drive partitions.

Knoppix provides the root kit scanning tool `chkrootkit`. This tool has a good database of known root kit signatures. However, it's often updated, so you should perform a two-stage process to check for root kits with chkrootkit:

1. **Run your current version of** `chkrootkit`:

    a. Disconnect your Knoppix computer network cable.

    b. Reboot your Knoppix computer.

    c. Run the current `chkrootkit` version.

    Running `chkrootkit` the first time without a network connection minimizes the risk of reinfection during the process.

2. **Run the current updated version of** `chkrootkit`:

    a. Reconnect your Knoppix computer network cable.

    b. Reboot your Knoppix computer.

    c. Update `chkrootkit` and run it again.

There's no sure thing when it comes to detecting malware. You must continue to be vigilant, check your logs (see Chapter 20), and maintain multiple levels of defense with such protection mechanisms as firewalls, regular software updates, and good passwords.

The following sections show how to run `chkrootkit` to scan for root kits.

Initial scanning

Running the `chkrootkit` utility without a network connection minimizes the damage any existing root kit could do while connected to the Internet.

Use the following steps to perform the initial root kit scan on a Knoppix computer without a network connection:

1. **Boot Knoppix from the *Knoppix For Dummies* DVD.**

    Chapter 2 shows you how to boot Knoppix from DVD.

2. **Click the Konsole terminal icon on the Kicker.**

3. **Check the Linux hard drive for root kits by entering the following command:**

    ```
    sudo chkrootkit -r /dev/file
    ```

For example, the following command checks /dev/hda2:

```
sudo chkrootkit -r /dev/hda2
```

chkrootkit checks for every type of root kit that it has a signature for and lists the results for each test. If chkrootkit finds a root kit, it lists the results. For instance, if it finds the Slapper worm, it shows the following:

```
Checking `slapper'... Warning: Possible Slapper Worm
            installed
```

4. **If you find a root kit, rescan your computer.**

The following section describes the rescanning process.

If you don't find a root kit, you can stop here.

Downloading the latest chkrootkit

Follow these steps to retrieve and install the latest chkrootkit version from the Internet:

1. Open Firefox and go to www.chkroot kit.org/download.

2. Click the Latest Source Tarball link.

   The Opening chkrootkit.tar.gz dialog opens.

   Linux uses the tape archive (tar) utility to store multiple files in one file. tar files are similar to the zip files familiar to the Windows world.

3. Select Save to Disk and click OK.

   The tarball is saved to your current working directory and you return to the download page.

4. Click the tarball's MD5 Signature link.

   Firefox displays a single text line with the checksum. You use this in the following steps to verify the tarball's authenticity.

5. Open a shell by clicking the Terminal icon on the Kicker.

6. Type the following command to calculate the checksum of the downloaded file.

   ```
   md5sum chkrootkit.tar.gz
   ```

   The long string of numbers should exactly match the numbers displayed in Firefox.

   If the numbers don't match, repeat Steps 3 through 6 and contact the www.chk rootkit.org Webmaster about a possible *man-in-the-middle attack*. You should definitely *not* use the chkrootkit you just downloaded in this situation.

7. Unpack the verified tarball.

   ```
   tar xzf chkrootkit.tar.gz
   ```

8. Start making sense and compile the chk-rootkit plug-ins.

   ```
   make sense
   ```

   These plug-ins provide extra protection, but chkrootkit can run without them.

Final scanning

You sleep better at night if you run the newest `chkrootkit` utility version after downloading it. Having run the utility and removed any malware makes it reasonable to reconnect to the Internet and run `chkrootkit` again.

Use the following steps to finish the delousing process:

1. **Reboot your Knoppix computer from your *Knoppix For Dummies* DVD.**

2. **Retrieve and install the latest** `chkrootkit` **version from the Internet.**

   The sidebar, "Downloading the latest chkrootkit," explains the process for updating the chkrootkit system.

3. **Type the following command to run the** `chkrootkit` **utility.**

   ```
   sudo chkrootkit-0.45/chkrootkit -r /dev/hdx
   ```

   For instance, if your Linux operating system is installed on `/dev/hda2`, run the following command:

   ```
   sudo chkrootkit-0.45/chkrootkit -r /dev/hda2
   ```

4. **Enter your password.**

   `chkrootkit` checks your computer.

5. **Delete any root kit files that are found.**

6. **Change all your user passwords**

   Changing the `root` password is especially important. The following command changes the `root` password:

   ```
   sudo passwd root
   ```

Chapter 19

Keeping Up with the Updates: Updating and Managing Packages

. . . .

In This Chapter

▶ Managing software with the graphical `KPackage`

▶ Updating Knoppix with `apt-get`

. . . .

*L*inux distributions are all about making Linux easier to use. Knoppix takes this idea a step further by pushing the use of live media to another level.

But Knoppix stands on the shoulders of those giants that came before. Knoppix is based on the popular, noncommercial, Debian GNU/Linux distribution. One of Debian's greatest contributions is the Debian Package Manager (DPM) system. DPM makes managing (installing, updating, querying, and removing) software a breeze.

This chapter describes how to use the DPM system to do several important administrative system tasks.

This chapter is oriented toward using a permanent Knoppix installation. The software on a permanent installation should be kept up-to-date to reduce security vulnerabilities and make use of the latest application improvements. You can perform updates on a live Knoppix instance, but it's time consuming — you have to spend time updating from scratch every time you boot from the *Knoppix For Dummies* DVD (or CD, if you download Knoppix from www. knoppix.net or www.knoppix.org).

Introducing the Debian Package Manager

Knoppix uses the *Debian Package Manager* (DPM). DPM is a combination of high-level applications that easily and intuitively control the low-level programs that actually do the work.

The DPM is based on the concept of *packages*. Software developers use many different file types (such as executable, configuration, graphics, and documentation) when building an application. The OpenOffice.org application suite, for instance, consists of hundreds of files. Not all applications use that many files, but the only practical way to distribute software is as a package.

Every Debian package is distributed as a single file. A package file contains an archive of all the files that make up the package. Debian package files are denoted by the .deb suffix. For instance, the Debian Mozilla-Firefox package is stored in the mozilla-firefox-*1.2.3*. deb file, where *1.2.3* represents the version number.

Working with DPM helps you

- ✔ Install packages
- ✔ Upgrade packages
- ✔ Remove packages
- ✔ Query packages

DPM consists of the following utilities:

- ✔ KPackage: A graphical interface to the DPM. Klaus likes Kpackage for its functionality and because you can find it on other Linux distributions.

  KPackage uses apt-get to download packages from the Internet and dpkg to install them. apt-get and dpkg are described in later sections.

- ✔ apt-get: A powerful utility whose main use is managing packages via Internet-based package repositories. See the section "An Ounce of Prevention Is Worth a Pound of Cure: Automatically Updating Knoppix" for more information about this system.

- ✔ dpkg: A text-based application that acts as an interface to dpkg-deb. You use dpkg from the command line interface (CLI) to interact with packages. dpkg-query and dpkg-reconfigure are supplementary versions of dpkg.

- ✔ dpkg-deb: A low-level utility that interacts with the DPM archives. dpkg provides the commands to dpkg-deb to manipulate packages.

- ✔ dselect: An interactive front end to dpkg and apt-get. However, dselect is very difficult to use and I don't recommend it.

Using KPackage

KPackage is part of the KDE suite of graphical interfaces. It's a graphical user interface (GUI) front end to the DPM and makes handling packages straightforward and easy. This section describes how to perform some common package-handling functions.

KPackage also acts as a front end for other Linux distributions' package managers, such as the Red Hat Package Manager (RPM).

Start KPackage by clicking the K-Menu and selecting System⇨KPackage (Package Manager). KPackage has to read the database of installed packages, and the process can take some time. Figure 19-1 shows the KPackage window.

The KPackage window shows information about the Debian packages installed on your Knoppix computer:

✔ The left panel shows installed packages, which are organized by the groups they belong to; groups are organized by function.

✔ The right panel shows the details of a selected package.

✔ The tab along the top of the window shows currently installed packages, updated packages, and new packages.

Updating packages

You can update your Knoppix computer with KPackage.

Since Knoppix adopted Unionfs, you can update both live and permanent Knoppix installations. The only limitations to updating live Knoppix instances is that you need at least 60MB of free ram disk to store the Debian package database. Using the live Knoppix with a persistent disk image (described in Chapter 3) works, too.

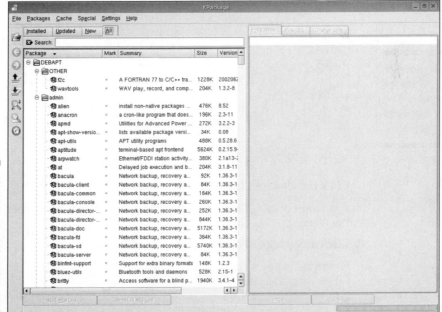

Figure 19-1:
The
KPackage
Debian
Package
Manager
showing
installed
packages.

The update process has two basic steps:

1. Update the package database.

2. Upgrade every package that has a newer version.

You can also upgrade, or even downgrade, individual packages.

Use the following instructions to update/upgrade your computer:

1. **Reboot (if necessary) and start Knoppix.**

2. **Make sure you have an Internet connection.**

3. **Click the K-Menu and select KNOPPIX⇨Utilities⇨Manager Software in Knoppix (kpackage)**

   The KPackage window opens.

4. **Click the Special menu tab and choose APT: Debian⇨Update.**

   Figure 19-2 shows KPackage looking for newer packages.

Figure 19-2:
KPackage
checking for
updated
packages.

5. **Click the Updated tab.**

   KPackage displays the available updates. Updates are prefaced by the big green U.

6. **Click any package to select it for installation.**

   Figure 19-3 shows some of the available updates in the left panel and the one selected for installation on the right.

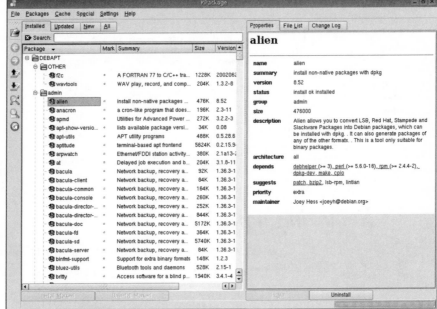

Figure 19-3:
KPackage
shows
the updated
list and
information
about a
package.

7. **Click Install.**

   The Install KPackage dialog opens.

8. **Click Install in the new dialog.**

   The installation process begins.

9. **Click Done when the process finishes.**

10. **Update your entire system by clicking the Special tab and choosing APT: Debian⇨Upgrade.**

    The Apt Upgrade dialog opens.

11. **Type Y to continue the upgrade process.**

    KPackage upgrades your system. Figure 19-4 shows a sample KPackage window that's ready to start updating your computer.

    If you want to stop the upgrade process, type N to quit.

12. **Choose File⇨Quit in the KPackage window to leave the utility.**

    The DPM installs the package, showing its progress as it does so. The Cancel button changes to the Done button when the installation finishes.

13. **Click Done to exit from the KPackage dialog.**

    Your software is installed and you can start using it.

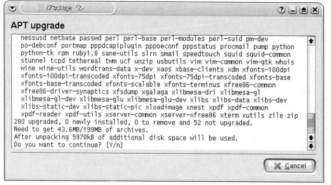

Figure 19-4:
The Apt Upgrade dialog ready to upgrade the computer.

Removing a package

Removing packages is even easier than installing them. The following steps describe the process:

1. **Start** KPackage **from the K-Menu.**

2. **Click the Installed tab in the KPackage window.**

   This shows the installed packages on your computer.

3. **Select the package in the left panel that you want to remove. (For example, click** alien.**)**

   The package information is displayed in the right panel (see Figure 19-5).

4. **Review the package information and decide whether you want to remove it.**

   Don't worry too much about removing packages and losing software and configurations:

   - You can generally reinstall a package without problem in the future.
   - The DPM saves package configuration files unless you explicitly tell it not to.

5. **Click the Uninstall button.**

   The KPackage <2> dialog opens and asks for the root password (if you aren't already logged in as such).

6. **If necessary, type the** root **password and press Enter.**

   The Uninstall – KPackage dialog opens, asking you to confirm package removal.

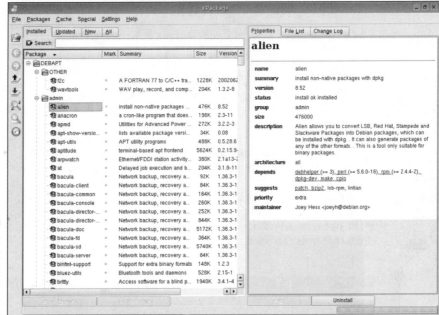

Figure 19-5:
Selecting
the alien
package to
remove.

You're given two extra package removal options:

- Remove Configuration Files permanently removes any of the package's configuration files.

- Test checks the removal of a package without actually erasing any files. (The package is left in place.)

7. Click the Uninstall button.

The dialog shows the progress of the removal process. The Cancel button changes to the Done button when the installation finishes.

8. Click Done when the removal process is finished.

Control returns to the KPackage window. Your package is removed. (The package's configuration files remain in place unless you asked for their removal.)

Getting package information

KPackage provides a great pool of package information. Click any package (installed or not) in the left panel, and the right panel displays its summary.

The following list describes the information that the KPackage tabs display:

- ✔ **Properties:** Package's name, version, package group membership, and a concise description.
- ✔ **File List:** Files that are part of the package.
- ✔ **Change log:** Changes that have been made to the package. For instance, removing and reinstalling the package shows how the process occurred.

For example, click the cron package and you get information about the package. Click the File List tab and you see all the cron package files. (Figure 19-6 shows an example of the files owned by the cron package.)

dpkg performs the same functions as KPackage but from a command line interface (CLI); actually, KPackage takes your input, spawns dpkg, and feeds it the options necessary to complete the task. You can do the same work with dpkg that you can with Kpackage.

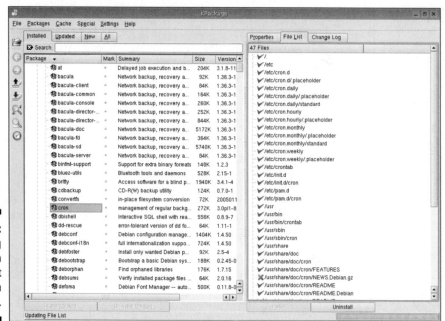

Figure 19-6:
Displaying
information
about
the cron
package.

An Ounce of Prevention Is Worth a Pound of Cure: Automatically Updating Knoppix

The `apt-get` utility installs and removes Debian packages. `apt-get` takes package management to the next level and works over the Internet.

Updating your computer regularly is one of the most important security measures you can take. Updating removes software bugs and vulnerabilities that hackers can use against you.

`apt-get` is easy to use. Simply connect your Knoppix computer directly to the Internet or to a private network with Internet access, and you're ready to go.

The following instructions describe how to use `apt-get` to update your Knoppix computer. These instructions perform the same process as the `KPackage` example. However, while `KPackage` is easy to use because of its graphical operation, `apt-get` lends itself to performing updates automatically.

Follow these steps to update your Knoppix computer:

1. **Log in to your computer.**

2. **Click the Terminal icon on the Kicker.**

3. **If your network accesses the Internet through a *proxy server*, insert your network's proxy address and port number into the `apt-get` configuration file by entering the following command:**

   ```
   sudo echo 'Acquire::http::Proxy "http://proxyaddress:portnumber"'\
   >> /etc/apt/apt.conf
   ```

4. **Enter the following command to start the update process:**

   ```
   sudo apt-get update
   ```

   `apt-get` updates its internal package lists but doesn't actually install any updated packages.

5. **Enter the following command to install any available upgraded packages:**

   ```
   sudo apt-get upgrade
   ```

   Your computer's software is updated with the latest and greatest packages.

The available DPM repositories are stored in the `/etc/apt/sources.list` file.

Debian package stores

Numerous Debian package repositories are scattered across the Net. `apt-get` is the one-stop-shopping utility of the Debian (and Knoppix) world:

✔ When you ask `apt-get` to install a package (or packages), it searches through the repositories (it keeps a list). `apt-get` finds the most recent package, downloads it, and then installs it.

✔ Many packages depend on other packages to install and operate correctly. In such cases, `apt-get` puts on its project manager hat, keeping track of dependencies and installing all dependent packages as necessary.

✔ Running `apt-get` in update mode to periodically update your computer automatically fixes bugs and security holes. In this mode, `apt-get` is a powerful security tool.

Chapter 20

Being Proactive: Logging, Detecting, and Auditing

In This Chapter

▶ Logging system events on your computer

▶ Examining your network traffic

▶ Detecting intrusions with Snort

▶ Scanning your network with Nmap

▶ Auditing your network with Nessus

*T*he best defense is a good offense. This philosophy is as true in computer security as it is in sports.

However, it's against the law to take the offensive against hackers in many countries (including the United States). It's also just plain dumb and unnecessary. I recommend a legal form of offense: actively *monitoring* and *updating* your Knoppix computer and network.

This chapter shows how to monitor your Knoppix computer, its network connection, and your local network. All three activities help keep you a step ahead of the bad guys (or at least prevent you from being a step behind).

You can use the setup steps in this chapter when you run a live Knoppix instance from the *Knoppix For Dummies* DVD (or from a CD that you download from www.knoppix.net or www.knoppix.org), but you must *repeat* the steps every time you reboot the PC unless you use the persistent settings utility to save your configuration. (Chapter 3 shows you how to use a persistent home directory.)

Dear Diary, Today 1 . . . :
Logging with syslog

Reading system and network log files is essential for maintaining a computer's health. Computer-system and intrusion-detection logs can

- ✔ Show what has occurred on a computer.
- ✔ Provide clues about possible security problems.

Reading logs is, of course, very boring. You must do it day after day, week after week, year after year. It's one of those never-ending chores that rarely provides any sense of accomplishment. But when something goes wrong, you'll give thanks to the log gods that you have them.

System logs help troubleshoot problems. `syslog` records events about many systems. Consult your logs when you're having difficulty getting hardware or software to work.

This section shows how to configure and use the nearly universal `syslog` system. I also introduce the Snort intrusion detection system (IDS).

Meta-view: Using syslog

Event logging is conceptually simple. Your logging system records events as they occur, and you periodically look through the logs. The reality is that every computer is as different as their users.

There are several keys to effective logging:

- ✔ **Be consistent:** Logs are useless without human eyes. Review your logs regularly.

- ✔ **Experience counts:** The more you practice, the better you get. Be consistent and pay

attention to detail and you get better at recognizing unusual and important events.

- ✔ **Refine your techniques:** Being consistent helps you gain experience, which makes you better and faster at digesting your logs. Use your increasing knowledge and skill to refine the system logging configuration. Fine-tuning `syslog` reduces logging unnecessary information, which helps you get the job done quicker.

The following section introduces the ubiquitous Linux `syslog` system.

Starting syslog

The `syslog` system is installed by default on Knoppix (and nearly every Linux and UNIX system). It's highly configurable and records most of the events that occur on a computer. `syslog` gives you very useful information.

Use the following instructions to start `syslog` on your Knoppix computer:

1. **Log in as a regular user.**
2. **Engage** `syslog` **to start automatically at boot time.**

   ```
   sudo update-rc.d sysklogd defaults
   ```

   Use this option for permanent Knoppix installations.
3. **Enter your password when prompted.**
4. **Start the** `syslog` **daemon.**

   ```
   sudo /etc/init.d/sysklogd restart
   ```

   The `/var/log/messages` file stores general logging messages.
5. **Look for verification that the daemon started.**

   ```
   cat /var/log/messages
   ```

   You see that `syslog` has recorded its own startup.

   ```
   Mar 11 13:00:40 cancun syslogd 1.4.1#16: restart.
   ```

You can continuously view the system log by using the `tail -f /var/log/messages` command. Entries are displayed as they're appended to the messages file. You can stop the process by pressing Ctrl+C.

`syslog` is controlled by the `/etc/syslog.conf` configuration file. The following section shows how to make some simple configuration changes.

Configuring syslog

The `/etc/syslog.conf` file configures the `sysklogd` daemon. The file uses a simple format with one rule per line:

```
Facility.Priority  Action  # OptionalComment
```

The basic rule format has two parts separated by *white space* (one or more spaces or tabs):

- *Selector* field

  The Selector field has two *parameters* that are separated by a period:

  - *Facility* determines what type of system information to log.

    Table 20-1 lists the syslog facilities and the information that the syslog facilities handle.

  - *Priority* tells syslog to log events that are either *at* or *above* the named priority level.

    Table 20-2 lists the priority levels from lowest *(log all events)* to highest *(log only the highest-priority event)*.

- The *Action field* defines the log information's *destination.*

  The destination usually is a file in the /var/log directory, but it can be a Linux-named *pipe,* a terminal/console, all logged-in users, or a remote syslog machine.

- The *pound symbol* (#) defines any following text on the line as a *comment* (notes and explanations that aren't part of the rule).

Table 20-1	syslog Facilities and Systems
Facility	**System**
auth or authpriv	Information about authentication-oriented commands, such as logins and switch user (su)
cron	cron jobs (cron schedules actions)
daemon	Daemon-created events
kern	Internal kernel events
Lpr	Print jobs
mail	Incoming and outgoing messages
news	Usenet (news) events
syslog	Events created by syslog itself; for example, starting or stopping the sysklogd daemon
user	Miscellaneous user processes
uucp	The old UNIX-to-UNIX copy mailing system
local0 – local7	Locally generated events

Syslog gets information

`syslog` uses information that the Linux kernel supplies to it. The kernel gets the information from

✔ The kernel's own internal events

✔ External applications and daemons

Linux uses a loosely defined `syslog` protocol that lets `syslog` and external programs "speak" the same language.

Table 20-2	syslog Priority Levels	
Level	*Function*	*Messages*
`panic/emerg`	Occurs only when the system is encountering severe problems	Only this level
`alert`	A program or subsystem needs immediate help	This level and above
`crit`	Information that an entire program or subsystem is having problems and may not be usable	This level and above
`error` or `err`	Information that part of a program or subsystem is having problems and may not be operational	This level and above
`warning` or `warn`	Warning messages	This level and above
`notice`	Events that may not indicate problems	This level and above
`info`	Informational information	This level and above
`debug`	Used for debugging purposes (software often can output low-level information for debugging)	*All* messages

---

The future of event logging

A lot of work is being done to update the `syslog` protocol. The updated `syslog`, `syslog-auth`, and `syslog-sign` protocols are being developed to both

✔ Update the current `syslog` protocol.

✔ Add authentication and encryption to system logging.

This is important work because of the importance of centralizing event logs in large organizations. (It's impossible to rely on employees to keep up with their logs.) You can find more information about the future of system logging from `www.ietf.org`.

In a `syslog.conf` rule, punctuation characters determine how configuration rules are handled:

✔ An *asterisk* (*) is a *wild card* that translates to all available options.

The following rule uses asterisks to record all events to the file `all.log`:

```
*.*                      /var/log/all.log
```

✔ *Commas* (,) let you specify multiple facilities with the same priority on a single line.

The following rule shows a rule that logs both `auth` and `authpriv` events to the `/var/log/auth.log` file:

```
auth,authpriv.*                    /var/log/auth.log
```

✔ The *equal sign* (=) tells `syslog` to record only events of a specific priority.

The following rule tells syslog to record only kernel events of informational priority into the `/var/log/kernel.log` file:

```
kernel.=crit                /var/log/kernel.log
```

Each rule in `syslog.conf` defines three functions:

✔ **Facility:** The Facility is the type of system event to be logged.

✔ **Priority:** The Priority determines the level of importance of an event.

✔ **Storage:** The Storage dictates the file or location where the event should be stored.

The following rules are from the default `/etc/syslog.conf` file:

✔ The following rule saves messages from the `auth` and `authpriv` facilities of all priorities to the `/var/log/auth.log` file:

```
auth,authpriv.*                    /var/log/auth.log
```

✔ The following rule is a catch-all that sends *everything not explicitly
specified* and *authorizations with no priority* to the `syslog` file.

```
*.*;auth,authpriv.none            -/var/log/syslog
```

✔ The following rules log messages (of any priority) from each facility to
their corresponding namesake log files in `/var/log`:

```
#cron.*                           /var/log/cron.log
daemon.*                          -/var/log/daemon.log
kern.*                            -/var/log/kern.log
lpr.*                             -/var/log/lpr.log
mail.*                            -/var/log/mail.log
user.*                            -/var/log/user.log
uucp.*                            /var/log/uucp.log
```

Using syslog

Make your New Year's resolution today. Resolve to make a habit of examining
logs daily (or more often). Look particularly hard at kernel and authentication events; also look for events with critical or higher priorities. With time,
you get used to the format and start to see patterns emerge.

After you gain some experience, you become capable of identifying problems
before they become problems. Reading logs is more of an art than a science,
but you can't get good at it without practice.

Sniffing Around with tcpdump

`tcpdump` is a simple-to-use network traffic–sniffing tool. You can use it to display the packet headers of packets flowing on your private network. This is
very useful for

✔ Debugging problems

✔ Tracking suspicious traffic

✔ Satisfying your curiosity about how networks work

Start by running `tcpdump` in its most simple, default way:

```
tcpdump
```

Wow, that was tough!

By default, `tcpdump` logs traffic on your default NIC, which is either

- `eth0` for wired connections
- `wlan0` for wireless connections

You see output similar to the following lines:

- The following two lines are information about tcpdump:

  ```
  tcpdump: verbose output suppressed, use -v or -vv for full protocol decode
  listening on eth0, link-type EN10MB (Ethernet), capture size 96 bytes
  ```

- The following line is an address resolution protocol (ARP) request from `veracruz`, which is looking for the Ethernet address of `cancun`.

  ```
  21:38:56.833675 arp who-has cancun.paunchy.net tell veracruz.paunchy.net
  ```

`tcpdump` continues running until you stop it:

- If you let `tcpdump` run, it shows every packet that runs by your computer.
- Stop `tcpdump` by pressing Ctrl+C.

Custom tcpdump configurations

Although `tcpdump` is simple to use, it's also highly configurable. Here are a couple of useful examples:

- To start `tcpdump` and monitor traffic from only one computer (in this case, `cancun`), form a command like this:

  ```
  tcpdump host cancun
  ```

- You can substitute a numeric IP address in place of the name, such as

  ```
  tcpdump host 192.168.1.100
  ```

- You can combine multiple options with `and`. This example tells `tcpdump` to show secure shell (SSH) packets (port 22) going to and from `cancun`:

  ```
  tcpdump host cancun and port 22
  ```

Substitute computer hostnames from your own private network in these examples and start getting used to `tcpdump`. It's a powerful tool that also shows you how networking works.

MAC and IP addresses perform two different network functions:

✔ *IP addresses* let computers on the Internet find each other, wherever in the world they're located. (Chapter 10 covers IP addresses.)

IP addresses are like *company street addresses.*

✔ *Media access control* (MAC) lets computers on the same network *switch* or *subnet* locate each other.

MAC is like an *office number* in a building.

Detecting Intrusions with Snort

Snort is an open source package that works like a virus-detection system for your network. Network-based probes and attacks produce unique signatures analogous to those produced by viruses. Detecting probes and attacks before they can deliver their payloads helps keep you a half-step ahead of the security curve. Snort gives you a chance to detect attacks and prevent their success.

Snort is an open source project. It was invented by Martin Roesch in 1998. It started as a simple, lightweight intrusion-detection system. *Lightweight* doesn't mean weak. Snort is one of the most powerful tools (commercial or open source) available in the industry. (I had the pleasure of sitting in on a two-day Snort seminar presented by Mr. Roesch. It was fascinating and eye-opening. There's a lot of nasty stuff out there.)

Meta-view: Using Snort

Snort uses a database of network probe and attack signatures to detect unauthorized activity:

✔ **Network probes:** Hackers probe networks to discover their layout and find vulnerabilities.

Two widely used network-probing systems are described in the sections "Scanning Your Network with Nmap" and "Auditing Your Network with Nessus" in this chapter.

✔ **Network attacks:** Hackers try to exploit detected vulnerabilities. You can find lots of exploits of software vulnerabilities on the Internet. You can also invent your own (0-Day exploits).

Snort has two operational methods to detect anomalies:

✔ Host-based detection looks exclusively at the network traffic on a single computer's network interface card (NIC).

This book concentrates on using Snort as a host-based network sniffer. This is the easiest to configure and use. It's also quite effective on small networks.

✔ Network-based detection looks at the traffic on an entire network segment.

The following sections show how Snort works and how to use it.

Snort is a system that uses a *daemon,* a *configuration file,* and a database of *signatures* to monitor your network traffic.

Snort isn't included in the Knoppix distribution. You download it from the Internet.

The following sections show how to download, install, and run Snort on a permanent Knoppix installation.

Downloading Snort

apt-get makes obtaining and installing Snort very easy. Follow these steps:

1. **Connect your Knoppix computer to the Internet.**

   Part IV shows how to connect to the Internet directly or through a network.

2. **Log in as a nonprivileged user.**

3. **Open a terminal window by clicking the Terminal icon on the Kicker.**

4. **Type the following command to download and install Snort:**

   ```
   sudo apt-get install snort
   ```

5. **Type Y when prompted.**

   apt-get does some housekeeping and then prompts you to either continue or cancel.

6. **Press Enter to install Snort.**

   apt-get shows the download and installation progress.

Configuring Snort

After Snort is installed, you're immediately prompted to configure it.

When prompted, use the following instructions to configure Snort for your Knoppix computer:

1. **Press Enter to continue into the configuration.**

   The next screen, shown in Figure 20-1, prompts you to use the eth0 network interface card (NIC) as Snort's default interface.

Figure 20-1:
Configuring
Snort to
listen on the
eth0 NIC.

2. **Enter the appropriate NIC:**

   • If you're using the default Knoppix network configuration, press Enter to accept the default (eth0).

   • If you have a WiFi device, type wlan0 and press Enter.

   • If you're using a modem connection, type ppp0 and press Enter.

   The next window shows a class B network address space of 192.168.1.0/16. This range cannot be routed on the Internet and is used for private networks. Most consumer switches and routers use the 192.168.1.0/24 address by default. Figure 20-2 shows the changes.

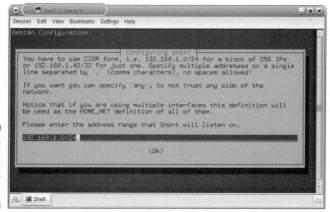

Figure 20-2:
Changing
the default
subnetwork.

3. **Enter the subnetwork range:**

   - If you're on a home network, the default `192.168.1.0/16` range should work, so press Enter (unless you know you're using another range).

   - If you're using another subnetwork address range, type the value and press Enter.

4. **Enter the username that should receive daily e-mail Snort summaries.**

   Change from `root` to an easily remembered name, such as `snortster`, as shown in Figure 20-3.

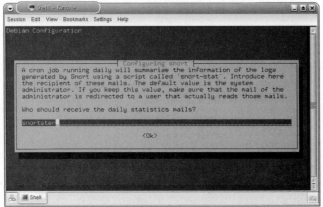

Figure 20-3:
Changing
the Snort
username.

5. **Press Enter.**

Snort accepts your configuration choices and finishes the installation.

Your NIC doesn't have to be fully connected to a network to "see" the network traffic. NICs can be placed into Promiscuous mode and operate without an IP address. When configured as such, your NIC displays all the network traffic that it encounters. Normally, your NIC only "sees" traffic addressed to it.

Running Snort

When Snort is installed and configured, all that's left to do is start the Pig (the nickname Snort's authors affectionately gave it, for obvious reasons) and resign yourself to monitoring its logs. Follow these steps:

1. **Start Snort.**

```
sudo /etc/init.d/snort start
```

   Snort monitors the packets flowing to your NIC and logs to several files in the `/var/log/snort` directory. Snort records a lot of uninteresting information but tries to distinguish possible intrusion attempts, recording them to the `/var/log/snort/alert` file.

2. **Start practicing monitoring the alert file by looking at its contents, which you access with the following command:**

```
sudo more /var/log/snort/alert
```

3. **Press the spacebar to progress one page at a time through the alert file (if it's more than a page long).**

Scanning Your Network with Nmap

The Nmap Security Scanner, or Nmap for short, is the most famous security tool in the world. It is featured in the movie *The Matrix Reloaded.* Trinity uses it to help defeat the evil matrix. (However, she should have used apt-get to update from version 2.54beta to at least 2.70, which is available as of March 2005. Oh well! The machines probably needed to update even more if the only energy system they could figure out was to use us puny humans as batteries. Couldn't they rehab an old nuclear power plant? I better not get started.)

How does Nmap work? It works by using the Internet protocols in ways they were never designed for. Nmap creates network packets and traffic in creative ways to trick the responding operating system into revealing information about itself and its network services.

You don't have to be a Hollywood starlet to use Nmap. It's a powerful yet easy-to-use scanning tool. Hackers use it to probe your network, and so can you.

Nmap was invented by Fyodor, a top security guru. He maintains a very useful and informative Web page at www.insecure.org. He is also the coauthor of the cyber-thriller *Stealing the Network: How to Own a Continent,* published by Syngress. This book is great for learning how real hackers and security professionals work.

Some organizations consider network scans to be a form of malicious hacking. It's best to practice on your own, private network. Avoid scanning computers and networks that you don't have explicit permission to scan.

Nmap is included in the Knoppix distribution. You can run a simple but effective scan of your home network as follows:

1. **Click the Konsole terminal icon on the KDE Kicker.**

   A Shell – Konsole window opens.

2. **Insert your network address into the following command:**

   ```
   nmap network_address
   ```

   For example, if your private network uses the nonroutable private network address space `192.168.1.0`, then the command is

   ```
   nmap 192.168.1.0/24
   ```

   Nmap returns a summary of every host that it finds on your network (such as network devices, computers, and routers).

3. **Focus your scan to detect the operating system of a machine:**

   ```
   sudo nmap -O network_address
   ```

   This command uses the `-O` option (that's the letter "oh," not a zero).

   Nmap returns a summary of every machine on the scanned network, including each machine's operating system and OS version number.

Nmap is pretty cool. These examples merely scratch the surface of its capabilities. Playing with Nmap on your own network to see what it reveals can be lots of fun. Use this information to learn about and tighten up your network.

Auditing Your Network with Nessus

Nessus is a network scanning and probing system. It first scans a machine or network and then uses the results to probe the machine or network. Nessus uses probes that are based on known vulnerabilities. The result is a system that mimics the process that a hacker might use to analyze and attack you.

Nessus is a client-server system. The server part scans and probes your network; the client controls the server. You can install the server on one machine and control it from another. However, I like to keep configurations as simple as possible and run the whole system on one machine.

The following sections show how to use Nessus to make your Knoppix computer a network scanning system.

Meta-view: Using Nessus

Knoppix installs Nessus by default. It works with the live Knoppix DVD. However, this section shows how to use Nessus on a persistent Knoppix installation because it's easier to keep Nessus updated on such a system.

Running Nessus isn't terribly difficult, but it does take some configuration. The following list outlines the overall process:

1. Register your service at `www.nessus.org` so you can receive automatic plug-in updates and start the Nessus server daemon.

2. Create a Nessus user and log in to the Nessus daemon.

3. Select the plug-ins and machines to probe.

4. Analyze the results.

Never use Nessus for "long-distance" scanning. That means you shouldn't scan over the Internet. You should never scan a network without consent from the network administrators of all involved networks. That effectively means that you should use Nessus only to scan your *private* network. Nessus plug-ins can sometimes crash Windows machines and routers that have bugs in their software.

System setup

Internet-based threats are constantly evolving and changing. The hackers get stopped by one protection mechanism and move to find other vulnerable machines. Security tools must evolve with the hackers. Nessus is no different and is constantly updated.

Registering your Nessus server

Follow these steps to register for automatic plug-in updates at `www.nessus.org/register`:

1. **Open Firefox and go to** `www.nessus.org/register`.

   The Web page shows a license agreement, as shown in Figure 20-4.

   There are two different licenses, depending on whether you *own* the network you intend to use Nessus on.

   Security tools are a double-edged sword that can either be used legitimately or be used illegitimately as hacker tools.

Figure 20-4:
The Nessus
plug-in
update
registration
page.

2. **Read and select the appropriate license agreement.**

3. **Click the I Accept button.**

   The Plugins Web page opens.

4. **Enter your e-mail address in the appropriate text box.**

5. **Click the Register button.**

You're sent an e-mail with a registration key. The following instructions complete the registration:

1. **Open your e-mail client and look for a message with the header "Nessus Plugin Feed."**

2. **Open the message.**

   It contains instructions similar to the following excerpt:

```
Your activation code for the Nessus plugin feed is
    8024-37D4-xxxx-yyyy-zzzz
To activate your account, simply execute the following command :
  nessus-fetch --register 8024-37D4-xxxx-yyyy-zzzz
```

3. **Click the URL link embedded in the message.**

   Another browser instance displays a Web page with a single text box.

4. **Enter the activation key in the text box like the one shown in Figure 20-5.**

Figure 20-5:
Entering
your Nessus
activation
key.

5. **Click the Registration button.**

The Web page displays a link where you can access the plug-ins.

Starting the Nessus server

You need to start the Nessus server before performing any scans. You also need to create a Nessus user that you'll use to control and monitor Nessus probes.

1. **Click the Terminal icon on the Kicker to open a shell window.**

   The Shell – Konsole window opens.

2. **Enter the following command to start the server:**

   ```
   sudo nessusd -a 127.0.0.1 -D
   ```

   The Terminal window displays a message about registering at www. nessus.org/register to get automatic plug-in updates.

Creating a Nessus user account

To use the Nessus client, you must first create a Nessus user account. Having an account allows you to log in to the Nessus server.

Follow these steps to create the Nessus user account with the nessus-adduser utility:

1. **Type the following command in the Shell – Konsole window.**

   ```
   sudo nessus-adduser
   ```

   You're presented with the Login: prompt.

2. **Enter a username (for instance, nessus).**

   The Authentication (pass/cert) [pass]: prompt appears.

3. **Press Enter to select the default** Authentication (pass/cert) [pass]: **option.**

   You're prompted to enter rules to restrict the Nessus user access.

   For this example, I choose not to enter any access rules.

4. **Press Ctrl+D to exit the user configuration.**

   You're prompted to accept the configuration.

5. **Press Enter to finish the configuration.**

You can use the new Nessus user to access and control the server.

Running Nessus

When Nessus is updated and you have a user account, you're ready to log in and start scanning with Nessus.

Selecting the machines to scan and probe

Before scanning, you need to start the Nessus client as follows:

1. **Click the K-Menu and select System➪Nessus.**

   The Nessus Setup window, shown in Figure 20-6, opens.

2. **Enter the username and password that you created in the previous section in the appropriate text boxes.**

3. **Click the Log In button.**

It takes some time to connect to and authenticate the Nessus server. After authentication, the Nessus Setup window switches to the Plugins tab, showing all the probes that Nessus is capable of. Figure 20-7 shows the Nessus Plug-in selection window.

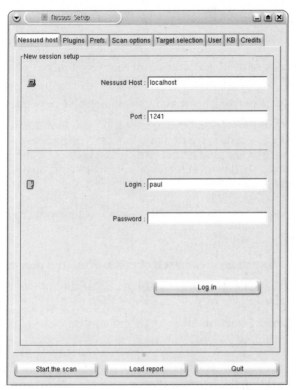

Figure 20-6:
The Nessus
Setup client
window.

Figure 20-7:
Nessus
shows the
available
plug-ins.

Selecting the probes

Nessus provides many scan and probe options. You can:

- ✓ Limit the scope of the scan, unless you're the system or network administrator for a heterogeneous network.

- ✓ Use all available plug-ins if you want an all-inclusive network scan.

   Nessus displays the warning dialog informing you that it has disabled all plug-ins that can crash systems and services. Nessus also displays a warning next to every plug-in that can crash systems or services. Please pay attention to such warnings so you can avoid wreaking havoc with your equipment and that of others.

For instance, if you want to scan a Windows machine, proceed as follows:

1. **Click the Disable All button.**

2. **Scroll down the submenu and select every Windows plug-in.**

   I also recommend clicking the *CGI Abuses, SNMP, Backdoors,* and *Remote File Access* options.

3. **Click the Target Selection tab.**

   Figure 20-8 shows the Target Selection window.

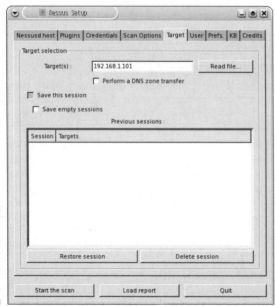

Figure 20-8:
The Nessus client Target Selection options.

4. **Enter the hostname (or IP address) in the Target(s) text box.**

5. **Start the scanning/probing process by clicking the Start the Scan button.**

   Nessus churns away on your network. Figure 20-9 shows the scan process dialog. The process takes a fair amount of time, so let it be and come back later.

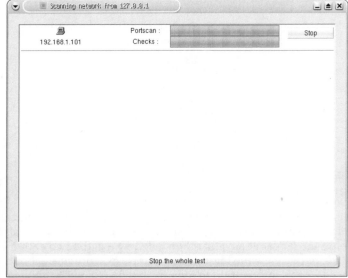

Figure 20-9: Nessus scanning your network.

Analyzing the results

After Nessus finishes, it displays an IP number. Here's how you get a look at the results:

1. **Click the subnetwork address in the upper-left corner of the Nessus client window.**

   In this case, it's 192.168.1.

2. **Click the Host IP address in the middle of the left side of the window.**

   In this example, it's 192.168.1.101. The Port and Severity subwindows display a list of the discovered vulnerabilities.

3. **Select Port Vulnerability from the list.**

   The severity of the vulnerability and the information about the problem are displayed.

   In this case, I click netbios-ssn (139/tcp) and select Security Hole. Figure 20-10 shows a severe vulnerability.

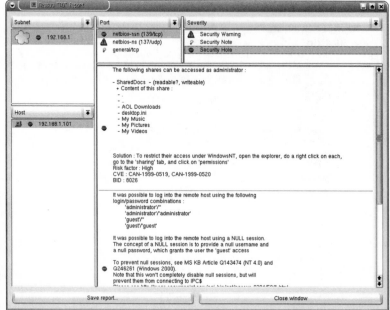

Figure 20-10:
Nessus
showing vul-
nerabilities
in the result
window.

Not all detected vulnerabilities are created equal. Some present severe risks to your computer and should be fixed immediately. Others are false positives that pose no danger at all. Still others fall between the two extremes. You should carefully view the information that Nessus provides about the bugs it detects. Use this information to identify and fix real vulnerabilities.

Oh no! I have open SMB shares and, worse, AOL on this machine! Where did it come from? (Oh yeah, I was helping relatives figure out their AOL problems — just say no!) And Nessus guessed some passwords! What was I thinking? (Well, I grooved a hanging curve ball for this example, but it's very demonstrative of Nessus's capability.)

Now, I'll go back to my Samba configuration and restrict access to these shares.

Nessus has provided me with information about some of my own vulnerabilities. This information illustrates why you must be vigilant, think ahead, and fix mistakes before they become problems. *Hasta la vista,* vulnerabilities!

Chapter 21

Remastering Your Knoppix Universe

*Y*ou are the master of your universe with Knoppix. Knoppix gives you the best of both worlds by letting you use both Windows and Linux on the same computer without installation hassles.

But you can go a step beyond mastery and *remaster* your universe. You can customize Knoppix and burn your own version on CD-ROM or DVD! That's pretty cool and very useful.

This chapter shows you how to build your own new, remastered Knoppix universe. Burn on!

 The example customized Knoppix version built in this chapter is used throughout Part V of this book. I use this example as the basis for several servers.

Customizing Knoppix

Why remaster your universe? You may be happy with things as they are, and there's nothing wrong with that. But you can enhance the beauty and functionality of a live Linux environment. Remastering lets you go wild with your environment.

But the devil is in the details. The customization process isn't extremely difficult, but it takes attention to detail. Fortunately, the details are in this chapter.

Cool ways to use a custom Knoppix CD

Add your own user account: Add a permanent username and password to your Knoppix disc. (Adding a real password adds security.) You can add productivity tools, information, and really almost anything to your account's home directory.

Put Knoppix on a diet: Eliminate unneeded software to make Knoppix fit on a mini CD-ROM or USB pen drive. You can keep your favorite tools and carry Knoppix around in your pocket.

Create "servers on a disc": Configure Knoppix as a network server and make a permanent copy on disc. You get more security and reliability for the following reasons.

✔ *Hackers can't touch the base system:* You create a fixed version of your software and configurations on read-only media that can't be modified. Every time you reboot, you're assured of starting from a known-good (secure) starting point.

✔ *Easy software updates:* Knoppix uses the Union File System (unionfs) to transparently stack ram disk and DVD (or CD-ROM) files together. unionfs allows you to effectively write to read-only media! unionfs lets you eat your cake and have it, too.

Before unionfs, you could remaster Knoppix but couldn't effectively update it. Not updating software outweighs booting from read-only media, so custom Knoppix servers have only recently become practical.

Knoppix 4.0 introduces the new "incremental image" feature. If you look on the Knoppix DVD, you see a directory called KNOPPIX containing, among other files, two files: KNOPPIX and KNOPPIX2. The KNOPPIX file contains the base Linux installation and has been used since Knoppix was first introduced. The KNOPPIX2 file is an incremental image that contains another Linux file system tree, which includes additional software. Knoppix 4.0 is capable of using Unionfs to stack up to eight incremental images — KNOPPIX1 through KNOPPIX8. This allows you to modify the base Knoppix system without modifying the base KNOPPIX image.

✔ *No yucky spinning things:* Extra reliability also comes from being able to boot directly from read-only discs. After you boot Knoppix, you're running from a 100% solid-state machine. There're no spinning discs to wear out — except when the system occasionally needs to access the DVD.

Hard drives are my bugaboo. Spinning disks of magnetic domains just seem out of place in the pure, esoteric world of electronic chips that are fast approaching the strange universe of quantum electronics.

Update Knoppix: You can boot Knoppix, update all the software packages that it contains, and then remaster it. This gives you up-to-date Knoppix with the latest and greatest software. Once again, pretty cool.

If you need a custom Knoppix version, you may not need to make it from scratch. Look for one of these shortcuts:

- ✔ **A remastered Knoppix version:** Dozens of specialized Knoppix versions are available. People with special needs and interests remaster Knoppix and distribute it. Check `www.knoppix.net/wiki/Knoppix_ Customizations` for information about customized Knoppix versions.

- ✔ **A script:** There are several remastering scripts, including scripts by Klaus Knopper himself. `www.ukuug.org/events/linux2004/knoppix. shtml` has more information about the scripts.

Now for less talk and more rock. The following section shows how to create a slimmed-down version of the vanilla Knoppix.

Creating a Smaller Version of Knoppix

This section describes how to create a smaller version of Knoppix. The example starts with the vanilla Knoppix that you boot by default from the *Knoppix For Dummies* DVD and takes out the graphics and other nonessential software. The end result is a version of Knoppix with a much smaller footprint.

The remastered Knoppix takes less than 200MB of disk space. That's small enough to easily fit on writable DVD, CD-ROM, and many USB flash drives. I concentrate on making Knoppix smaller because I think it's a good example in general, but also because I use the smaller version to create network servers in Part V.

Small is beautiful. Minimal Linux installations make better servers. Smaller is simpler, easier to maintain, and more secure.

Starting the customization process

This section gets down to the job of making a remastered Knoppix disc.

Resources

You need the following resources to perform the job:

- ✔ **A computer:** Well, duh, but I thought I'd mention it. You need to boot the Knoppix DVD from a computer that you use to perform the remastering process. That computer must include a Pentium processor and at least 256MB of memory.

- ✔ **Two CD-ROM/DVD drives:** This chapter requires two CD-ROM/DVD drives, one of which must be a writable CD-ROM or DVD. Most computers manufactured since 2000 (and some older computers) can read DVDs.

These instructions require two CD-ROM/DVD drives because you use a live Knoppix instance, which boots from and holds onto a CD-ROM/DVD drive. You'll need the second drive to burn your remastered Knoppix image.

If you have only one CD-ROM/DVD drive, you can still remaster Knoppix. In that case, you must use the copy-to-hard-drive cheat code when booting. The option copies the Knoppix image to your hard drive. You then reboot and use the boot-from-hard-drive boot option to boot from the Knoppix image stored on the hard drive. This two-step process boots a live Knoppix image but frees up your CD-ROM/DVD.

✔ **Knoppix:** You need the *Knoppix For Dummies* DVD from this book.

You can use other Knoppix versions, but these instructions are based on the *Knoppix For Dummies* DVD.

✔ **Disk space:** You need at least 15GB of free hard drive space to work in.

You *copy* part of the DVD, *modify* the duplicate, and *re-create* the modified DVD.

✔ **Writable media:** You need to be able to write the modified Knoppix image to a CD or DVD.

If using a virtual PC, you can use the disc image (ISO file) from a virtual machine instead of physically creating a new disc. The commercial VMware — `www.vmware.com` — and open source User-mode Linux — `www.usermodelinux.org` — provide great virtual environments.

✔ **Patience:** Remastering isn't the simplest of processes, but it's one of the most rewarding. Leave yourself enough time to patiently slog through this example.

Remaster Knoppix from a *live* instance for:

✔ **Convenience:** You might not have installed Knoppix permanently.

✔ **Safety:** Installing from the bootable disc is safer because mistakes can make a permanent Knoppix instance (hard disk–installed) inoperable. If you're running from a bootable Knoppix instance, none of your mistakes are permanent.

✔ **Simplicity:** Remastering from DVD or CD-ROM requires more steps but is easier to understand. I also think it's conceptually easier to go from disc to disc rather than from hard drive to disc.

The following sections describe each phase of the remastering process.

These instructions were derived from the HOWTO found at `www.knoppix.net/wiki/Knoppix_Remastering_Howto`. However, what I call the `Target` directory in this chapter is referred to as the `Master` directory in many Knoppix remastering HOWTO documents. I like `Target` better because the combination of `Source` and `Target` somewhat reduces my confusion.

Meta-view: Remastering

Remastering is an involved process. Therefore, the meta-view is very important for understanding the overall process. This meta-view is longer than others in the book, and I've provided more explanation for each step.

The overall process for remastering Knoppix goes like this:

1. Boot Knoppix live from the DVD and create a swap file.

   You can remaster from a permanent Knoppix instance. However, I prefer to work from a live instance so I don't have to worry about accidentally erasing files or configurations and so that I always work from the same baseline. (Permanent installations tend to get modified quickly and are more difficult to use in the remastering process.)

2. Mount a hard drive partition.

   You need at least 16GB of hard drive space to complete the remastering process. You need more space to create a swap file if you have less than 1GB of RAM to work with.

   You need to find space if working from a live Knoppix instance. You can either use qtparted to steal space from a Windows partition or use a second disk (for instance, a USB hard drive).

3. Create a Knoppix Source and Target directory on the hard drive.

   You copy the Linux file system from the working DVD to the Source directory. Once copied, you chroot to the Source directory and make your modifications.

   The Target directory serves as the platform for recreating the Knoppix DVD structure.

4. Configure the Knoppix Source directory.

   Copy the contents of the DVDs KNOPPIX directory to the Source directory on the hard drive.

5. Customize Knoppix.

   Run Knoppix just like you normally do, but with the intention of modifying it to perform some function or purpose. Customize it a little or a lot. Customize to your heart's content. Customize all day long. You can refine it until you're satisfied with its configuration and operation. It's all up to you. Freedom, baby, freedom.

6. Create an ISO image of the source/KNOPPIX directory in the Target directory.

   When you're satisfied with your customization, save it in *compressed loop* (cloop) format. Using the cloop format is Klaus's innovation that makes Knoppix Linux so useful. cloop compresses a complete Debian installation (the entire root file system) into a single file. That file compresses many gigabytes to fit onto the DVD.

   Paul Russel, the author of ipchains/iptables packet filters, invented cloop for the LinuxCare Live Rescue business card–sized CD. Klaus rewrote most of the code when he ported cloop to the Linux 2.4 and 2.6 kernel.

7. Configure the Knoppix Target directory.

   You use the Source directory to customize Knoppix. When you're finished, you use the Target directory to create a bootable image containing the modifications.

8. Create an ISO image of the entire Target directory.

(continued)

(continued)

This bootable image is your new personal Knoppix universe, err, distribution.

9. Burn the ISO image to CD-ROM or DVD.

Make your customized Knoppix portable by saving it to recordable media (such as DVD+RW, DVD-RW, or CD-R).

You're ready to boot your personal Knoppix from the new CD-ROM or DVD.

The fun starts when you boot into your new personalized Knoppix. Impress friends and family, get dates, and be popular. To be honest, remastering Knoppix might not help you do any of that, but it helps you transcend from normal nerd to *über* status.

Social status aside, remastering your Knoppix universe is just plain cool.

Booting Knoppix and getting started

Boot Knoppix from the *Knoppix For Dummies* DVD as follows:

1. **Insert the disc into your computer's read-only CD-ROM/DVD drive.**

   You need two CD-ROM/DVD drives to remaster Knoppix using these instructions. You boot from one drive and burn the image to the other. You boot Knoppix from the read-only drive so you can burn the remastered image to the writable drive.

2. **Turn the power on.**

   This chapter's example strips graphics from the remastered Knoppix. Therefore, you want to boot into non-graphical mode.

3. **Type the following at the boot prompt.**

   ```
   knoppix 2
   ```

   Knoppix boots into run level 2. That mode is non-graphical.

After Knoppix boots, you end up with a command line interface (CLI) and can proceed with the remaster process.

Create and mount a hard drive partition

You need a work area to remaster Knoppix. This section describes how to free up space on your hard drive to use for the remastering process.

The following list provides some common disk partitions:

- **IDE disk:** Integrated Drive Electronics (IDE) drives are most common. PCs provide two IDE interfaces:
  - The first IDE interface appears as /dev/hda and /dev/hdb.
  - The second IDE interface appears as /dev/hdc and /dev/hdd.

  Each interface connects to one or two drives (either hard drives or CD-ROM/DVD drives).

✔ **SCSI:** Small Computer System Interface (SCSI, pronounced "scuzzy") provides higher performance but at greater cost.

SCSI devices show up as files `/dev/sda` and `/dev/sdb`.

✔ **USB disks:** USB flash drives and hard drives are very popular because they're so convenient.

Enter the `df` command to list your disk partitions. You can add up all the kilobyte usage of all the KNOPPIX directories to find the required disk space.

I recommend purchasing an external USB hard drive if you don't have enough space on your hard drive to complete this chapter's example.

Find at least 16GB of usable space and use the following instructions to prepare the space for this example.

1. **Find at least 16GB of free space on a Linux or Windows partition:**

   • If necessary, Chapter 4 shows you how to free up space from an existing hard drive.

   • You don't need to free up space if you're adding a second, internal IDE hard drive, adding an external USB hard drive, or running from a permanent Knoppix installation with at least 16GB of spare drive space.

2. **Mount the partition:**

   ```
   mount -o suid,dev /dev/partition /mnt/partition
   ```

   For example, use the following command for the IDE `hda5` partition:

   ```
   mount /dev/hda5 /mnt/hda5
   ```

After you allocate your working space, continue to the next section to create working directories.

Create directories

You need to create two directories to organize your work after you have enough hard drive space.

Knoppix documentation uses the naming convention of `Source` and `Master` for these directories. However, I depart slightly from that convention because I confuse easily; I use `Target` instead of `Master` because it just sounds better to my ear.

Enter your hard drive partition into the following two commands to create the directories:

```
mkdir -p /mnt/partition/knx/source/KNOPPIX
mkdir -p /mnt/partition/knx/target/KNOPPIX
```

For example, use the following commands for the IDE hda5 partition.

```
mkdir -p /mnt/hda5/knx/source/KNOPPIX
mkdir -p /mnt/hda5/knx/target/KNOPPIX
```

These directories help keep the input to the remaster process separate from the output. The next section shows how to configure the Source directory.

Configure the Knoppix Source directory

Configuring the Source directory means copying the default Knoppix source file tree to the Source directory:

```
cp -Rp /KNOPPIX /mnt/partition/knx/source
```

For example, use the following command for the IDE hda5 partition:

```
cp -Rp /KNOPPIX /mnt/hda5/knx/source
```

When you boot Knoppix live from disc, the /KNOPPIX directory is created and populated with the Knoppix file system. The preceding command copies the Knoppix file system to the Source directory you created in the previous section. You customize Knoppix by modifying the files in the Source directory.

The following section describes how to modify the Source directory to create a new Knoppix.

Customizing Knoppix

This is the section where you actually modify the Source directory you create and populate in the previous sections.

There are many ways you can modify the Source directory. However, the example in this chapter creates a simpler, smaller version of Knoppix, which is the basis for several servers that you can build with Part V of this book.

The following steps modify the Source directory to create a customized version of Knoppix:

1. **Change Linux's root directory to the Source directory:**

```
chroot /mnt/partition/knx/source/KNOPPIX
```

For example, use the following command for the IDE hda5 partition:

```
chroot /mnt/hda5/knx/source/KNOPPIX
```

2. Create and mount the `proc` file system:

```
mount -t proc proc /proc
```

The `proc` file system isn't attached to any physical disk. `proc` is a logical file system that displays and interacts with the internal Linux kernel structures. In this case, you need to mount it so you can activate networking.

3. Type the appropriate command to use a DNS for your network:

- If your network supports DHCP, enter the following command:

```
echo "nameserver ip_address" >> /etc/resolv.conf
```

Most consumer DHCP servers use the default address of 192.168.1.1 for name resolution, so type the following:

```
echo "nameserver 198.168.1.1" >> /etc/resolv.conf
```

- If your network doesn't support DHCP, insert a valid name server IP address into the following command:

```
echo "nameserver ip_address" >> /etc/resolv.conf
```

For example, the following command uses the IP address `198.59.115.2` (a name server from the ISP Southwest Cyberport):

```
echo "nameserver 198.59.115.2" >> /etc/resolv.conf
```

You can use the following command to view the 20 largest Debian packages.

```
dpkg-query -W --showformat='${Installed-Size} \
    ${Package}\n'|sort -n |tail -20
```

You can use the results to select packages to remove.

If you want to reduce the size of the remastered Knoppix image you're building, see the sidebar "Putting Knoppix on a diet."

4. Update your packages:

```
apt-get update
apt-get upgrade
```

5. Press Enter when prompted about how to upgrade certain packages.

6. Leave some bread crumbs:

```
touch /REMASTERED
echo "Welcome to My Knoppix" > /etc/issue
```

These changes aren't essential. They just make it obvious when you're running your customized version of Knoppix instead of the full version.

7. Unmount the `/proc` file system by entering the following command:

```
umount /proc
```

8. Exit from the `chroot` environment by entering `exit`.

From small acorns, a mighty OS grows

The Linux file system starts from the `root` directory. Think of the file system as a tree full of

✔ **Branches (directories and subdirectories):** All branches start from the `root`. When you boot Linux from the Knoppix DVD, it creates a file system from the DVD and ram disk.

✔ **Leaves (files):** Every file and application that you access comes from the file system. The

`chroot` command tells Linux to change its root file system to the working `Source` directory.

Chapter 7 describes some of the ins and outs of the Linux file system.

Congratulations, you've just effectively remastered Knoppix. Changing the `Source` directory changes Knoppix. The following sections simply create the special files necessary to create a bootable disc containing these changes.

Configure the Knoppix Target directory

Knoppix works so well because it's able to combine several seemingly incompatible elements so they work together. Those elements originally included a bootable CD-ROM (now a DVD), a compressed file system, and numerous utilities.

The compressed file system allowed Klaus Knopper to include software on a single CD-ROM that normally required several. He created his overall distribution and then compressed its file system into a single file. He used the `cloop` (compressed loop) file system to format the file. This innovation was one of the keys to making Knoppix so usable.

The following instructions show how to create your own `cloop` file from the Source directory:

1. **Copy the base Web page, which you see after booting Knoppix, from the /cdrom file system to the Target directory:**

```
cp /cdrom/index.html /mnt/partition/knx/target
```

   Substitute your IDE partition as necessary. The following example shows a PC with the `hda5` partition.

```
cp /cdrom/index.html /mnt/hda5/knx/target
```

2. **Copy all the files except the original KNOPPIX file from the /cdrom file system to the Target directory:**

```
cd /cdrom
find . -size -10000k -type f -exec cp -p --parents '{}' \
    /mnt/partition/knx/target/ \;
```

The following example uses the partition `hda5`.

```
cd /cdrom
find . -size -10000k -type f -exec cp -p --parents '{}' \
    /mnt/hda5/knx/target/ \;
```

The backslashes in the preceding command have different functions:

- The first backslash (\) is a continuation mark. It tells the shell to treat the two lines as one command.

- The second backslash tells the Bash shell to ignore the semicolon (;) at the very end of the command.

The `find` command's `-size -10000k` option locates all files smaller than 10MB; the existing `KNOPPIX` file is nearly 800MB, so it isn't copied (there's no need to copy this file because you're going to build your own). The `-type -f` option tells `find` to operate only on files, excluding such objects as directories and soft links.

The `-exec` option tells `find` to execute the subsequent text as a separate command. In this case, the subcommand is copy (`cp`): `cp -p --parents '{}' /mnt/hda5/knx/target/ \;`.

- The `-p` option preserves the original file attributes (such as ownership and time stamp).

- `--parents` tells `cp` to prepend the source directory path to the destination path.

- The `'{}'` option is replaced by every file that `find` locates.

- The `/mnt/hda5/knx/target/` command is the destination to copy each file to.

- The `\;` tells `find` that the `cp` command has ended.

You can copy the same files without using the `find` command: Change to the `/cdrom` directory by typing `cd /cdrom` and then run the command `cp`.

3. **Make all the files on the target directory writable.**

```
chmod -R u+w /mnt/partition/knx/target
```

The following example uses the `hda5` partition:

```
chmod -R u+w /mnt/hda5/knx/target
```

4. **Remove the file containing the original Knoppix checksums:**

```
rm -f /mnt/partition/knx/target/KNOPPIX/md5sums
```

The following example uses the `hda5` partition.

```
rm -f /mnt/hda5/knx/target/KNOPPIX/md5sums
```

Putting Knoppix on a diet

You need to reduce the size of Knoppix if you want to remaster Knoppix to fit on a USB memory stick or demo CD. Use the following instructions to remove unneeded packages. The following instructions show how to remove several Debian packages. The packages removed in the following instructions are suggestions, not requirements. You should select the packages to remove.

1. Type the following command to remove a Debian package.

```
apt-get update
apt-get -y remove -purge package-name*
```

For instance, the following command removes several Debian packages that you probably don't need. (The back slashes (\) are continuation characters.):

```
apt-get update
apt-get remove --purge \
apache* autofs* blue* cvs* emacs* gimp* hpijs* \
isdn* openoffice* samba* squid*
```

I think these are packages are expendable. This isn't a comprehensive list — I just picked low-hanging fruit. For instance, OpenOffice.org takes lots of space, so removing it provides a big bang for your buck. I picked the other packages because I knew removing them would not adversely affect running Knoppix.

You should consider exiting from the package removal process by pressing Ctrl+C if you encounter a prompt that gives you the opportunity to tell your computer Yes, do as I say!. This prompt means that important system files are selected for removal, and you might render your remastered system-to-be inoperable if you proceed.

2. Optionally enter this command to remove most of the X Window System and KDE graphical environment:

```
apt-get remove --purge xfree86-common  kde-base*
```

In this case, specifying xfree86-common and kde-base not only removes those packages but also removes tons of other packages that depend on them. This command removes lots of software and reduces the overall size of the live Knoppix instance to less than 200MB.

3. Enter the following commands to clean up after yourself after you have removed all the packages in the previous step.

You must type the back quotes (`) before and after the deborphan option:

```
apt-get remove `deborphan`
deborphan | xargs apt-get remove
```

The checksums are used to ensure the integrity of the disc files. Remastering creates new files with new checksums.

5. **Enter the following commands to create a new compressed KNOPPIX file:**

```
mkisofs -R -U -V "Knoppix remastered" \
-publisher "Knoppix Heavy Industries" \
-hide-rr-moved -cache-inodes -no-bak -pad \
/mnt/partition/knx/source/KNOPPIX |  \
nice -5 /usr/bin/create_compressed_fs - 65536 > \
/mnt/partition/knx/target/KNOPPIX/KNOPPIX
```

For example, the following command uses the hda5 partition.

```
mkisofs -R -U -V "Knoppix remastered" \
-publisher "Knoppix Heavy Industries" \
-hide-rr-moved -cache-inodes -no-bak -pad \
/mnt/hda5/knx/source/KNOPPIX |  \
nice -5 /usr/bin/create_compressed_fs - 65536 > \
/mnt/hda5/knx/target/KNOPPIX/KNOPPIX
```

Wow, that's one big, bad-boy command (and probably took ten or more minutes to run). The numerous options to the mkisofs, nice, and create_compressed_fs commands specify technical choices that aren't important to know, so I don't describe them here. For clarification, here's the command without the options:

```
mkisofs file | nice create_compressed_fs - > filename
```

The overall operation creates an ISO file from the Source Knoppix directory. The ISO file isn't written to disk but instead is streamed (*piped* in Linux terminology) to the nice and create_compressed_fs command combination. nice simply tells Linux to run the create_compressed_fs utility at a slightly higher priority than normal. create_compressed_fs is a Knoppix utility that creates a compressed file system, which in this case is the KNOPPIX file containing the compressed Knoppix file system.

6. **Re-create the md5sums file:**

```
find /mnt/partition/knx/target -type f \
-not -name md5sums \
-not -name boot.cat \
-not -name isolinux.bin \
-exec md5sum '{}' \; \
>  /mnt/partition/knx/target/KNOPPIX/md5sums
```

The following example uses the hda5 partition.

```
find /mnt/hda5/knx/target -type f \
-not -name md5sums \
-not -name boot.cat \
-not -name isolinux.bin \
-exec md5sum '{}' \; \
>  /mnt/hda5/knx/target/KNOPPIX/md5sums
```

In the preceding command, the backslashes have two functions:

- The backslash preceding the semicolon (\;) is an *escape character*. (The escape character tells the bash shell to pass the next character to the command.) Without the escape character, bash processes the following character and the command does not function as desired.
- The other backslashes (\) are continuation characters.

In this case, find locates all the files except md5sums, boot.cat, and isolinux.bin, and then the md5sum command recomputes their checksums and stores them in a new md5sums file.

Burning the disc

The ISO file system standard (from the International Organization for Standardization) is used extensively in the Linux world. The mkisofs command creates an ISO file (with the .iso suffix) from one or more files and directories. You can

- Mount ISO files directly on your computer by using the mount command with the -loop option (for instance, mount -o loop knoppix.iso /mnt).
- Create DVDs and CD-ROMs from ISO files.

The rest of this chapter shows you how to create an ISO image and burn it to a disc.

Create an ISO image

The next step creates a file that contains the new Knoppix version that you just created.

This example uses a writable CD-ROM rather than a DVD because CD-ROMs are cheaper and more common.

Follow these steps to create an ISO image of your customized Knoppix distribution:

1. Change to the Target directory.

```
cd /mnt/partition/knx/target
```

For instance, type the following command if you're using the hda5 hard drive partition.

```
cd /mnt/hda5/knx/target
```

2. Type the following command to create the remastered ISO file:

```
mkisofs -pad -l -r -J -v -V "KNOPPIX" \
-no-emul-boot -boot-load-size 4 \
-hide-rr-moved -boot-info-table \
```

```
-b boot/isolinux/isolinux.bin \
-c boot/isolinux/boot.cat \
-o /mnt/partition/knx/myknoppix.iso \
/mnt/partition/knx/target
```

The following command assumes you're using the hda5 partition.

```
mkisofs -pad -l -r -J -v -V "KNOPPIX" \
-no-emul-boot -boot-load-size 4 \
-hide-rr-moved -boot-info-table \
-b boot/isolinux/isolinux.bin \
-c boot/isolinux/boot.cat \
-o /mnt/hda5/knx/myknoppix.iso \
/mnt/hda5/knx/target
```

Yikes! You just broke your record for unbelievably long command lines! But it's worth it. Remastering Knoppix, combined with the Union file system, is extremely powerful.

The preceding step customizes this basic mkisofs command:

```
mkisofs output input
```

✔ *input* is the Target directory (the preceding example uses the directory that's created in this chapter)

✔ *output* is a filename, ending in .iso, that contains your custom Knoppix distribution. The new ISO file contains

- • Files that make your new CD-ROM bootable

- • The Knoppix file system that you customized and converted into a compressed KNOPPIX file

You've just successfully remastered Knoppix! The ISO created in the preceding steps is Knoppix remastered.

You can use your newly remastered Knoppix ISO file to boot a virtual machine. I use VMware to create and test my images; I also use a spare "real" PC. VMware is a commercial product, but you can download a 30-day trial copy from www.vmware.com. User-mode Linux is an open source project found at www.usermodelinux.org that effectively creates virtual PCs.

Create a bootable CD-ROM

This section finishes the remastering process. You create a CD-ROM containing your custom Knoppix. Follow these steps:

1. **Insert a CD-R or CD-RW into your drive.**

2. **Type the following command to find the writable CD-ROM drive on your computer:**

```
cdrecord dev=ATAPI -scanbus
```

The output shows which device is the CD writer.

3. **Type this command to burn the remastered Knoppix ISO file to disc:**

```
cdrecord -v dev=0,0,0 myknoppix.iso
```

Substitute 0,0,0 with your device number if necessary. (Actually, cdrecord defaults to 0,0,0.)

Burn, baby, burn!

The last step is trivial: Reboot your computer with the new CD-ROM you just created.

Create a bootable DVD

This section finishes the remastering process. You create a DVD containing your custom Knoppix. Follow these steps:

1. **Insert a writable DVD into your drive.**

2. **Type the following command to find the writable DVD drive on your computer:**

```
growisofs -dvd-compat -Z /dev/dvd=/mnt/dev/knx/myknoppix.iso
```

For instance, enter the following command for the hda5 partition:

```
growisofs -dvd-compat -Z /dev/hdc=/mnt/hda5/knx/myknoppix.iso
```

The last step is trivial: Reboot your computer with the new DVD you just created.

Part VII
Advanced Knoppix Devices

The 5th Wave   By Rich Tennant

Don't get your hopes up, Ted. The other end may not be plugged in.

In this part . . .

Knoppix is so easy to use that it sometimes seems as though you can't do real work with it. That's not true. Knoppix provides a full-fledged Linux platform to perform advanced tasks, such as building servers. This part shows how to configure Knoppix to provide several interesting and useful services.

Chapter 22 describes how to use Knoppix as both a diskless client and server. One of the most basic and original Linux functions is sharing files over a network, and Chapter 23 shows how to do that. Chapter 24 delves into the new arena of digital TV recordings. Yes, if computers don't consume enough of your time already, you can finish the job with MythTV and this chapter!

Chapter 22

Going Diskless: Using Diskless Computers

Computers are found in every niche of life. You find them at work, at school, at home, and almost everywhere in between. Computers are almost as common as coffee in coffee shops (and coffee shops seem to be turning into ISPs). Computers are as common today as telephones, radios, and televisions were in past generations.

But the ever-present computer presents a problem: configuration. If you look at a million computers, you find almost as many individual configurations. That creates a problem when you administer and maintain lots of computers.

Is there a solution? Yes. Radios, telephones, and televisions don't require much configuration or maintenance; just plug 'em in and turn 'em on. One radio is pretty much like any other radio. Diskless computers bring this simplicity to the computing world.

Introducing Diskless Computing

People want to *use* computers without working to install and maintain them. Commercial and noncommercial organizations spend lots of money purchasing, installing, and maintaining their employees' computers. Neither individuals nor corporations want to spend time and money on nonessential tasks. Something must be done.

Spreading PXE dust on your network

Diskless computing requires a client to retrieve its operating system from a server on a network. But when you start a computer, it doesn't know how to communicate with the server — the diskless client-to-be doesn't know where to find its brain. So how does it work?

It works with a little help from PXE "dust." The *Pre-boot eXecution Environment* was invented by the Intel Corporation as part of its Wired for Management (WfM) initiative. It's designed to help the client computer boot over a network.

PXE is built into most network interface cards (NICs) manufactured since 2001. Our Knoppix-based network boot process works as follows:

1. The PXE-enabled NIC broadcasts a DHCP request and receives an IP address to use.

2. PXE also requests and then receives the boot server's IP address and the name of the network boot program (NBP) to use.

    The boot server can be the DHCP server or a separate machine. The server contains the operating system that the client loads. For the purposes of this chapter, the DHCP and boot server are the same machine.

3. The client computer uses the Trivial File Transfer Protocol (TFTP) to download the NBP from the boot server.

4. NBP starts on the client and uses TFTP to download a configuration file from the boot server.

    The configuration file contains information that is used later to start the operating system.

5. The NBP downloads the Linux operating system kernel.

6. NBP starts the kernel.

    After the Linux kernel starts, the NBP is no longer needed.

7. The Linux kernel broadcasts a DHCP query and gets the boot server IP address and the NFS address of the root file system.

8. Linux mounts the network root file system from the server via NFS (Network File System).

9. Linux starts the `init` process.

10. The `init` process executes the startup scripts found in `/etc/rc.d`.

    Your diskless computer finishes booting and becomes a full-fledged workstation. The only difference between it and a regular "fat" computer is the location of its storage, which is physically located on the server and accessed over the network.

The following list shows alternatives to the traditional personal computing model of installing and configuring an operating system and applications on a local hard drive:

- **Use a common operating environment:** Some organizations provide a common operating environment (COE) and require their people use it. You can typically customize your COE computer, but everyone starts from the same point, and usually some restrictions limit what you can do. This reduces but doesn't eliminate configuration variations.

- **Use thin clients:** *Thin clients* provide a graphical environment to share a central computer with other users. (Sun Microsystems' SunRay system is an example of a thin client.)

This effectively returns to the early days of computing, when everyone shared a single computer. You logged into your account with a terminal (or worse, used punch cards) and the computer did your work (and everyone else's).

✔ **Go diskless:** *Diskless computers* boot over a network, without their own hard drives or operating systems.

Diskless computers are what their name implies: diskless. (How's that for a recursive explanation, GNU?)

Diskless computers can keep everyone happy:

- *Users* get their own computers but don't have to maintain them.

  Users get all the gigabytes of memory and gigahertz of processing power of today's PCs, but not a local disk or operating system. A network server provides each user's computer with its operating system and storage space.

- *Management* maintains only a few central servers (or maybe just one). They only configure and update a limited number of machines.

The following sections show how to build a simple Knoppix diskless server and client.

Setting Up a Diskless Client-Server

Building a Knoppix diskless server is simple; creating a diskless client is even simpler. Knoppix supplies a script that automates the process. You just plug 'n' chug.

This section shows how to use live Knoppix as both a diskless client and server.

The *Knoppix For Dummies* DVD includes the Knoppix Terminal Server (KTS) utility. We use the KTS to configure a Knoppix diskless server in this chapter. The KTS uses the Knoppix DVD (or the Knoppix CD-ROM that you can download from www.knoppix.org) to provide the root file system to diskless clients.

Configuring and using the diskless server and client is described in the following sections.

Accounting for any DHCP servers

The Knoppix Terminal Server provides its own DHCP service. Many private networks also provide their own DHCP service. The two might interfere with each other.

You *can* create the diskless server without accounting for existing DHCP services, but you might encounter trouble. If you encounter interference (or want to prevent it), you can do the following to account for the existing DHCP server:

✔ **Configure the server to ignore your diskless clients.** You can configure many DHCP servers to either

- Work with pre-authorized NICs.

- Prevent access to specific NICs.

When configuring your diskless server, preventing specific machines — your diskless client(s) — from being serviced is the best idea.

Use the manufacturer's instructions to specify the media address control (MAC) of the NICs you want to use as diskless clients.

Every network interface card (NIC) has a unique *MAC address*. The MAC allows networks to distinguish one device from another.

✔ **Use or create a separate subnetwork.** Place the diskless server and clients on a network segment not served by the DHCP server. Separating the DHCP servers eliminates interference.

✔ **Turn it off.** If you use a router with your home DSL or cable modem, it probably provides DHCP. You can use the manufacturer's instructions to turn off the service.

Turning off your router's DHCP means you must reconfigure the rest of your network with *static IP addresses*. Chapter 10 shows how to configure your Knoppix computer to use static IPs.

Linksys routers and wireless access point/routers can permit or deny DHCP access based on MAC addresses. Use the Wireless MAC Filter options.

The following example assumes the diskless server and its clients use the same private network as an existing DHCP, which is how my own network works. I eliminate interference by configuring my private network router to ignore my diskless client when doling out IP addresses.

Configuring the server

Booting the diskless server is simple: Turn on the power to your PC and insert the *Knoppix For Dummies* DVD.

After the server boots, follow these instructions to configure the computer as a diskless server:

1. **Click the K-Menu and select KNOPPIX⇨Services⇨Start KNOPPIX Terminal Server.**

   The Information about the KNOPPIX Terminal Server dialog opens.

2. **Click OK.**

   The Terminal Server dialog opens with the Setup (Re)Configure Server and (Re)Start option selected. Figure 22-1 shows the Terminal Server window.

Figure 22-1:
The initial
Terminal
Server
menu.

3. **Click OK.**

   The Choose Network Device Connected to Client Network dialog opens.

4. **Select the appropriate NIC for your diskless client and click OK.**

   The IP Address Range for Clients dialog opens, as shown in Figure 22-2.

   However, if the Terminal Server notices that the NIC doesn't have an IP address, it opens the Configure LAN dialog from which you can define static network parameters.

5. **If your existing DHCP server overlaps with the Terminal Server, change the diskless server DHCP address range to values different from the existing DHCP server.**

   You don't need to change the diskless server DHCP range if your network is configured with both of these common default ranges:

   • DHCP server: 192.168.1.100 to 192.168.1.150.

   • Terminal Server: 192.168.1.201 to 192.168.1.250.

6. **Click OK.**

   The Client Hardware dialog shows a menu of NIC cards.

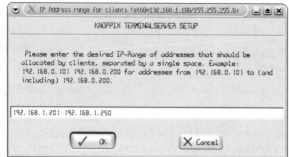

Figure 22-2:
The
Terminal
server's
DHCP
address
range.

7. Select all the NIC card types that you want to be able to boot from this server.

The kernel module for every NIC you select is inserted into the PXE boot image that the server provides to clients; the boot image contains all the necessary software that a client needs to load Linux and start the boot process. However, you should select only the NIC card types that you expect your clients to use. Otherwise, selecting too many NIC card types makes the boot image too big to be booted via PXE.

8. Click OK.

The Options dialog opens (see Figure 22-3).

Figure 22-3:
The
available
services in
the Options
dialog.

9. Click OK to select the default services.

The Client Boot Options dialog opens. You shouldn't need to specify any specific options here.

10. Click OK.

The Starting Server dialog tells you

- The Terminal Server is about to be started.

- What you will see if you display the process table (ps -ef).

11. Click Yes.

Your diskless server starts and is ready to serve clients.

Configuring the client

Configuring a diskless client is even easier than setting up the server. Use the following instructions to boot a PC from the diskless server:

1. Connect a PC, with a PXE-capable NIC, to the same network as the diskless server.

Alternatively, boot from the boot floppy available from www. rom-o-matic.net if your NIC is not PXE-cabable.

2. Turn the PC on.

3. Press the appropriate function key to edit BIOS (Basic Input/Output System).

Some computers dedicate a function key to executing a network boot. For instance, VMware virtual machines use the F12 key to start a network boot.

4. Change the boot sequence to place the network-boot first in the queue.

5. Save the new BIOS configuration and continue the boot process.

Figure 22-4 shows the typical Knoppix boot prompt, which in this case is also the diskless boot prompt. This sequence is exactly the same as when you boot Knoppix live from the *Knoppix For Dummies* DVD, as described in Chapter 2. You're effectively booting from the Knoppix DVD, after all.

6. Press Enter when you encounter the boot: prompt.

Your diskless client boots just like the *Knoppix For Dummies* DVD.

You can use your diskless client as if you were running Knoppix live from the DVD. As with the DVD, any changes you make or files you save are lost when you reboot the machine. The following section shows you how to save your files and settings.

Using persistent settings

Chapter 3 provides instructions for saving a private directory. The process saves your files and settings on permanent media (such as USB memory sticks and floppy diskettes).

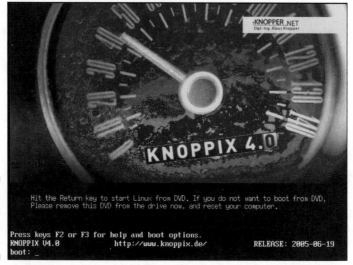

Figure 22-4:
The Knoppix
diskless
boot prompt.

The KTS provides the root file partition to diskless clients from the Knoppix DVD. You can increase your Knoppix Terminal Server's performance by creating and using a hard drive–based DVD image. Serving up the diskless client's file system from a hard drive is faster than from a DVD or CD-ROM.

You need to perform the following steps from a permanent Knoppix installation. You must also have at least 5GB of free space on your hard drive.

The following instructions describe how to speed up your KTS.

1. **Insert the *Knoppix For Dummies* DVD into your computer.**

2. **Type the following command to create an exact image of the DVD on your hard drive.**

   ```
   dd if=/dev/cdrom of=/knoppix-4.0.iso
   ```

   This process can take a number of minutes.

3. **Unmount the DVD.**

   ```
   umount /cdrom
   ```

4. **Mount the newly created image as follows.**

   ```
   mount -t loop /cdrom
   ```

You can boot your diskless clients from the hard drive–based Knoppix image.

Chapter 23

Building a File Server

Knoppix is best known as *the* Live Linux distribution. When it comes to living Linux, Knoppix is *numero uno.* Boot from a disc and you get a workstation running a full-blown KDE desktop from which you can run applications like OpenOffice.org and Mozilla Firefox.

This capability makes Knoppix famous, but it doesn't stop there. Knoppix is also a great platform from which to provide network services. It installs many types of server software by default. Boot Knoppix (live or from a permanent hard-disk installation) on a networked computer and configure the service, and you have yourself a network server.

This chapter describes how to build a file server; actually, it shows how to configure the default Knoppix installation to serve out files and directories (folders). File servers let you share information across networks, which is useful even if you have a private network consisting of only two computers. Whether your network is large or small, file sharing helps you obtain efficiency and convenience.

This chapter's examples assume a permanent Knoppix installation. You can use a live Knoppix instance if you want to learn about this technology. However, a hard disk installation is more useful if you want to create an actual file server, unless you simply want to share the read-only Knoppix DVD.

Introducing Linux File Sharing

The concept behind file sharing is simple:

   ✔ The server lets clients access its file systems and directories through a network.

- ✔ The file system and/or directory can be made either *read-only* or *read-write*.

   NFS provides only host-based access control.

   Samba provides both machine-based and user-based access control.

Linux provides two file-sharing systems:

- ✔ *Samba* mimics Windows file servers.

   Samba dances in the Windows world by "speaking" the Windows language: *Server Message Block* (SMB).

- ✔ *Network File System* (NFS) is a proven protocol for sharing files with Linux and UNIX computers.

   Use *Samba* if you need to mix Knoppix and Windows on a network.

Exporting Resources with Samba

You don't have to worry about the North American Free Trade Agreement or European Union trade standards when you export files with Knoppix. As the song says (I think), "All you need is Samba."

The following sections describe the more important parts of the Samba suite and provide two example configurations.

Essential Samba components

Samba is a suite of programs, configuration files, and documentation. It's the sum of its parts, as they say. The following sections describe the most important parts of the whole.

Knoppix Samba packages

Samba software is stored in several Debian packages. These are the most important packages:

- ✔ **samba:** This package includes the Samba server daemons (smbd and nmbd), utilities, and documentation files.

- ✔ **smbclient:** You use the client utilities to interactively use or mount remote Samba services.

- ✔ **samba-common:** This package contains supporting software used by both the client and server (such as the base configuration file, libraries, and miscellaneous files).

✔ **sambastart-knoppix:** This contains the utility to start Samba on Knoppix computers.

✔ **SWAT:** The *Samba Web Administration Tool* utility provides a Web-based configuration interface with which to configure Samba. Use your browser to connect to SWAT and configure any and all aspects of Samba.

The main Samba components are

✔ The smbd daemon (which provides the file- and printer-sharing service to clients)

✔ The nmbd daemon (a NetBIOS name server that answers a Windows computer's attempts to located Windows file shares)

✔ The smb.conf configuration file, which controls the smbd and nmbd daemons

The Samba configuration file

Samba configurations are stored in the smb.conf file. The configuration file is divided into sections, which contain parameters and comments. *Shares* define what resources Samba exports.

Samba uses these three special shares:

✔ [global]: The [global] section or share defines Samba's overall behavior. You define options such as authentication methods in the [global] share.

✔ [homes]: Most people use Samba to export user home directories to their private networks. The [homes] share is designed to facilitate this action and typically exports the /home directory.

✔ [printers]: Clients copy files to be printed to a temporary location on the print server, and the server then prints the file. The temporary directory is called a *spool directory* (or simply a *spool*). You can use Samba to export a spool directory.

You populate shares with parameters that define the behavior or the share. Some of the most popular parameters are described in the upcoming examples.

The Samba suite provides man pages and documentation. The quickest way to find information is to use the man command. For instance, run man smb.conf, man smbd, and man nmbd to find information about the Samba configuration and Samba daemons. The /usr/share/samba directory holds informational documents about Samba.

Meta-view: Building a Samba server

Using Samba to serve out files is conceptually simple: Decide on the file system or directories to export and configure Samba to serve it up.

Samba itself is simple to configure for basic operations; you can make very complex configurations if you need to provide complex file services.

This chapter concentrates on simple Samba configurations. Simpler is better when you're first getting started. The following steps describe the overall configuration process:

1. Configure a file system to be exported.

   Samba exports entire file systems and/or directories to one or more networked devices. You must decide the files, directories, or file systems to export.

2. Configure the Samba server to export shares.

   After you get your file system ready, you need to tell Samba what to export.

3. Connect one or more clients to the Samba server.

This chapter uses two example Samba configurations:

✔ **Exporting the DVD/CD-ROM drive**

The DVD/CD-ROM uses a very simple configuration because it's *read-only*. You have less exposure to hackers when exporting read-only media, so you have less to worry about.

✔ **Exporting the user account home directory**

Exporting your home directory presents more opportunities for mischief and requires more care.

The following examples describe how to export both types of file systems.

Example 1: Exporting your DVD/CD-ROM drive

Exporting the DVD/CD-ROM drive as your file system has the advantage of using a read-only file system, so the worst that a misconfiguration can do is let someone see your DVD.

Samba provides *file access lists* (acls) that let you permit or deny access to files and directories. However, Linux's file/directory acls take precedence over Samba's. If Samba says you can access a file but Linux's file permissions say otherwise, you're denied access. Therefore, you must pay close attention to file permissions.

You must also be careful when selecting what to export. Any mistakes that you make on non-exported file systems are protected by your computer's passwords and firewall. Stated another way, what goes on in Knoppix stays in Knoppix — until you start exporting files. When you start exporting, you can export your mistakes, and hackers and even regular people can see your dirty laundry.

Preparing your /cdrom file system

You needn't configure anything at this point. You need only to insert a DVD or CD-ROM into your drive if you haven't already done so.

Configuring Samba to export the DVD/CD-ROM drive

The next step is to configure Samba. Configuring Samba boils down to working with the smb.conf file, which is stored in the /etc/samba directory. You can manually edit smb.conf or use the graphical SWAT configuration system. SWAT lets you use a browser to configure Samba.

You don't have to worry about me making any silly SWAT puns, even if it was one of the greatest TV shows of the 1970s. (Just kidding.)

Before you can install SWAT, you have to know how to manually configure the /etc/samba/smb.conf file.

Building the smb.conf file to export the /cdrom directory

To start manually configuring Samba, save the original Samba configuration file and create a new one. Using a new file lets you easily create a simple configuration that illustrates Samba's basic capabilities.

Use the following instructions to create a new smb.conf file to work from.

1. **Boot your Knoppix computer.**

   Boot a live or permanent instance.

2. **Click the Terminal icon on the Kicker.**

3. **Switch to the root user.**

   ```
   su -
   ```

4. **Enter the root password when prompted (you won't be prompted if you're running from a live Knoppix instance).**

5. **Rename the default smb.conf file by typing**

```
mv /etc/samba/smb.conf /etc/samba/smb.conf.orig
```

Knoppix supplies a sample Samba configuration file designed to help create a print server. This example creates a new configuration file, so the preceding command pushes the printer sample off to the side.

6. **Create a new smb.conf file by entering the following command:**

```
kwrite /etc/samba/smb.conf
```

7. **Enter the following text in the KWrite window:**

```
[global]
    security = share
    workgroup = MSHOME
    server string = File server

[cdrom]
    comment = DVD/CD-ROM drive
    path = /path
```

The [global] options provide the following capabilities:

- security: Using the share option removes password authentication from the share. The client must supply a valid username and password if you specify the user option.

- workgroup: Windows file shares use the concept of workgroups to organize computers that share a common purpose. The default Windows XP Home Edition workgroup is MSHOME. Specifying MSHOME means Windows computers can easily browse your Knoppix Samba share from the Network Neighborhood.

- server string: This is an optional option. It provides information about your Samba share.

The [cdrom] share options pertain only to the /cdrom export. The options provide the following capabilities:

- comment: This option provides information about the share.

- path: This defines the directory or file system to export (in this case /cdrom).

8. **Save the file by choosing File⇨Save.**

9. **Choose File⇨Quit to exit the editor.**

This process creates a simple configuration file that exports the DVD/CD-ROM drive.

Starting Samba

The `/etc/init.d/samba` script starts and stops the `smbd` and `nmbd` daemons. To start Samba, switch to the root user and enter the following command in a command line interface (CLI):

```
/etc/init.d/samba start
```

You can stop Samba as follows:

```
/etc/init.d/samba stop
```

When you make configuration changes, you can reload the configuration file as follows:

```
/etc/init.d/samba reload
```

Or you may prefer to restart the daemons:

```
/etc/init.d/samba restart
```

Run the following command to make Samba start automatically when you boot your Knoppix computer:

```
sudo update-rc.d samba defaults
```

Running this script places links in the `/etc/rc2.d` through `/etc/rc5.d` directories, which point to the `/etc/init.d/samba` script. Those links execute the Samba startup script to start the daemons.

Now you can connect a Linux or Windows computer client to your Knoppix Samba server. Chapter 16 describes how to connect Linux and Windows computers to Samba and Windows file shares.

Example 2: Exporting user home directories

This example exports your Knoppix `/home` directory containing user account directories. Exporting home directories is very useful if you want to access your personal files from multiple computers on a private network.

The following sections describe how to prepare the `/home` directory and configure Samba to export it.

Preparing your /home directory

Exporting your `/home` directory requires more work than exporting a DVD or CD-ROM because you don't want to unnecessarily expose your sensitive information to the outside world.

By default, Knoppix configures the /home directory and the user home directories stored in /home with these permissions:

- ✔ **Directory owner:** read, write, and execute
- ✔ **Group owner:** read and execute
- ✔ **Everyone else:** read and execute

Run the command ls -ld /home to see the /home directory permissions:

```
dr-xr-xr-x  3 root root 4096 Apr  1 15:20 /home
```

This information means that the owner root, the group owner root, and others (every user) have read and execute permission.

The following command lists the directories that reside in the /home directory and lists their permissions:

```
ls -l /home
```

In my case, I see the following:

```
drwxr-xr-x  17 psery psery 4096 Apr  1 20:37 /home/psery
```

The permissions for the /home/psery directory (my user account directory) allow the owner psery (me) read, write, and execute permissions; the group owner, psery, and everyone else gets read and execute permission. By default, only the psery user has access to the psery group, so the default permissions should be secure enough. However, giving everyone read and execute permission is a little risky when exporting to the network.

Consider eliminating group read, execute, and especially write permissions to increase security. Recent Linux vulnerabilities have allowed any unprivileged users to arbitrarily change group ownership. I've successfully tested the exploit on several of my Linux machines running the 2.6 kernel. If you wish, run chmod -R 750 /home to eliminate this vulnerability. See www.securityfocus.com/bid/10662 for more information about the exploit.

Exporting the /home directory

You can modify the smb.conf file to perform a more useful function: configuring Samba to export users' home directories.

To modify the previous example's smb.conf file to export both the cdrom and /home directory, follow these steps:

1. Create a new smb.conf by entering the following command:

```
sudo kwrite /etc/samba/smb.conf
```

2. **Enter the following text in the KWrite window:**

```
[global]
   workgroup = MSHOME
   server string = File server
   security = user
   encrypt passwords = true

...

[homes]
   comment = Home directories
   path = /home
   read only = yes
   create mask = 0700
   directory mask = 0700
   browseable = yes
```

Here's a summary of the changes that the preceding commands make to the original smb.conf file.

- security = user: This option forces Samba to require a valid username and password to access a share. (security = share requires only a valid password to access a share.)

- encrypt passwords = true: The smbpasswd file contains your Samba passwords. It's best to encrypt those passwords to protect them from prying eyes.

  Recent versions of Windows require encrypted passwords so you have to use this option.

- [homes]: This option defines a new share used to export the /home directory, which contains user account home directories.

- comment = Home directories: This option adds a simple comment to the [home] share.

- path = /home: This exports the /home directory for the [home] share.

- read only = yes: Setting this parameter to yes keeps you from writing to the home directory shares. I include this option because it makes your Samba server safer while you learn and experiment. Change to no when you're ready to start writing to your home share.

- create mask = 0700: This is a security-oriented option that forces all files created under a Samba share to grant read, write, and execute permission to owners of the file and no access otherwise.

- directory mask = 0700: This option works the same as the previous option except it works on new directories.

- `browseable = yes`: When set to yes, anyone can view (browse) the share name. However, they may or may not be able to view the contents of the share depending on its acls.

3. **Save the file by choosing File⇨Save.**

4. **Choose File⇨Quit to exit the editor.**

5. **Set a Samba password as follows.**

   ```
   smbpasswd -a username
   ```

   For example, I type the following command to set the Samba password for my username:

   ```
   smbpasswd -a psery
   ```

   Your new Samba configuration sets the `security` parameter to `user`. That configuration requires anyone trying to connect to a share to authenticate with a local password. In this example, I use my own username `psery`; you should use your own username.

6. **Enter your password and then enter it again to confirm it.**

You don't have to use the same password as your Linux account. Samba's password authentication is independent of Linux's authentication.

You have reconfigured Samba to export both your DVD/CD-ROM drive and your home directories.

Restarting Samba

Assuming that you constructed the first example, you need to restart (or reload) Samba to force `smbd` and `nmbd` to reread and enact the new configuration. You can either

✔ Enter the following command in the terminal window:

```
/etc/init.d/samba restart
```

✔ Reload the configuration without restarting the daemons:

```
/etc/init.d/samba reload
```

When you browse your Knoppix Samba server, you should see and be able to read and write to its user home directories.

Using SWAT to configure Samba

The Samba Web Administration Tool (SWAT) is a powerful graphical configuration system that works through a Web browser. Install SWAT, point Konqueror or Mozilla at it, and configure away.

Installing SWAT

SWAT comes in Debian package form.

Use the following instructions to install and use SWAT:

1. **Connect your Knoppix computer to the Internet.**

   Part IV shows how to connect Knoppix computers to the Internet.

2. **Click the Terminal icon on the Kicker.**

3. **Type the following commands to install SWAT:**

   ```
   sudo apt-get update
   sudo apt-get install swat
   ```

   The first command updates the Debian package database to ensure you can run the second command.

   The Samba Web Administration Tool (SWAT) text-based dialog opens, informing you that your `smb.conf` file will be overwritten.

4. **Press Enter to let SWAT overwrite the Samba configuration file, and SWAT installs.**

You must configure Knoppix to start SWAT when you want to configure Samba, which is the subject of the next section. Big surprise!

Configuring Knoppix for SWAT

Linux uses the `xinetd` system to start generic network services. The `xinetd` system is a network service (a daemon) that

- ✔ Listens to incoming connections.
- ✔ Activates a network service if the request matches the `xinetd` configuration for the service.

The `inetd` configuration file is `/etc/inetd.conf`, and you must modify it so SWAT requests are listened to. Here's how:

1. **Click the Terminal icon in the Kicker.**

2. **Edit `/etc/inetd.conf` by typing the following command:**

   ```
   sudo kwrite /etc/inetd.conf
   ```

3. **Remove the `#<off>#` string at the beginning of the SWAT line at the bottom of the file.**

4. **Save the file by choosing File⇨Save.**

5. **Exit by choosing File⇨Quit.**

6. **Restart `inetd` by typing the following command:**

   ```
   sudo /etc/init.d/inetd restart
   ```

`inetd` rereads the modified `inetd.conf` file and is ready to start SWAT.

Configuring Samba with SWAT

This section describes how to use the Mozilla Firefox browser to configure Samba via SWAT.

1. **Click the Mozilla Firefox icon on the Kicker.**

   Mozilla Firefox opens.

2. **Type `http://127.0.0.1:901` in the Location text box and press Enter.**

   SWAT listens on the loopback interface (IP address 127.0.0.1) on port 901. Pointing your browser to that address connects Firefox to SWAT, which opens an authentication dialog.

3. **Enter `root` in the User text box, enter the `root` password in the Password text box, and click OK.**

   Your browser displays the introductory SWAT page shown in Figure 23-1.

You can configure any aspect of Samba by clicking the appropriate section button. The section configuration page opens, and you can select and change options and parameters. Click the Status button to see the state of Samba or to restart it.

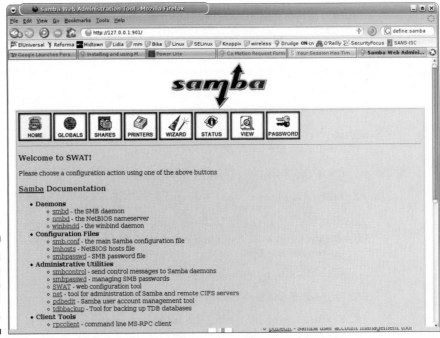

Figure 23-1:
The Welcome to SWAT! page.

Exporting Resources with NFS

NFS exports files to Linux and UNIX computers. NFS is simple to configure and use. This section describes how to configure a simple NFS share.

Windows computers can't mount NFS shares without extra software.

Essential NFS components

NFS is a software system that efficiently shares files across a network. Much of NFS is built into the Linux kernel. It is a leaner, meaner fighting machine.

Knoppix installs the Debian packages you need to configure and run an NFS server. The most important packages are

- **nfs-common:** Organizes files common to all aspects of NFS
- **nfs-client:** Contains software used to access NFS share
- **nfs-kernel-server:** Provides the software used to export an NFS share

NFS requires these parts:

- **NFS kernel modules:** This software inserts the NFS capability into the Linux kernel and provides most of the NFS functionality.
- **NFS daemons:** These programs run in the background on the server and handle client authentication and activate the kernel server processes.
- **Portmap daemons:** These daemons make it possible for both the NFS client and server to interact.
- **NFS client configuration:** The `/etc/fstab` file is used to tell the client what shares to mount from which server.
- **NFS server configuration:** The `/etc/exports` file tells the NFS server which directories to export to which clients.

You can configure NFS by creating and editing the `/etc/exports` file. Needless to say (but that won't stop me), the `exports` file contains the directories and file systems to export. The syntax is simple:

```
object    options
```

- `object` is the file system or directory to export. By default, an object is exported read-only to everyone.
- `options` adds restrictions to who can access the object from where. Options are, well, optional.

> ✔ You can add *comments* by starting the line with the # symbol and writing comments after it. The NFS server ignores all text after the # symbol up to the next line break.

NFS is automatically installed by Knoppix and every other major Linux distribution. You just configure it, start it, and use it.

Example: Exporting read-only user home directories

Linux file permissions take precedence over NFS acls. You need to properly configure the resources you intend to export before you export them.

Synchronizing user identifications on the client and server

You can configure NFS to allow general access to objects on the server. However, this isn't generally a good idea from a security viewpoint.

Now you need to configure the NFS client to work with the NFS server.

Configuring NFS to export the /home directory

Configuring NFS to export your home directories is a very complex task — *not!* Configuring NFS is simple because NFS uses only a few configuration options.

The following instructions configure NFS:

1. **Boot your Knoppix computer.**

   Boot a live or permanent instance.

2. **Click the Terminal icon on the Kicker.**

3. **Create and edit /etc/exports by entering the following command:**

   ```
   sudo kwrite /etc/exports
   ```

4. **Enter the following text in the KWrite window.**

   ```
   /home    a.b.c.d (ro)
   ```

   where `a.b.c.d` is the IP address of the host or network that you want to give access to the NFS share.

   The following example gives the `192.168.1.0` network read-only access to the /home directory.

   ```
   /home    192.168.1(ro)
   ```

This example entry uses the following components:

- `/home`: This is the directory to export. All of its child directories are exported, too.

- `192.168.1`: The `192.168.1` specifies the subnetwork that the NFS server serves. In this case, the server lets any computer with an IP address within the range of 192.168.1.1 through 192.168.1.254 mount the share.

  You can also specify one or more individual addresses, separated by commas (for example, `192.168.1.1,192.168.1.2, ...`) to let only specific machines connect to the NFS server.

  Use an asterisk (*) to allow all computers that can see your server to connect to the network. Change the IP address to an asterisk to allow access for all computers on your network. (For example, use the `/home *(ro)` configuration to allow all computers to access the `/home` directory.) Be careful, though: If you misconfigure your firewall, for instance, you could make an NFS server accessible to the entire Internet!

- `(ro)`: This option means read-only. All directories in `/home` are designated as read-only. Change this option to `(rw)` to make the shares read-write.

You can use other options when constructing the exports file. Consult the exports man page for more information (`man exports`).

5. **Save the file by choosing File⇨Save.**

6. **Close the file by choosing File⇨Close.**

7. **Open the /etc/hosts.allow file by choosing File⇨Open.**

8. **Enter the following filename in the dialog that opens.**

```
kwrite /etc/hosts.allow
```

   Kwrite opens the `/etc/hosts.allow` file.

9. **Enter the following text in the KWrite window.**

```
portmap : 192.168.1. : ALLOW
```

10. **Choose File⇨Save to save your changes.**

11. **Choose File⇨Quit to exit the editor.**

NFS is almost ready to export the `/home` directory. The next section shows how to complete the process.

Meta-view: Building an NFS server

You need to do the following to configure NFS:

1. Configure a file system on the server to export.

2. Configure NFS on the server.

3. Synchronize user IDs on the client and server.

4. Start the NFS daemons.

This chapter provides detailed instructions describing how to perform these steps with NFS.

Starting NFS

The operational side of NFS has two parts: the NFS daemons and the Portmap daemon.

The daemons need to be started so you can connect to the server. Here's how:

1. **Enter the following command to start the Portmap daemon:**

   ```
   /etc/init.d/portmap start
   ```

2. **Start the NFS daemons:**

   ```
   /etc/init.d/nfs-kernel-server start
   ```

3. **Verify that the NFS and Portmap daemons were started:**

   ```
   ps -ef | tail
   ```

   You should see Portmap and several NFS daemons running, like these:

   ```
   daemon 8047  1  0 21:52 ?  00:00:00 /sbin/portmap
   root   9428  1  0 22:13 ?  00:00:00 [nfsd]
   root   9422  1  0 22:13 ?  00:00:00 [nfsd]
   root   9431  1  0 22:13 ?  00:00:00 [nfsd]
   root   9433  1  0 22:13 ?  00:00:00 [lockd]
   root   9435 10  0 22:13 ?  00:00:00 [rpciod/0]
   root   9438  1  0 22:13 ?  00:00:00 /usr/sbin/rpc.mountd
   ```

   Several of the duplicate NFS daemons are not shown to protect the innocent — er, to save space.

   The `lockd`, `rpciod`, and `rpc.mountd` daemons are all related to and help the NFS daemons.

4. **Tell NFS to export the file system(s) in the `/etc/exports` file:**

   ```
   exportfs -r
   ```

You can mount the NFS share from any computer on your private network.

Chapter 24

I Want My MythTV

In This Chapter

▶ Installing MythTV
▶ Using the software
▶ Networking video

A myth has been floating around that you need to purchase digital video recorders (DVRs) from giant corporate conglomerates. DVRs are the modern-day successors to video cassette recorders (VCRs). DVRs digitally record television and provide features well beyond the capabilities of VCRs. For instance, you can record a TV program while watching another recording.

Another myth says that you have to subscribe to expensive services so you can schedule recordings on your DVR. These are indeed myths.

MythTV is an open source project that turns your computer into a DVR. Download and install the software, add a TV tuner, mix in Internet-based programming information — and you have yourself a DVR!

You can watch TV programs from your MythTV server with any computer on your network. This chapter shows you how.

If you want to sit down and watch TV with as little work as possible, there are two good reasons to buy or rent a ready-made DVR instead of using MythTV:

✔ MythTV takes time to set up. (You may need every step in this chapter.)

✔ *You* are your own MythTV tech-support staff.

If you want to watch TV from your Knoppix/MythTV DVR, continue on!

Introducing MythTV

MythTV is a system that combines

- A computer TV tuner
- Graphical software to view and record TV programs from the tuner
- Program listings that you get from the Internet

You get the following capabilities from MythTV:

- **Free program listing downloads:** Tribune Media Services provides the free DataDirect service in North America. DataDirect provides two weeks of scheduling data that you download from http://labs.zap2it.com. You can get program listings in other countries from the XMLTV service. Commercial DVRs, such as TiVO, require you to subscribe to their program-listing services.

- **Multiple TV tuners:** You can use one or more tuners in your computer to record shows. Commercial DVRs get expensive as you add tuners; computer-based tuners cost as little as $40.

- **Control live TV broadcasts:** You get the same capability as with the commercial DVR services, such as pausing and rewinding live TV.

  The DVR automatically records the show you're watching, so you can rewind what's already occurred.

- **Watch TV anywhere:** Well, at least watch TV on any MythTV client on your private network.

- **And much more:** You can create sophisticated, multiple-DVR configurations if you want them. You can install MythTV on more than one server and manage those servers from a single computer.

MythTV is an open source project started by Robert Kulagowski. What began as a homebrew project snowballed into an incredible system with a huge following. You can find everything you want to know about the process at www.mythtv.org.

This chapter shows what you can do with MythTV. The following section starts the journey that ends with a cool and fun personal video recorder (PVR).

MythTV has a few technical limitations:

- It can't run over older, slower wireless networks, such as 802.11b.
- There currently isn't a reliable MythTV system for HDTV (high definition television).

   ✔ MythTV program information currently is available for these countries:

   • *English language:* United States, Canada, the UK, and Australia

   • *German:* Tvtoday

   • *Other languages:* Sweden (`tv.swed.sc`), France, Finland (the birth-place of Linux!), Norway, Spain, Holland, Denmark, Portugal, Estonia, and Japan.

Stay tuned for the introduction of new MythTV regions and features.

Building a MythTV Client-Server

MythTV is based on the *client-server* model: Clients connect to a server.

   ✔ The server controls, records, and plays TV shows; it also displays live TV. The MythTV server is called the *back end.*

   ✔ The client is called the *front end.* You watch programs on the front end.

MythTV supports multiple back ends that work together; you can spread the load. This chapter concentrates on configuring one system that combines both the MythTV server and client.

These instructions assume you're running from a permanent Knoppix instal-lation. You can create a MythTV installation from a live Knoppix instance; however, you have to use persistent settings to save yourself the frustration of reconfiguring every time you boot.

Step 1: Make your computer ready for TV

MythTV works with analog — non-digital — cable TV service. It also uses common computer-based TV tuners and scheduled broadcast guides.

TV tuner

MythTV requires at least one TV tuner in your Knoppix computer DVR-to-be. Chapter 14 shows you how to install it.

Program listing guide

To program MythTV, you download your local TV schedule from the Internet.

Meta-view: Installing MythTV

This chapter covers the process to install MythTV:

Step 1: Make your computer ready for TV.

✔ Install and configure a TV tuner.

✔ Register with the TV program listing service and fill out the Lineup Wizard.

Step 2: Install the software.

✔ Download, compile, and install the LAME library.

LAME libraries are not distributed with Knoppix because of potential legal problems with the MPEG encoder.

✔ Download, compile, and install MythTV software.

✔ Add the QT3/MySQL library.

Step 3: Configure the database.

✔ Start the MySQL database.

✔ Configure the MythTV MySQL database.

✔ Set the database passwords.

Step 4: Configure the server (back end).

✔ Prepare the MythTV back end.

✔ Configure the general parameters, capture cards, video sources, and input connections.

✔ Start the back end.

✔ Download current TV program listing information and automate future program downloads.

There's probably a free TV program listing guide for your country:

✔ If you're in the United States, the fine company Zap2it.com provides a free service for downloading program listings. (Use the following instructions to sign up for Zap2it.com.)

✔ For other countries, check the www.mythtv.org Web site to find a program listing service.

Zap2it.com registration

If you're in the United States, follow these steps to register for Zap2it.com:

1. **Open Firefox.**

2. **Browse to http://labs.zap2it.com.**

3. **Click the New User? Sign-Up link.**

4. **Call in your lawyers, guns, and money and read the Subscription Agreement.**

5. **Click Accept.**

6. **Type your username, password, and e-mail address in the appropriate text boxes.**

7. **Type the following in the Certificate Code text box:**

   ```
   ZIYN-DQZO-SBUT
   ```

   You can obtain this code from the MythTV HOWTO found at www.mythtv.org/docs/mythtv-HOWTO-5.html#ss5.4.

8. **Enter more information as it's requested.**

   Zap2it.com provides a great service, so spending the time filling in all this information is worth the effort.

9. **Click the Subscribe button.**

   Figure 24-1 shows a typical final registration page.

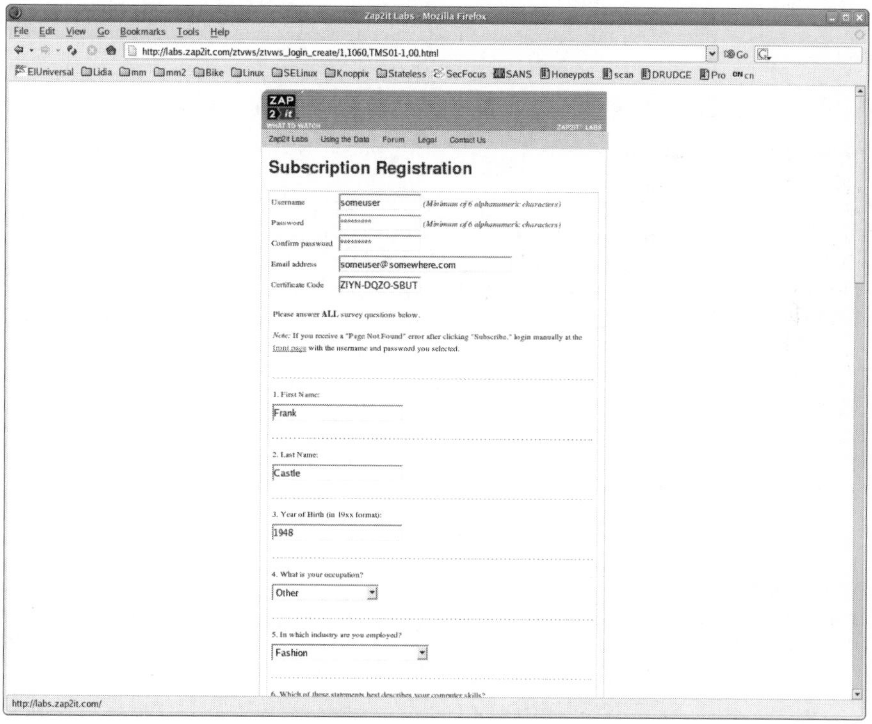

Figure 24-1:
Your finished registration.

Zap2it.com Lineup Wizard

After you register with Zap2it, your browser displays the Zap2it Labs Lineup page. From this page, you can download your local TV lineup. The downloaded lineup provides up to two weeks of program listings. You use the lineup to program MythTV to record TV programs. Use the following instructions to download the Zap2it program listing:

1. **On the Zap2it Labs Lineups Web page, click the Add a Lineup button.**

    The Lineup Wizard - Step 1 page opens. Figure 24-2 shows the screen.

2. **Enter your zip code (U.S. residents) in the text box and click Next.**

    This information helps locate your provider. The Lineup Wizard - Step 2 page opens.

3. **Select the type of television feed you use by clicking the appropriate button and then click Next.**

    You proceed to the Lineup Wizard - Step 3, which shows your local television provider.

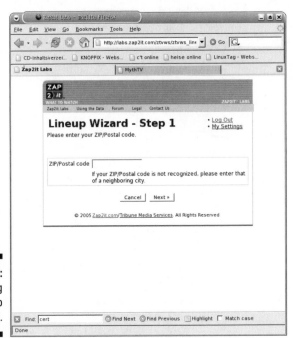

Figure 24-2:
Starting
the Lineup
Wizard.

4. **Select your provider and click Next.**

   Figure 24-3 shows the Lineup Wizard - Step 4 dialog, including the available channels from my local cable TV provider.

5. **Change the selected channels to suit your needs; then click Finish.**

   By default, all of the channels are selected. Deselect these channels:

   - Channels whose lineup doesn't change often (like news, weather, and shopping channels)

   - Channels you never watch

   The configuration process finishes and you're shown information about your selections (see Figure 24-4). You can return to this page later to view or change your lineup.

Your registration information is sent to the e-mail address you entered when you registered with Zap2it.

After you register and configure your Zap2it service, you can proceed to installing and configuring MythTV. MythTV uses the Zap2it program listing information to schedule and record your shows.

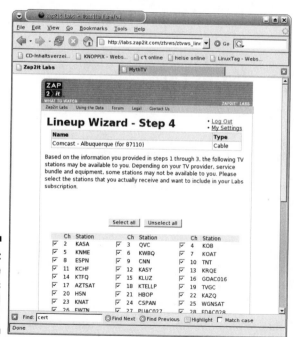

Figure 24-3:
My cable
provider's
channel
lineup.

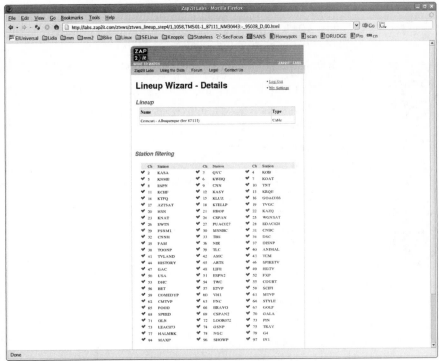

Figure 24-4:
Your Zap2it
Labs lineup.

Step 2: Install the software

MythTV requires both its own *software* and other supporting *libraries*.

This section installs the MythTV suite. You download the LAME supporting library and the MythTV software and then *compile* and install the software.

Compiling is the process of converting human-readable source code into an executable format that Linux can run.

LAME

LAME provides an essential library that lets MythTV read and write into the ubiquitous MP3 format. (MP3 is the common standard for encoding audio and video information.)

The acronym *LAME* started life in true GNU recursive-acronym form and stood for *LAME Ain't an MP3 Encoder.* Now it just means LAME.

Knoppix doesn't bundle LAME libraries with your system for legal reasons. You must download, compile, and install LAME before installing MythTV.

Download and unpack

The following instructions download and unpack the LAME source code:

1. **Log into your Knoppix computer as a regular user (non-root).**

   Chapter 6 shows you how to log in.

2. **Click the Mozilla Firefox icon to open the browser.**

3. **Enter `http://www.sourceforge.net/projects/lame` in the Firefox location text box and press Enter.**

   This takes you to the LAME Project home page.

4. **Click the Download link for Lame under the Latest File Releases heading.**

   The Project: LAME (Lame Ain't an MP3 Encoder): File List Web page opens.

5. **Click the Download lame-*x.y.z*.tar.gz link (where *x.y.z* is the version number).**

   A download page opens.

   Every LAME RPM includes a version number and creation date. Newer versions have higher version numbers and, of course, new dates.

   The Web page shows a list of mirrors.

6. **Under the Download heading, click the link for the closest mirror.**

   The Opening dialog appears; the Open With button should be selected.

7. **Click OK.**

   Firefox's Download dialog opens and shows the download progress. After the download completes, a dialog opens with a name like File:/tmp/lame-*x.y.z*.tar.gz, where *x.y.z* is the LAME version number.

   For instance, the dialog is named File:/tmp/lame-3.96.1.tar.gz if downloading LAME version 3.96.1

8. **Click the Extract button.**

   The Extract dialog opens.

9. **Double-click the Home directory icon in the left-side subwindow of the dialog.**

10. **Click the tmp directory icon in the right-side subwindow of the dialog.**

11. **Click the All Files button.**

12. **Click the Extract button in the lower right of the dialog.**

    The utility unpacks and stores the LAME tarball in the `lame-x.y.z` directory (folder) in your home directory.

13. **Close the (still) open dialogs that started during this process.**

    You've downloaded and unpacked the LAME source code!

Compile and install

Use the following instructions to compile and install the LAME code:

1. **Click the Terminal icon on the KDE Kicker.**

2. **Switch to the LAME directory by inserting the LAME directory name into the following command:**

   ```
   cd directory_name
   ```

   For example, the following command switches to the LAME source code directory:

   ```
   cd ~/tmp/lame*
   ```

3. **Configure the Makefile to compile and install the code by typing the following command:**

   ```
   ./configure
   ```

   The sidebar "Compiling files fast" explains how Makefiles work.

4. **Type the following command to compile the code:**

   ```
   make
   ```

5. **Install the LAME library:**

   ```
   sudo make install
   ```

6. **Enter your user account password, if prompted.**

   You enter your user password if you have a permanent Knoppix installation.

7. **Return to your home directory by typing this command:**

   ```
   cd
   ```

MythTV

The current MythTV software must be downloaded to your computer from the Internet.

Download and unpack

The following steps show how to download and unpack the MythTV source code:

1. **Use Firefox to navigate to www.mythtv.org.**

2. **Click the Downloads link on the left side of the window.**

3. **Click the MythTV link under the Downloads Main Categories heading.**

4. **Click the MythTV link.**

The Opening mythtv-*x.y*.tar.bz2 dialog opens, where *x.y* is the current MythTV version. The Open With button should be activated.

The MythTV version was 0.17 as of this writing.

5. **Click OK.**

   The file:/tmp/mythtv-x.y.tar.bz2 - Ark dialog opens.

6. **Choose Action⇨Extract.**

   A Knoppix - Konqueror window opens. It shows your home directory, including the new `mythtv-x.y` directory (folder). This shows that you've downloaded MythTV and you can compile the software.

Compile and install

The following steps compile the MythTV software after downloading it.

You must compile and install the LAME library before you compile and install MythTV.

Use the following instructions to compile and install MythTV:

1. **Enter the following command to switch to the MythTV directory.**

   ```
   cd mythtv-x.y
   ```

   where `x.y` is the MythTV version number. For instance, enter the following command if using MythTV version 0.17.

   ```
   cd mythtv-0.17
   ```

2. **Type the following command to configure the MythTV Makefile:**

   ```
   ./configure
   ```

   The sidebar "Compiling files fast" explains how Makefiles work.

3. **Create the Makefile by typing the following command:**

   ```
   make mythtv.pro
   ```

4. **Compile and install the source code by typing the following command:**

   ```
   sudo make
   sudo make install
   ```

   The compilation process can take a long time on a slow computer.

5. **If you're running from a permanent Knoppix installation, enter your password if prompted.**

   After the process completes, you've configured, compiled, and installed the MythTV software.

Compiling files fast

When you compile and install code, Makefiles contain instructions that compilers use to compile source code into an executable format. Without a Makefile, you enter many instructions by hand.

Using Makefiles doesn't directly convert source code into executable programs. There's an in-between step: the compiler converts each source code file into an object code file. Object files are binary formatted (no longer human readable). The object code files need to be linked (*stitched together,* if you will) with the appropriate libraries (such as LAME) into an *executable*

file. The executable file, composed of the object and libraries, is what you actually use to run an application such as MythTV.

Running the `make` command starts this process:

1. `make` checks the Makefile for instructions to compile the code.

2. `make` follows the instructions to convert the source code into object code.

3. `make` converts the object code into a single, executable file.

QT3/MySQL database library

MythTV interacts with the MySQL database, which requires the QT3/MySQL database library.

To add the QT3/MySQL library to your Knoppix computer, follow these steps:

1. **Ensure that your Debian package database is up to date:**

   ```
   sudo apt-get update
   ```

2. **If prompted for your user password, enter it.**

3. **Install the QT3/MySQL database library:**

   ```
   sudo apt-get install libqt3c102-mt-mysql
   ```

4. **If prompted to continue, press Enter.**

   If you're prompted to update any of your graphical systems during the `apt-get` installation, press Enter to select the default option.

Step 3: Set up the database

MythTV uses the MySQL database to store its configuration and program listing information. Knoppix bundles MySQL, so you just configure and start it; MythTV provides an SQL script that helps configure the database.

The following example uses the default MythTV MySQL database usernames and passwords. This is a potential security hazard; the passwords are well known, so they don't provide any protection. However, a basic MythTV system works within one Knoppix computer. This chapter shows you how to tighten security for MythTV on a private network.

The following sections get MySQL ready to work with MythTV.

Start the MySQL database

MythTV interacts with the MySQL database, which runs as a daemon. The MySQL daemon accepts Structured Query Language (SQL) requests. The following instructions start the MySQL daemon and configure the daemon to start automatically whenever you boot your Knoppix computer.

After the QT3/MySQL library is installed, you can start the MySQL database. Follow these steps:

1. **Type the following command:**

   ```
   cd
   ```

   This step makes sure of your starting place (your home directory) from which you execute the following instructions.

2. **Start MySQL by typing this command:**

   ```
   sudo /etc/init.d/mysql start
   ```

3. **Configure the MySQL script with this command to start at boot time:**

   ```
   sudo update-rc.d mysql defaults
   ```

Configure the MythTV MySQL database

MythTV bundles an SQL script that sets up the mythconverg and other essential MythTV database settings. This script saves you some work.

The following instructions run the script and test the basic database functionality:

1. **Create a database for MythTV:**

   ```
   mysql -u root < ~/mythtv-x.y/database/mc.sql
   ```

   where $x.y$ is your MythTV version number.

   The following example shows how to configure the mythconverg database when using MythTV 0.17.

   ```
   mysql -u root < ~/mythtv-0.17/database/mc.sql
   ```

The file mc.sql contains SQL statements that create an SQL user called mythtv and give it access to a database called mythconverg. The mythtv user can access the database only from this (local) machine.

2. Test the new database with this command:

```
mysql -u mythtv -p mythconverg
```

3. When prompted for a password, enter mythtv (it's the default MySQL mythtv user password).

4. Type the status command.

You should see information about MySQL and the mythconverg database, similar to Listing 24-1.

Listing 24-1:   Typical Status Command Output

```
mysql  Ver 12.22 Distrib 4.0.24, for pc-linux-gnu (i386)

Connection id:          28
Current database:       mythconverg
Current user:           mythtv@localhost
SSL:                    Not in use
Current pager:          stdout
Using outfile:          ' '
Server version:         4.0.24_Debian-2-log
Protocol version:       10
Connection:             Localhost via UNIX socket
Client characterset:    latin1
Server characterset:    latin1
UNIX socket:            /var/run/mysqld/mysqld.sock
Uptime:                 1 day 9 hours 48 min 36 sec

Threads: 4  Questions: 249145  Slow queries: 0  Opens: 165  Flush tables: 1  Open
            tables: 53  Queries per second avg: 2.047
```

5. Type the following command to show the available databases:

```
show databases;
```

You see the mythconverg database.

6. Exit from the database by typing exit at the mysql> prompt.

The MythTV configuration parameters are stored in the mysql.txt file in the mythtv directory in your home directory.

Step 4: Configure the server

After you install and compile all necessary software and prepare the MySQL database, you must configure the server before you can watch TV with the client. In this section, you configure the MythTV server *(back end)*.

Use the up- and down-arrow keys on your keyboard to navigate through the MythTV setup windows. If you use the mouse for navigation, you can't see the pointer on the screen.

Getting started

You need to do some prep work on the MythTV user account before configuring the back end. Follow these steps:

1. **Create a user account to use with MythTV.**

   ```
   sudo useradd -m -d /home/mythtv mythtv
   ```

   You use this account's home directory to store your videos.

2. **Start the configuration process by typing the following command:**

   ```
   sudo mythtv-setup
   ```

   The Setup window opens, showing the languages it understands. The window fills your entire monitor screen.

3. **Select your language (by pressing the up- and down-arrow keys) and press Enter.**

4. **If you want to delete existing Knoppix video settings, press the down-arrow key to select either of the following options and then press Enter:**

   - *Yes, Delete My Card Settings:* Removes any video card capture settings you've entered.

   - *Yes, Delete My Channel Settings:* Removes any TV channels you've entered.

Chapter 14 shows how to install video cards and configure these settings.

After starting the MythTV setup program, the Main mythtv-setup menu window appears.

The sidebar, "Introducing the mythtv-setup utility," lists the Main menu's submenus.

Pressing Esc at this point exits from mythtv-setup.

Main menu setup

The following functions on the Main menu set up the MythTV server.

When you're working within a submenu, pressing Esc returns you to the previous window. Pressing Esc several times eventually sends you back to the Main menu and finally exits from the mythtv-setup utility.

General

Follow these instructions to configure the general-purpose MythTV settings:

1. **From the Main mythtv-setup menu window, press Enter to select the General menu.**

   Figure 24-5 shows the Host Address Backend Setup window with the default IP address and ports.

   The local host address of 127.0.0.1 is internal to your Knoppix computer and isn't visible on your LAN.

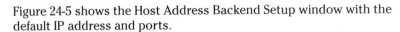

Host Address Backend Setup

IP address for veracruz: 127.0.0.1

Port the server runs on: 6543

Port the server shows status on: 6544

Master Server IP address: 127.0.0.1

Port the master server runs on: 6543

Cancel   < Back   Next >

Figure 24-5: Default IP and port settings.

2. **Press Enter to open the Host-specific Backend Setup dialog.**

3. **Type the home directory into the Directory to Hold Recordings text box:**

   ```
   /home/mythtv
   ```

4. **Enter `/home/mythtv` into the Directory Live TV Buffers text box.**

   The Tab key works the same as the right-arrow key. Shift-Tab provides the same action as the left-arrow key.

5. **Press Enter to open the Global Backend Setup window.**

6. **Use the TV Format submenu to select your TV broadcast format options:**

   a. Use the left- and right-arrow keys to select your country's TV format; then press the down-arrow key *twice*.

   In the United States, select *NTSC* (National Television Standards Committee).

   This puts you in control of the *Channel Frequency* option.

   b. Use the left- and right-arrow keys to select your TV channels.

   In the United States, select either *US-cable* or *US-broadcast*.

7. **Scroll down to the Time Offset for XMLTV listings.**

   The time offset identifies your local time zone.

8. **Use the left-arrow and right-arrow keys to select your offset from *Greenwich Mean Time* (GMT).**

   Table 24-1 lists time offsets for most of the United States. To find the time offset for other regions, check `www.timeanddate.com/worldclock`.

Table 24-1	Common United States Time Offsets		
Time Zone	*Major City*	*Standard Time Offset*	*Daylight Saving Time Offset*
Eastern	New York	–0500	–0400
Central	Chicago	–0600	–0500
Mountain	Denver	–0700	–0600
Pacific	Los Angeles	–0800	–0700

MythTV automatically adjusts for Daylight Saving Time.

Figure 24-6 shows my finished MythTV server configuration.

9. **Press Enter to finish configuring the Global Backend Setup window.**

   You've effectively finished editing the general options.

10. **Press Enter to skip through each of these sections:**

    • WakeOnLan setting

    • Job Queue (host specific)

    • Job Queue (Global)

    • Job Queue (Job Commands)

    When you return to the Main menu, you've configured the MythTV general settings.

Global Backend Setup

TV format: NTSC

VBI format: None

Channel frequency table: us-cable

Time offset for XMLTV listings: +0700

☑ Master Backend Override
☐ Follow symbolic links when deleting files

The TV standard to use for viewing TV.

Cancel   < Back   Next >

Figure 24-6:
Configuring
the Global
Backend
Setup
settings.

Introducing the mythtv-setup utility

The Main mythtv-setup menu has five submenus:

✔ **General:** Configure general operating options, such as the IP address and ports that the back end works with.

This chapter shows how to set the General submenu so MythTV runs over a *network*.

✔ **Capture cards:** Configure your video card.

✔ **Video sources:** Define how to get your TV program listing information.

In the United States, use Zap2it.com for program listing information.

✔ **Input connections:** Define the device file that interfaces with the video card.

✔ **Channel editor:** Edit the channel information, such as whether to use a channel or not.

Capture cards

You need to tell MythTV what kind of video card you're using. The following instructions show you how:

1. **From the Main menu, press the down-arrow key to select the Capture Cards submenu and then press Enter.**

   The Capture Cards window opens.

2. **Press Enter to select the (New Capture Card) option.**

   The Capture Card Setup window appears.

3. **Select the video card settings:**

   • To accept the default video card settings, just select Finish and press Enter.

   • If you need to customize MythTV for an unusual video card (such as HDTV), follow the steps in the "Advanced video cards" sidebar.

   This TV card configuration process is similar to the process of configuring xawtv in Chapter 14.

   After you select Finish, control returns to the Capture Cards window, which shows you the new configuration called [V4L: /dev/video0].

4. **Press Esc to return to the Main menu window.**

Advanced video cards

If you need to customize MythTV for an unusual video card, such as HDTV, follow these steps:

1. On the Connect to Source menu, use the up-/down-arrow keys to select an option that you need to change.

   For instance, select the appropriate option value if you use a video card such as High Definition or Digital Video Broadcast (DVB).

2. Press the left-/right-arrow keys to select the appropriate value for the option.

3. Repeat Step 1 and Step 2 for each option you need to change.

4. After you make all of the changes you need for your video card, press the down-arrow key until you get to the Finish button and then press Enter.

Video sources

This section shows you how to tell MythTV to log in to the service and get your local broadcaster's channel information.

If you followed the instructions to sign up for Zap2it.com's free program listing service, earlier in this chapter, it's payout time!

Follow these steps to tell MythTV how to download TV program listings:

1. **Scroll down to the Video Sources menu option and press Enter.**

   The Video Sources window opens.

   At this point, you have only one choice: (New Video Source).

2. **Press Enter to select (New Video Source).**

   The Video Source Setup window opens.

3. **Press the down-arrow key twice to move to the XMLTV Listings Grabber.**

4. **Type the name you want to call your configuration in the Video Source Name text box and press the down-arrow key.**

   For instance, type iwantmymythtv.

5. **Select your country's option:**

   - If you live north of the Rio Grande, press the down-arrow key to select the default value *North America*.

   - For other regions, use the right-/left-arrow keys to find your country's option and then press the down-arrow key.

6. **Enter your Zap2it username and password.**

   If you're a lucky Zap2it.com user in North America, follow these steps:

   a. *Type your Zap2it.com username in the UserID text box and press the down-arrow key.*

   b. *Type your account password in the Password text box and press the down-arrow key.*

   A dialog shows a progress bar as MythTV downloads channel information from Zap2it.com.

   Figure 24-7 shows an example of the final video source setup for a TV video card.

7. **Press Enter to finish the video source setup.**

   You return to the Video Sources window, which lists your new configuration.

8. **Press Esc.**

   The setup returns to the Main menu.

Figure 24-7:
Entering your video source information.

Video source setup	
Video source name:	iwantmymythtv
XMLTV listings grabber:	North America (DataDirect)
User ID:	me	Password:	iamnotanumber
	Retrieve Lineups
Data Direct Lineup:	Comcast-Cable--87110-NM30443:-
Channel frequency table:	default

Use default unless this source uses a different frequency table than the system wide table defined in the General settings.

Cancel   < Back   Finish

Input connections

After you configure MythTV's program listing source, you must associate it with your video card.

MythTV uses a modular design philosophy that separates its functional components into individual pieces. This makes it more robust and flexible.

MythTV lets you use multiple video sources and video cards. Configure each card separately and then link them together. This section shows you how.

The following steps connect a video card to your program listing provider:

1. **From the MythTV Backend Main menu, press the down-arrow key to highlight the Input Connection option and press Enter.**

    The Input connections window opens, showing four options.

2. **Press Enter to select the first option, [V4L: /dev/video0] (Television)->(None).**

    The Connect Source to Input window opens.

3. **Press the down-arrow key twice.**

    You find yourself at the Video Source submenu.

    The menu is set to (None), meaning no video source has been selected.

4. **Press the right- and left-arrow keys to select the source you created in the previous "Video sources" section.**

    For instance, select `iwantmymythtv`.

5. **Press Enter and you go back to the Input Connections window.**

    The first video input option is now associated with the video source: [V4L: /dev/video0](Television)->iwantmymythtv.

6. **Press Esc.**

    You return to the Main menu, and the MythTV back end is ready to go!

7. **Press Esc to exit from the mythtv-setup utility.**

Start the back end

Start the MythTV back end by typing the following command:

```
sudo mythbackend
```

The MythTV server starts and displays the following response:

```
Starting up as the master server.
2005-04-12 21:05:25.867 mythbackend version: 0.17.20050130-1 www.mythtv.org
2005-04-12 21:05:25.868 Enabled verbose msgs : important general
2005-04-12 21:05:27.866 Reschedule requested for id -1.
2005-04-12 21:05:27.903 Scheduled 0 items in 0.0 = 0.01 match + 0.03 place
2005-04-12 21:05:27.914 Seem to be woken up by USER
```

You can now view the server from the MythTV client: the `mythfrontend` application.

Download program listings

When the MythTV back end and MySQL database are ready to go, download your TV service provider's schedule. The `mythfilldatabase` application downloads up to two weeks of schedule information.

Type the following command from a CLI to get the program listing information.

```
mythfilldatabase
```

This utility downloads program listings and inserts them into the `mythconverg` database. You see a series of text-based dialogs as the `mythfilldatabase` utility does its work. Listing 24-2 is an example.

Listing 24-2: Typical mythfilldatabase Text Dialogs

```
Watching your new MythTVRefreshing Tomorrow's data
Retrieving datadirect data...
Grabbing data for Tue Apr 12 2005 offset 1
From : Wed Apr 13 04:00:00 2005 To : Thu Apr 14 04:00:00 2005 (UTC)
--20:57:48--  http://datadirect.webservices.zap2it.com/tvlistings/xtvdService
        => `-'
Resolving datadirect.webservices.zap2it.com... 206.18.98.160
Connecting to datadirect.webservices.zap2it.com[206.18.98.160]:80... connected.
HTTP request sent, awaiting response... 401 Unauthorized
Connecting to datadirect.webservices.zap2it.com[206.18.98.160]:80... connected.
HTTP request sent, awaiting response... 401 Unauthorized
Authorization failed.
Grab complete.  Actual data from --20:57:49--
        http://datadirect.webservices.zap2it.com/tvlistings/xtvdService
```

The download process takes at least a few minutes over a typical cable-TV Internet connection.

Automatic program downloads

Automating your MythTV program listing downloads means configuring the standard Linux `crond` daemon to periodically run the `mythfilldatabase` utility. Type the following command to insert the cron instruction that will automatically download the program listings:

```
sudo echo "minute hour * * * /usr/local/bin/mythfilldatabase" \
>> /etc/crontab
```

Minute can be 0 to 59. *Hour* can be 0 (midnight) to 23 (11 p.m.).

For example, the following command runs at 11:01 p.m. every day:

```
sudo echo "1 23 * * * /usr/local/bin/mythfilldatabase" \
>> /etc/crontab
```

The asterisks are *wildcards* that make the command run every day.

The `crond` is configured to run `mythfilldatabase` nightly.

Realizing the Myth: Watching TV with the MythTV Client

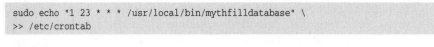

Start the MythTV front end and you can watch live TV, schedule recordings, and watch those recordings.

This is really it! No kidding!

Starting the front end

You need to tell the MythTV front end where the back end is. (There's a pun there, but I should stop while I'm ahead.) To start the front end, type the following command and press Enter:

```
mythfrontend
```

The front end places you in its *Main menu.* The Main menu has these options:

✔ **Watch TV:** This means what it says. Select this option and press Enter, and MythTV switches to full-screen video mode and displays the current channel.

Use the up-arrow and down-arrow keys to change channels.

> ✔ **Media Library:** You access your recordings from this menu after you start recording.
>
> ✔ **Manage Recordings:** Schedule and modify recordings.
>
> ✔ **Information Center:** Information about live and recorded programs.
>
> ✔ **Utilities/Setup:** Make general configuration changes.

Securing MySQL

Don't leave yourself completely vulnerable to hackers. Configuring MythTV isn't a simple job, so I minimize the process as much as possible and use the default settings throughout this chapter. The default settings are no secret, so you should assume that anyone who can get an interactive shell on your computer can access your MythTV setup. You're still protected by your basic security measures, but it's better to be safe than sorry.

The following instructions change the default `mythtv` password and set the currently nonexistent MySQL root user password (this *isn't* your Knoppix root account):

1. **Log into the database as `root`:**

   ```
   mysql -u root
   ```

   The root user in this case is different from your Knoppix Linux root user. The MySQL root user password should be different from your Linux root user in case the database is compromised. (SQL databases have been notorious for various vulnerabilities.)

2. **Set the `root` password.**

   In the following command, replace `iamnotanumber` with a password of your own creation:

   ```
   SET PASSWORD FOR 'root'@'localhost' = PASSWORD('iamnotanumber');
   ```

3. **Change the MythTV password.**

   In the following command, replace `amianumber` with a password of your own creation:

   ```
   SET PASSWORD FOR 'mythtv'@'localhost' = PASSWORD('amianumber');
   ```

4. **Save the changes:**

   ```
   flush privileges;
   ```

5. **Exit from the database interface by typing this command:**

   ```
   quit
   ```

6. **Run mythtv-setup, as described in the section, "Step 4: Configure the server," and reset the database password.**

You've set the basic security for the database and are at least protected from trivial exploits (such as a lack of passwords).

Watching live TV

The MythTV front end selects Watch TV when you start. Just press Enter to see live TV.

If another Main menu option is selected, press the up-arrow key to select Watch TV and then press Enter.

You can use your computer keys like a remote control:

- ✔ **Up-arrow key:** Change to the next higher channel.
- ✔ **Down-arrow key:** Change to the next lower channel.
- ✔ **Left-arrow key:** Rewind the current program.
- ✔ **Right-arrow key:** Fast-forward from a rewind.

  MythTV is great, but it can't see into the future. If you rewind the program you're watching, you can fast-forward back to the current time.

- ✔ **S:** View program listings.
- ✔ **Esc:** Return to TV viewing mode after switching to configuration mode.

Recording programs

MythTV records TV programs. This section describes how to schedule programs to record.

Scheduling TV programs to record

Follow these steps to schedule a recording with MythTV:

1. **On the MythTV Main menu, select the Manage Recordings option and press Enter.**

   The Manage window opens. The default selection is Schedule Recordings.

2. **Press Enter to select the default (Schedule Recordings).**

   The Schedule window opens, and the Program Guide is the default option.

3. **Press Enter to select the default (Program Guide).**

   The Program Guide gives you a grid of TV programs and times.

4. **Select the TV program you want to record and press Enter.**

   Use your up-/down-arrow keys to navigate the schedule.

TIP

A dialog opens, giving you many recording and other options.

The following steps schedule one recording of the selected show:

   a. *Press the right-arrow key.*

   The Do Not Record This Program option changes to Record Only This Showing.

   b. *Press the down-arrow key until you get to the Save These Settings option.*

   c. *Press Enter.*

   The TV program is scheduled to be recorded, and you return to the Program Guide.

5. **After you finish scheduling the recordings you want, press Esc until the Main menu appears.**

6. **On the Main menu, select the option to leave `mythfrontend` and then press Enter.**

   When the time comes, your program is recorded.

Watching recordings

When you're ready to watch a recorded MythTV program, follow these steps:

1. **Select the Media Library option from the Main menu.**

   You see the recorded programs.

2. **Press the right-/left-arrow keys to select a program.**

3. **Press Enter to select and view the program.**

Network access

You can watch MythTV over a network if you configure the server (back end) and client (front end) for network connections.

Back end configuration

To make a MythTV back-end accessible over your network, follow these steps:

1. **Open the back end General menu by typing the `mythbackend` command.**

2. **Change the *IP* and *Master Source IP* addresses to the server's LAN IP address.**

   The default value is `127.0.0.1`; the LAN IP address may be `192.168.1.1`.

3. **Enter the following command to make the `mythbackend` daemon reread its configuration:**

```
sudo killall -HUP mythbackend
```

Stop the `mythbackend` daemon by typing `sudo killall -9 mythbackend`.

Front end configuration

If a MythTV back end is accessible over a network, you can connect, control, and view it from a front end. Follow these steps to configure the front end:

1. **Open the `mythfrontend` configuration.**

2. **Change the front end IP address to match the back end address.**

Part VIII
The Part of Tens

The 5th Wave   By Rich Tennant

HELP DESK

TECHNICAL

ETHICAL

In this part . . .

All *For Dummies* books have a Part of Tens, which gives a few brief top-ten lists for quick reference. This book is no different. In this part, you can find ten great Knoppix hacks and ten resources for more information.

Chapter 25

Ten Knoppix Hacks

In This Chapter
▶ Fixing freeze-ups
▶ Communicating safely
▶ Customizing your system

*N*o *For Dummies* book is complete without a Part of Tens chapter or two. I take this opportunity to dole out ten of the most useful hacks in Knoppix. That's *hacks* as in performing a useful and fun task, not maliciously breaking into someone's computer system to wreak havoc.

The following sections show how to do some fun and useful tasks. Enjoy!

Fixing Freezes and Stopping Processes

Knoppix provides utilities for stopping and restarting processes. This section describes how to fix a frozen KDE desktop or a confused Knoppix computer. It also shows how to end individual windows.

Fixing freezes

Sometimes Knoppix loses its brain. Not all software is bulletproof. Processes can go crazy and freeze your computer. This doesn't happen often, but you should know how to restart the computer or KDE if it does.

Restarting KDE

Sometimes the problem lies with a bad, bad graphical process. In that case, you can restart KDE rather than the whole computer. You can use any of the following methods to restart KDE:

▶ Click the K-Menu and choose KNOPPIX⇨Utilities⇨Choose/Restart KNOPPIX desktop. KDE disappears, thinks, and then reappears as good as new.

- Press Ctrl+Alt+Backspace to restart the X Server.
- Press Ctrl+Alt+F1 and enter the `init 2; sleep 2; init 5` command.

  This command drops Knoppix into non-graphical mode, waits 2 seconds, and returns to graphics (KDE) mode.

Restarting Knoppix

If restarting KDE fails to fix your problem, the next step is to restart Knoppix. Use the following steps to restart Knoppix:

Before rebooting, ensure that any *queued data* (such as OpenOffice.org files) is written to disk. Follow these steps:

1. **Press Ctrl+Alt+F1.**

   You enter a virtual console.

2. **Flush all file system buffers to hard drive.**

   You can press *either* of these key combinations:

   - Alt(right)+SysReq+S
   - Alt(right)+PrintScreen+S

3. **Switch back to the KDE desktop by pressing Ctrl+Alt+F5.**

Use the following instructions to halt your Knoppix computer.

1. **Click the K-Menu and select Logout.**

   Wait for the End Session for "knoppix" dialog.

2. **Click the Restart Computer button when the dialog opens.**

If you can't restart Knoppix from the KDE menu, you can try the following method.

1. **Switch to a virtual terminal by pressing Ctrl+Alt+F1.**

2. **Enter the `reboot` command.**

Klaus Knopper mentions that you may find it interesting to find out what caused the problem. If you can open a terminal shell window, type `dmesg`:

- If you see a lot of lines saying `cloop read error`, your CD or DVD has scratches or is badly burnt, and you should get a new one.
- A `kernel panic` message is a bad software error that usually happens in device drivers, or it may mean misconfigured hardware.

If you can't use the menu to restart Knoppix, you have to power cycle your computer. *Power cycle* means physically turning your computer power off and then on again.

Kill (Bill's) Windows

All Linux geeks know how to kill — kill processes, that is.

Traditionally, to kill a Linux process, you open a terminal window, run `ps -ef` to list all processes, and either

- ✔ Use the `kill` command to end the poor process's life.
- ✔ Pipe the list through the `grep` filter, like this: `ps -ef | grep` *someprocess*.

Knoppix lets you kill processes without being a Linux geek and spending your Friday nights using and writing about Linux — d'oh! Knoppix provides the easy-to-use `Xkill` utility for killing a process. Follow these steps:

1. **Click the K-Menu and choose Utilities➪Tools➪Xkill (Xkill).**

   A square cursor with a bouncing KDE gear appears on your desktop.

2. **Move the new cursor over any application window or dialog that you want to kill.**

3. **Click the window and it dies.**

Uma would be proud.

Using OpenSSH to Communicate Securely

OpenSSH lets you securely transfer files, interactively communicate across networks, and tunnel other communications. (*Tunneling* means piggybacking the communication from other applications on OpenSSH.) OpenSSH is the Swiss army knife of secure communication: It keeps your communication safe from the bad guys, and it's easy to use.

OpenSSH is an open source encrypted communication system based on the *Secure Shell* (SSH) protocol.

Commands

OpenSSH allows you to run applications and utilities on a remote SSH server without having to first log into the server. The following sections describe how to execute remote commands.

Sending commands

Knoppix comes with the OpenSSH client installed. The client provides an interactive shell that communicates with the server via an encrypted channel.

You use the client like a local command line interface (CLI):

1. **Click the Konsole terminal icon on the KDE Kicker.**

2. **Type this command to connect to an OpenSSH server using protocol 2 (protocol 1 is broken and should not be used):**

```
ssh  -2 remotehost
```

   You're connected to the server with the username that you're logged into the client with.

3. **Enter your password when prompted.**

   You're securely connected to `remotehost`.

Type `man ssh` to view information about how to use the OpenSSH client and its options.

Receiving commands

Knoppix installs an OpenSSH server. Starting the server lets you "SSH" into your Knoppix computer from remote computers:

✔ Start the server *manually* from a terminal window:

```
sudo /etc/init.d/ssh start
```

✔ Set the server to start *automatically* every time you boot your permanent Knoppix computer:

```
sudo update-rc.d ssh defaults
```

   If you want the OpenSSH server to start automatically with a live Knoppix DVD or CD, use a persistent Knoppix image. (See Chapter 3.)

After the server starts, you can use the SSH client on another computer to communicate with your Knoppix box.

Execute remote commands

Use OpenSSH to execute remote commands without logging into an interactive shell. This provides a convenient way to

🗸 Perform simple tasks that don't require a full interactive shell.

🗸 Automate processes that you need to perform on remote machines.

For example, type `ssh` *`username@remotehost`* `echo hello` and you get the response `hello`. In this case, the remote host executes the command `echo hello` and displays the results on the standard output, which gets piped back to your OpenSSH client.

The remote server must be configured to tunnel X Window graphics back to the client; however, the OpenSSH server is configured, by default, to pipe X back to the client.

In the following example, the remote computer runs `xclock`, but OpenSSH displays it on the client's machine:

```
ssh -X username@remotehost xclock
```

File transfer

OpenSSH provides options to securely transfer files to and from an SSH server.

scp

The `scp` client copies files in either direction.

Sending

The following command securely copies a file from your client to a remote computer running the OpenSSH server:

```
scp filename username@remotehost:
```

Change `filename`, `username`, and `remotehost` to your own values. For instance, the following example copies the file `.bashrc` from your current working directory (it's installed by default in every user account's home directory) to the home directory of the user `paul` on a remote computer called `cancun`:

```
scp .bashrc paul@cancun:
```

You can copy the file to another directory by appending the directory's name after the colon. For example, type the command `scp` `filename username@` `remotehost:tmp filename` to copy `filename` to the user's `tmp` directory. Alternatively, type `scp` `filename username@remotehost:/tmp` to send the file to the `/tmp` directory on the remote machine.

Receiving

To securely copy a file from another computer running the OpenSSH server, change `filename`, `username`, and `remotehost` in the following command to your own values:

```
scp username@remotehost:filename .
```

For example, to copy the file `.bashrc` from your home directory on the remote computer `xcaret` to the directory of the computer you're currently logged into, type the following command.

```
scp paul@xcaret:.bashrc .
```

Type your password when prompted, and the file is copied to your current location.

The period (`.`) at the end of the preceding command tells OpenSSH to copy the file into your current working directory.

sftp

The interactive `sftp` works like the *FTP* (file transfer protocol) system:

✔ Type `sftp remotehost` for an interactive `sftp>` prompt.

✔ Type `help` for a list of commands.

✔ Use the `get` and `put` commands to *retrieve* and *send* files.

Tunneling

OpenSSH creates encrypted tunnels that you can run arbitrary services through. For instance, if your ISP offers Internet Message Access Protocol (IMAP) but not SSL-based IMAP, then you can't retrieve your e-mail securely. However, with OpenSSH, you can tunnel IMAP through an encrypted link and create your own security.

The following instructions use the Thunderbird e-mail client with a tunnel:

1. **Click the Terminal icon in the Kicker.**

2. **Type the following command to create an SSH tunnel for IMAP (port 143) to your ISP:**

```
ssh -N -f -L 1433:localhost:143 -l
    username@mail.myisp.com
```

Enter your ISP password when prompted, and the tunnel connects.

The SSH tunnel command's options are

- -N: Prevents executing remote commands.

- -L *1433:mail.myisp.com:143*: Forwards communication from port 1433 on the local machine's loopback (lo) interface to port 143 on the remote host, mail.myisp.com. IMAP uses port 143 by default.

  I use port 1433 on the front end because it's above port 1024. Only root can connect to ports below 1024, which are privileged. You can select any arbitrary, unprivileged port, but 1433 reminds me that I'm connecting to port 143. (I tacked on an extra 3.)

- -l *username*: Specifies the username to log into the remote machine with.

- &: Tells your local computer to detach from the terminal the process that the ssh tunnel command creates. The process runs independently without requiring your interaction.

  If you don't use the ampersand, the process remains responsive in the terminal window.

3. **Enter your user account password (when prompted) on the remote machine.**

4. **Edit your ISP server connection properties to use *server 127.0.0.1* and *port 1433*.**

   This tells your e-mail client to read e-mail on the loopback (lo) interface on port 1433; it doesn't affect any network or dialup settings. OpenSSH pipes input and output through that interface and port, and your e-mail client simply connects to it there.

   Chapter 12 shows you how to edit the properties of the Thunderbird e-mail client.

You can now securely read your e-mail via the SSH tunnel. Your private information can travel safely over the insecure Internet without being exposed to prying eyes.

In the preceding example, OpenSSH protects only e-mail you *receive.* If you want to protect e-mail you *send,* you can

- ✔ Configure another OpenSSH pipeline to encrypt outgoing messages.
- ✔ Use Transport Layer Security (TLS) and Secure Sockets Layer (SSL) for outgoing mail (if your ISP supports them).

System Setup

Knoppix provides utilities to help you configure your Knoppix computer. This section describes how to configure your monitor, mouse, time, and language.

If you're running Knoppix from a live DVD or CD, the tips in the rest of this chapter work best with a persistent home directory (see Chapter 3).

Monitor madness

Knoppix configures your monitor by default whether you use a live instance or a permanent installation. You can also create custom display configurations by using the Knoppix utility described in this section.

Screen gems

Knoppix does a good job of automatically configuring your monitor for color depth and maximum resolution. But you may want to customize the video settings for your own preferences. Knoppix gives you a utility to manually adjust your graphics.

Use the following instructions to change your video settings:

1. **Click the K-Menu and select Control Panel.**

2. **Click Peripherals and select the Display option.**

   The Control Center, shown in Figure 25-1, shows your current resolution.

   You shouldn't have to change your monitor's refresh rate (the second option in the Control Center's Display menu). The difference between values like 75Hz and 70Hz (or even 60Hz) is negligible.

3. **Click the Screen Size pull-down menu and select a new value.**

4. **Click Apply.**

   Knoppix implements the new resolution, and the Confirm Display Setting Change – Control Center dialog asks you to accept or reject the new settings.

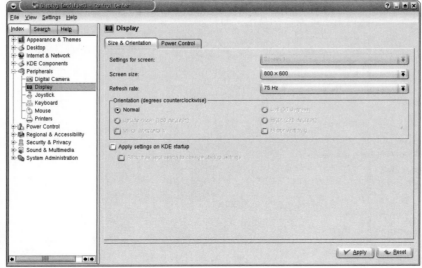

Figure 25-1:
The Control
Center
showing
the display
resolution.

5. **Click the Accept Configuration button.**

6. **Choose File⇨Quit to exit from Control Center.**

   Your new screen resolution is saved as the default value.

Click locally, act globally

Reduce global warming (or at least room warming)! Computers are annoying when they waste power. I hate when my computer doesn't put its monitor to sleep and drives my electric bill up. The KDE Control Center can tell your computer monitor to behave.

The following instructions reduce your use:

1. **Click the K-Menu and select Control Center.**

   The Control Center window opens.

2. **Click Peripherals and select the Display option.**

   The Display window opens.

3. **Click the Power Settings tab.**

4. **Select the Enable Display Power Management option.**

   The Display subwindow shows the available power-saving options. Figure 25-2 shows the default settings.

5. **Change the values as you want and click Apply.**

6. **Choose File⇨Quit to exit from Control Center.**

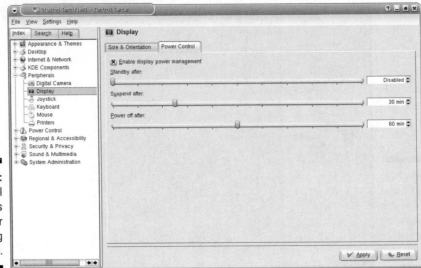

Figure 25-2:
The Control
Center's
power
saving
settings.

Your monitor will use less juice now.

Turn back time

You can set your Knoppix's date, time, and time zone by using graphical or text-based utilities. This section describes how to use the utilities.

Manually setting the date and time

Twice a year, Daylight Saving Time rears its ugly head. Spring forward, fall back, keel over, and so on. I don't like springing forward and falling back because I have to reset clocks and readjust to the time difference. It's jet-lag-in-a-box.

I think we should switch to *metric* time. Ten-hour days, ten-day weeks, ten-month years, and so on. I'll leave it to the brainiacs to figure out the details — but I can figure out that a ten-day week would have *four-day* weekends! Woo-hoo!

When you have to reset your computer's date and time, the KDE Control Center comes to the rescue once again. Follow these steps:

1. **Click the K-Menu and select Control Center.**

2. **Click System Administration and select Date & Time.**

   If you're running from a live Knoppix instance, click the Terminal icon and enter the command sudo kcontrol to start the utility as a privileged user.

3. **Click the Administrator Mode button, and the Run as Root – KDE su dialog opens.**

4. **Enter the `root` password and click OK.**

5. **If you want to change the time zone, click the Current Time Zone pull-down menu and select your corner of the Earth.**

6. **Change the date and time by clicking the appropriate values or typing the values directly into the text boxes.**

7. **Choose File⇨Quit to exit from Control Center.**

You're now up-to-date.

You can set your date and/or time from the command line. Open a terminal window and type `date`. You see the current date and time, such as `Fri Apr 8 21:02:55 MDT 2005`. You can set the date and time by using the basic format `date` *mmddhhmm* (*month, day, hour,* and *minute*). For example, set the date and time to 4:30 p.m., April 9, of the current year by typing `date 04091630`. (The date utility uses a *24-hour* clock.)

Automatically setting the date and time

Some computers have a good clock, some don't. Either way, the network time protocol (`ntp`) can keep your computer up-to-date.

Knoppix comes with the `ntpdate` command preinstalled. Follow these steps to automate your time-setting process with `ntpdate` and `cron`:

1. **Click the Mozilla Firefox icon on the Kicker.**

2. **Navigate to `http://ntp.isc.org/bin/view/Servers/NTPPoolServers`.**

   This Web page provides a list of open-access NTP time servers grouped by country. Open-access time servers are designed to be used by anyone anywhere. Each URL provides access to at least one server — you don't have to know which server actually supplies your time request.

3. **Click the Terminal icon in the Kicker.**

4. **Type the following command to switch to the Super User.**

   ```
   su -
   ```

5. **Enter the `root` password when prompted.**

6. **Type the following line:**

   ```
   echo "1 * * * * root /usr/sbin/ntpdate \
      us.pool.ntp.org" >> /etc/crontab
   ```

   This example tells `cron` to run the `ntpdate` command at 1 minute after every hour.

Run man crontab for more information about cron.

7. **Configure the cron daemon to start automatically, as follows:**

```
update-rc.d cron defaults
```

8. **Start the cron daemon.**

```
/etc/init.d/cron start
```

Your computer updates its time every day — or more often if you want.

The Debian package ntp supplies the ntpd daemon. Running ntpd keeps your computer constantly up-to-date.

Learning another language

Knoppix is multilingual. (This is fortunate for me; I speak only English, and Knoppix's native language is German, and it's hard enough writing in my native language.) Fortunately, Knoppix is truly an international Linux distribution.

You can easily boot Knoppix into your own language by using a *Cheat Code*. To use U.S. English, boot Knoppix and enter the following at the boot: prompt.

```
knoppix lang=us
```

Knoppix knows the following languages (use the associated lang= Cheat Code to use that language):

Language	*Cheat Code*	*Language*	*Cheat Code*
Danish	da	Italian	it
Dutch	nl	Lithuanian	lt
English	us (or lang=en)	Latvian	lv
Estonian	et	Norwegian Bokmål	nb
Finnish	fi	Norwegian Nynorsk	nn
French	fr	Northern Sami	se
German	de	Swedish	sv
Icelandic	is		

Permanent Knoppix installations inherit the language they were booted into. For instance, boot Knoppix live and use the lang=en Cheat Code. If you proceed to install Knoppix permanently on your hard drive, then that installation will use English.

Mouse tales

Options on the General tab can choreograph every step you take with your mouse:

- **Button Order:** Click the right- or left-handed button. Left handers rejoice! (Activating left-handed mouse buttons can make your desktop appear to freeze. Don't forget to *right-click* icons and options.)

- **Double-click:** Double click to activate an icon.

- **Single-click:** Single click to activate an icon.

- **Automatically select icon:** Set the time threshold after which holding the mouse cursor over an object selects the object.

- **Cursor Theme:** Click to select alternative cursors.

- **Advanced:** This tab changes mouse options such as speed.

- **Mouse navigation:** This tab lets you configure your keyboard to move and use the mouse cursor and mouse commands.

Training your mouse

The KDE Control Center controls all things (well, a few things at least). One is the ability to configure your mouse.

Follow these steps to make your mouse squeak just the way you want:

1. **Click the K-Menu and select Control Center.**

2. **Click Peripherals and select Mouse.**

   The Mouse - Control Center subwindow opens.

3. **Select a mouse option and select the value you want.**

   The sidebar, "Mouse tales," lists useful options under the General tab.

4. **Click Apply.**

   The dialog says you must restart KDE to use the changes.

   Many changes are applied as soon as you click Apply.

5. **Click OK.**

6. **Choose File⇨Quit to exit from Control Center.**

   When you restart KDE, all of the changes are applied.

Chapter 26

Ten Knoppix Resources

In This Chapter
▶ Using Knoppix documentation
▶ Using online resources

*T*his chapter provides information about useful and helpful resources. The resources range from general-purpose UNIX man pages to specific Knoppix documentation. Other resources are Internet-based, like Klaus Knopper's Web page.

Use the following information as a starting point to learn more about Knoppix. I use all of these resources to learn more about Knoppix.

Help Files

This section introduces some of the simplest but most useful Linux resources. All these resources provide both general and specific information about Linux.

Man pages

Man (as in *manual*) pages provide information about specific topics, utilities, protocols and commands.

Using man pages is simple: type `man` and the name of the topic you're interested in. For instance, type `man ls` to display the man page on the `ls` command.

Man pages are organized into nine general topics. The topics are *numbered*, as listed in Table 26-1.

Table 26-1		Topic Levels
Topic	*Level*	*Contents*
Executable commands	1	These are programs, shell scripts, and shell commands.
System calls	2	System calls are kernel functions.
Library calls	3	Libraries contain common programming functions. Rather than rewrite common functions over and over again, programs use library functions.
Special files	4	Linux uses special files to interact with hardware, such as keyboards, mice, and monitors.
File formats	5	These pages provide Information about file formats and conventions.
Games	6	Woo-hoo! Games! Linux command-line games are, well, fun I guess. Obviously, some man pages are getting long in the tooth.
Miscellaneous	7	This is a catch-all category for information that doesn't fit into any other category.
System administration	8	This level includes some system administration–related man pages. You can find a page for the `adduser` utility, for instance.
Kernel	9	Only one man page currently exists in this section: the man page for `ksoftirqd`, which deals with the soft IRQ daemon. 'Nuff said.

Levels are important when a single man page (such as a command, a configuration file, or a library) contains multiple man pages. You can specify which level to access by using the following syntax:

```
man level manpage
```

For instance, type the following command to display the Level 1 version of the `crontab` man page.

```
man 1 crontab
```

Alternatively, type the following command to display the level 5 version of the `crontab` man page.

```
man 5 crontab
```

The two man pages display different information about the `crontab` system. The former displays information about the `crontab` command, and the latter about the `crontab` configuration file `/etc/crontab` file.

You can use the `man` command to search for man pages even if you don't know the specific man page. Type the following command to find man pages based on a topic.

```
man -k topic
```

For instance, enter the following command to find man pages related to the `crontab` system.

```
man -k crontab
```

Debian includes documentation and examples for many packages in the `/usr/share/doc/packagename` directory.

Knoppix DVD documents

The *Knoppix For Dummies* DVD contains the entire Knoppix distribution. The distribution contains a wealth of information about itself.

Internet-based Resources

You can find a wealth of information about Knoppix (and about a few other subjects, or so I hear) on the Internet. The following sections describe some of the most popular and useful Knoppix-oriented Web pages.

Klaus's page

Klaus Knopper (creator of the Knoppix distribution) maintains his own Web page at `www.knopper.net` (shown in Figure 26-1).

Figure 26-1:
Klaus
Knopper's
Web site.

The following list shows some of the information Klaus distributes through his site:

- **Knoppix:** Information about Knoppix and its upcoming releases.

- **Courses and seminars:** Information about Knoppix and general software classes and seminars.

- **Products and solutions:** Information about Klaus's consulting services.

- **Links:** Discover links to other Knoppix-related sites.

North American Web page

The Knoppix Web site, `www.knoppix.net`, is the most useful Web page for English-speaking users in North America. This fine site provides a wealth of information and interaction possibilities. Figure 26-2 shows the Web page.

The following list shows some of this Web page's more useful information.

- ✔ **Download Knoppix:** Links to Knoppix mirrors throughout the world.
- ✔ **Documentation:** Numerous documents for using and developing Knoppix.
- ✔ **Forums:** User forums for discussing and finding information about Knoppix.
- ✔ **Bug reports**
- ✔ **General information:** Find contact information and much more about Knoppix.

This Web site has proved invaluable to the writing of this book.

Figure 26-2:
Visit www.
knoppix.net.

The European Web page

The European Knoppix Web page, `www.knoppix.org`, is another valuable Web site. Its default language is German, but you can also set it to these languages:

- ✔ **English**
- ✔ **French**
- ✔ **Japanese**
- ✔ **Polish**
- ✔ **Romanian**
- ✔ **Spanish**

Click the appropriate flag icon (as shown in Figure 26-3) to change to the associated language.

Figure 26-3:
The
European
Knoppix
Web site.

Online documents

The Knoppix-centric Web pages described in this chapter include documentation you may find useful. Check out the How-Tos, FAQs (frequently asked questions), and other documents those Web sites offer.

I extensively used the documents found at `www.knoppix.net/wiki/Main_Page` for this project. (I'm sorry, guys, I think I wore out a couple of your hard drives.)

Knoppix forums

One of the most frequently expressed knocks against Linux and open source software is that they lack customer support. This is just plain false. In the open source world, "customer support" doesn't typically come in the form of a subscription service. Instead, you find a wealth of support from user forums.

You can find the right forum and ask any question at `www.knoppix.net/forum`. You aren't guaranteed an immediate response; however, my experience is that this and many other forums are excellent. Take some time to formulate your question and submit it to the appropriate forums.

These are some of the most useful Knoppix forums at `www.knoppix.net/forum`:

- **Customizing & Remastering:** Use the information you find here (and in this book!) to customize and/or remaster Knoppix.
- **Games:** Increase Knoppix fun by interacting with this forum.
- **General Support:** This is a forum for people who have general or miscellaneous questions.
- **Hardware & Booting:** Find answers to your hardware problems.
- **Hdd Install/Debian/Apt:** You find answers to questions about installing Knoppix to your hard drive in this forum. Installing Knoppix means you effectively install Debian GNU/Linux; you can find information about Debian here, too.
- **Ideas:** You have a good idea? Submit it here and see where it goes.

- ✔ **Knoppix DVD:** A lot of work went into creating and improving the Knoppix DVD. Read about the process and interact with the ongoing development process.

- ✔ **Klik:** Klik is an interactive programming method. Find more information about it here.

- ✔ **Laptops:** This forum provides information about installing Knoppix to your laptop.

- ✔ **MS Windows & New to Linux:** This forum helps smooth the difficulties you may find if you're either new to Linux or switching from the Microsoft Windows world.

- ✔ **Network:** Look for solutions to your networking problems here.

- ✔ **News:** Knoppix developments and announcements are posted at this site.

- ✔ **Other Live CDs:** Find out information about Knoppix derivatives and independent live Linux distributions.

- ✔ **Tips & Tricks:** Submit your own Knoppix hacks here and make the Knoppix world better.

- ✔ **The Lounge:** Use this forum if you just want to talk with other Knoppix types.

You can find a wealth of information in these forums. You get to interact with many smart, helpful, and friendly people!

Google

Using Google to find stuff is a no-brainer. (Whenever a noun becomes a verb, you know it has arrived.) *Google* is the famous search engine that set the standard for searching the Internet. It's at www.google.com.

Google derived its name from the mathematical term *googol*. Googol is the name for the number 1 followed by 100 zeros — $1 - 10^{100}$ in mathematical parlance. Googol is a number which is larger than the estimated number of particles in the universe. Needless to say, that's a fairly big number. In 1938, Dr. Edward Kasner was looking for a name for that number and asked his 8-year-old nephew Milton Sirotta to think of one. The rest is history. Smart kid.

Appendix

About the DVD

This appendix describes what you get on the companion DVD and the minimum computer configuration you need in order to use Knoppix Linux.

The companion *Knoppix For Dummies* DVD contains the full Knoppix 4.0

The companion DVD contains most applications described in this book. However, you must download a few applications such as MythTV from the Internet. I describe where to find and how to download and install such applications.

System Requirements

Make sure that your computer meets (or exceeds) the minimum system requirements listed here. Please note that you can run Knoppix on older, slower equipment if you run in text-mode (enter **knoppix 2** at the boot prompt):

- ✔ An Intel-compatible Pentium PC running at least 500 MHz, less for non-graphical mode.

- ✔ For reasonable performance using the graphical X Window System, we recommend at least 256MB, but you can get away with only 192MB of main memory. You can never have too much memory, and we recommend that you increase your computer's memory, if possible.

- ✔ Since a "Live" Knoppix instance uses RAM in place of a hard drive, you should have at least 256MB of memory. You can run Knoppix in text-mode on as little as 16MB of memory!

- ✔ Zero MB of hard disk space. Zero? Yes, zero! Of course, that's only if you run Knoppix directly from DVD. You should have available at least 3GB of disk space if you want to make a permanent installation.

- ✔ You should also have a DVD drive, an LCD display or multisync monitor, a keyboard, and a mouse.

The instructions for booting the Knoppix operating system directly from the DVD are in Part I.

Instructions for installing it to hard drive are detailed in Part II.

What You Find

The companion DVD includes the full version of Knoppix Linux and much more. In other words, it contains a ton of stuff. The following list summarizes the DVD's contents:

- The KDE Desktop graphical environment
- The rich, great-looking OpenOffice.org desktop productivity suite
- Mozilla's powerful and cutting-edge Firefox browser
- The easy-to-use Mozilla Thunderbird e-mail client
- Many multimedia applications
- Numerous graphical tools
- System administration tools and utilities
- Network services
- Games

If You Have Problems with Your DVD

We test the companion DVD on as many computers and configurations as possible. Unfortunately, we can't test enough computers to ensure that our DVD will work across the board.

Call the Wiley Product Technical Support phone number at 800-762-2974 if you have problems using the companion DVD. Outside the United States, call 1-317-572-3994. Alternatively, browse www.wiley.com/techsupport — Wiley Product Technical support on the Internet — to obtain support. Wiley Publishing, Inc. provides technical support for only for physical manufacturing flaws in the Knoppix DVD. You must contact a program's vendor or author for application-specific support.

Call 800-225-5945 to place additional orders or to request information about other Wiley products.

Index

• *O* •

Notes

Notes

Notes

Notes

Wiley Publishing, Inc.
End-User License Agreement

READ THIS. You should carefully read these terms and conditions before opening the software packet(s) included with this book "Book". This is a license agreement "Agreement" between you and Wiley Publishing, Inc. "WPI". By opening the accompanying software packet(s), you acknowledge that you have read and accept the following terms and conditions. If you do not agree and do not want to be bound by such terms and conditions, promptly return the Book and the unopened software packet(s) to the place you obtained them for a full refund.

1. **License Grant.** WPI grants to you (either an individual or entity) a nonexclusive license to use one copy of the enclosed software program(s) (collectively, the "Software") solely for your own personal or business purposes on a single computer (whether a standard computer or a workstation component of a multi-user network). The Software is in use on a computer when it is loaded into temporary memory (RAM) or installed into permanent memory (hard disk, CD-ROM, or other storage device). WPI reserves all rights not expressly granted herein.

2. **Ownership.** WPI is the owner of all right, title, and interest, including copyright, in and to the compilation of the Software recorded on the disk(s) or DVD "Software Media". Copyright to the individual programs recorded on the Software Media is owned by the author or other authorized copyright owner of each program. Ownership of the Software and all proprietary rights relating thereto remain with WPI and its licensers.

3. **Restrictions on Use and Transfer.**

    (a) You may only (i) make one copy of the Software for backup or archival purposes, or (ii) transfer the Software to a single hard disk, provided that you keep the original for backup or archival purposes. You may not (i) rent or lease the Software, (ii) copy or reproduce the Software through a LAN or other network system or through any computer subscriber system or bulletin- board system, or (iii) modify, adapt, or create derivative works based on the Software.

    (b) You may not reverse engineer, decompile, or disassemble the Software. You may transfer the Software and user documentation on a permanent basis, provided that the transferee agrees to accept the terms and conditions of this Agreement and you retain no copies. If the Software is an update or has been updated, any transfer must include the most recent update and all prior versions.

4. **Restrictions on Use of Individual Programs.** You must follow the individual requirements and restrictions detailed for each individual program in the "What's on the CD" appendix of this Book. These limitations are also contained in the individual license agreements recorded on the Software Media. These limitations may include a requirement that after using the program for a specified period of time, the user must pay a registration fee or discontinue use. By opening the Software packet(s), you will be agreeing to abide by the licenses and restrictions for these individual programs that are detailed in the "What's on the CD" appendix and on the Software Media. None of the material on this Software Media or listed in this Book may ever be redistributed, in original or modified form, for commercial purposes.

GNU GENERAL PUBLIC LICENSE

TERMS AND CONDITIONS FOR COPYING, DISTRIBUTION AND MODIFICATION

0. This License applies to any program or other work which contains a notice placed by the copyright holder saying it may be distributed under the terms of this General Public License. The "Program", below, refers to any such program or work, and a "work based on the Program" means either the Program or any derivative work under copyright law: that is to say, a work containing the Program or a portion of it, either verbatim or with modifications and/or translated into another language. (Hereinafter, translation is included without limitation in the term "modification".) Each licensee is addressed as "you".

   Activities other than copying, distribution and modification are not covered by this License; they are outside its scope. The act of running the Program is not restricted, and the output from the Program is covered only if its contents constitute a work based on the Program (independent of having been made by running the Program). Whether that is true depends on what the Program does.

1. You may copy and distribute verbatim copies of the Program's source code as you receive it, in any medium, provided that you conspicuously and appropriately publish on each copy an appropriate copyright notice and disclaimer of warranty; keep intact all the notices that refer to this License and to the absence of any warranty; and give any other recipients of the Program a copy of this License along with the Program.

   You may charge a fee for the physical act of transferring a copy, and you may at your option offer warranty protection in exchange for a fee.

2. You may modify your copy or copies of the Program or any portion of it, thus forming a work based on the Program, and copy and distribute such modifications or work under the terms of Section 1 above, provided that you also meet all of these conditions:

   a) You must cause the modified files to carry prominent notices stating that you changed the files and the date of any change.

   b) You must cause any work that you distribute or publish, that in whole or in part contains or is derived from the Program or any part thereof, to be licensed as a whole at no charge to all third parties under the terms of this License.

   c) If the modified program normally reads commands interactively when run, you must cause it, when started running for such interactive use in the most ordinary way, to print or display an announcement including an appropriate copyright notice and a notice that there is no warranty (or else, saying that you provide a warranty) and that users may redistribute the program under these conditions, and telling the user how to view a copy of this License. (Exception: if the Program itself is interactive but does not normally print such an announcement, your work based on the Program is not required to print an announcement.)

   These requirements apply to the modified work as a whole. If identifiable sections of that work are not derived from the Program, and can be reasonably considered independent and separate works in themselves, then this License, and its terms, do not apply to those sections when you distribute them as separate works. But when you distribute the same sections as part of a whole which is a work based on the Program, the distribution of the whole must be on the terms of this License, whose permissions for other licensees extend to the entire whole, and thus to each and every part regardless of who wrote it.

Thus, it is not the intent of this section to claim rights or contest your rights to work written entirely by you; rather, the intent is to exercise the right to control the distribution of derivative or collective works based on the Program.

In addition, mere aggregation of another work not based on the Program with the Program (or with a work based on the Program) on a volume of a storage or distribution medium does not bring the other work under the scope of this License.

3. You may copy and distribute the Program (or a work based on it, under Section 2) in object code or executable form under the terms of Sections 1 and 2 above provided that you also do one of the following:

    a) Accompany it with the complete corresponding machine-readable source code, which must be distributed under the terms of Sections 1 and 2 above on a medium customarily used for software interchange; or,

    b) Accompany it with a written offer, valid for at least three years, to give any third party, for a charge no more than your cost of physically performing source distribution, a complete machine-readable copy of the corresponding source code, to be distributed under the terms of Sections 1 and 2 above on a medium customarily used for software interchange; or,

    c) Accompany it with the information you received as to the offer to distribute corresponding source code. (This alternative is allowed only for noncommercial distribution and only if you received the program in object code or executable form with such an offer, in accord with Subsection b above.)

    The source code for a work means the preferred form of the work for making modifications to it. For an executable work, complete source code means all the source code for all modules it contains, plus any associated interface definition files, plus the scripts used to control compilation and installation of the executable. However, as a special exception, the source code distributed need not include anything that is normally distributed (in either source or binary form) with the major components (compiler, kernel, and so on) of the operating system on which the executable runs, unless that component itself accompanies the executable.

    If distribution of executable or object code is made by offering access to copy from a designated place, then offering equivalent access to copy the source code from the same place counts as distribution of the source code, even though third parties are not compelled to copy the source along with the object code.

4. You may not copy, modify, sublicense, or distribute the Program except as expressly provided under this License. Any attempt otherwise to copy, modify, sublicense or distribute the Program is void, and will automatically terminate your rights under this License. However, parties who have received copies, or rights, from you under this License will not have their licenses terminated so long as such parties remain in full compliance.

5. You are not required to accept this License, since you have not signed it. However, nothing else grants you permission to modify or distribute the Program or its derivative works. These actions are prohibited by law if you do not accept this License. Therefore, by modifying or distributing the Program (or any work based on the Program), you indicate your acceptance of this License to do so, and all its terms and conditions for copying, distributing or modifying the Program or works based on it.

6. Each time you redistribute the Program (or any work based on the Program), the recipient automatically receives a license from the original licensor to copy, distribute or modify the Program subject to these terms and conditions. You may not impose any further restrictions on the recipients' exercise of the rights granted herein. You are not responsible for enforcing compliance by third parties to this License.

7. If, as a consequence of a court judgment or allegation of patent infringement or for any other reason (not limited to patent issues), conditions are imposed on you (whether by court order, agreement or otherwise) that contradict the conditions of this License, they do not excuse you from the conditions of this License. If you cannot distribute so as to satisfy simultaneously your obligations under this License and any other pertinent obligations, then as a consequence you may not distribute the Program at all. For example, if a patent license would not permit royalty-free redistribution of the Program by all those who receive copies directly or indirectly through you, then the only way you could satisfy both it and this License would be to refrain entirely from distribution of the Program.

   If any portion of this section is held invalid or unenforceable under any particular circumstance, the balance of the section is intended to apply and the section as a whole is intended to apply in other circumstances.

   It is not the purpose of this section to induce you to infringe any patents or other property right claims or to contest validity of any such claims; this section has the sole purpose of protecting the integrity of the free software distribution system, which is implemented by public license practices. Many people have made generous contributions to the wide range of software distributed through that system in reliance on consistent application of that system; it is up to the author/donor to decide if he or she is willing to distribute software through any other system and a licensee cannot impose that choice.

   This section is intended to make thoroughly clear what is believed to be a consequence of the rest of this License.

8. If the distribution and/or use of the Program is restricted in certain countries either by patents or by copyrighted interfaces, the original copyright holder who places the Program under this License may add an explicit geographical distribution limitation excluding those countries, so that distribution is permitted only in or among countries not thus excluded. In such case, this License incorporates the limitation as if written in the body of this License.

9. The Free Software Foundation may publish revised and/or new versions of the General Public License from time to time. Such new versions will be similar in spirit to the present version, but may differ in detail to address new problems or concerns.

   Each version is given a distinguishing version number. If the Program specifies a version number of this License which applies to it and "any later version", you have the option of following the terms and conditions either of that version or of any later version published by the Free Software Foundation. If the Program does not specify a version number of this License, you may choose any version ever published by the Free Software Foundation.

10. If you wish to incorporate parts of the Program into other free programs whose distribution conditions are different, write to the author to ask for permission. For software which is copyrighted by the Free Software Foundation, write to the Free Software Foundation; we sometimes make exceptions for this. Our decision will be guided by the two goals of preserving the free status of all derivatives of our free software and of promoting the sharing and reuse of software generally.

BUSINESS, CAREERS & PERSONAL FINANCE

0-7645-5307-0

0-7645-5331-3 *†

Also available:

- Accounting For Dummies †
  0-7645-5314-3
- Business Plans Kit For Dummies †
  0-7645-5365-8
- Cover Letters For Dummies
  0-7645-5224-4
- Frugal Living For Dummies
  0-7645-5403-4
- Leadership For Dummies
  0-7645-5176-0
- Managing For Dummies
  0-7645-1771-6

- Marketing For Dummies
  0-7645-5600-2
- Personal Finance For Dummies *
  0-7645-2590-5
- Project Management For Dummies
  0-7645-5283-X
- Resumes For Dummies †
  0-7645-5471-9
- Selling For Dummies
  0-7645-5363-1
- Small Business Kit For Dummies *†
  0-7645-5093-4

HOME & BUSINESS COMPUTER BASICS

0-7645-4074-2

0-7645-3758-X

Also available:

- ACT! 6 For Dummies
  0-7645-2645-6
- iLife '04 All-in-One Desk Reference
  For Dummies
  0-7645-7347-0
- iPAQ For Dummies
  0-7645-6769-1
- Mac OS X Panther Timesaving
  Techniques For Dummies
  0-7645-5812-9
- Macs For Dummies
  0-7645-5656-8

- Microsoft Money 2004 For Dummies
  0-7645-4195-1
- Office 2003 All-in-One Desk Reference
  For Dummies
  0-7645-3883-7
- Outlook 2003 For Dummies
  0-7645-3759-8
- PCs For Dummies
  0-7645-4074-2
- TiVo For Dummies
  0-7645-6923-6
- Upgrading and Fixing PCs For Dummies
  0-7645-1665-5
- Windows XP Timesaving Techniques
  For Dummies
  0-7645-3748-2

FOOD, HOME, GARDEN, HOBBIES, MUSIC & PETS

0-7645-5295-3

0-7645-5232-5

Also available:

- Bass Guitar For Dummies
  0-7645-2487-9
- Diabetes Cookbook For Dummies
  0-7645-5230-9
- Gardening For Dummies *
  0-7645-5130-2
- Guitar For Dummies
  0-7645-5106-X
- Holiday Decorating For Dummies
  0-7645-2570-0
- Home Improvement All-in-One
  For Dummies
  0-7645-5680-0

- Knitting For Dummies
  0-7645-5395-X
- Piano For Dummies
  0-7645-5105-1
- Puppies For Dummies
  0-7645-5255-4
- Scrapbooking For Dummies
  0-7645-7208-3
- Senior Dogs For Dummies
  0-7645-5818-8
- Singing For Dummies
  0-7645-2475-5
- 30-Minute Meals For Dummies
  0-7645-2589-1

INTERNET & DIGITAL MEDIA

0-7645-1664-7

0-7645-6924-4

Also available:

- 2005 Online Shopping Directory
  For Dummies
  0-7645-7495-7
- CD & DVD Recording For Dummies
  0-7645-5956-7
- eBay For Dummies
  0-7645-5654-1
- Fighting Spam For Dummies
  0-7645-5965-6
- Genealogy Online For Dummies
  0-7645-5964-8
- Google For Dummies
  0-7645-4420-9

- Home Recording For Musicians
  For Dummies
  0-7645-1634-5
- The Internet For Dummies
  0-7645-4173-0
- iPod & iTunes For Dummies
  0-7645-7772-7
- Preventing Identity Theft For Dummies
  0-7645-7336-5
- Pro Tools All-in-One Desk Reference
  For Dummies
  0-7645-5714-9
- Roxio Easy Media Creator For Dummies
  0-7645-7131-1

 **WILEY**

SPORTS, FITNESS, PARENTING, RELIGION & SPIRITUALITY

0-7645-5146-9

0-7645-5418-2

Also available:
- Adoption For Dummies
  0-7645-5488-3
- Basketball For Dummies
  0-7645-5248-1
- The Bible For Dummies
  0-7645-5296-1
- Buddhism For Dummies
  0-7645-5359-3
- Catholicism For Dummies
  0-7645-5391-7
- Hockey For Dummies
  0-7645-5228-7

- Judaism For Dummies
  0-7645-5299-6
- Martial Arts For Dummies
  0-7645-5358-5
- Pilates For Dummies
  0-7645-5397-6
- Religion For Dummies
  0-7645-5264-3
- Teaching Kids to Read For Dummies
  0-7645-4043-2
- Weight Training For Dummies
  0-7645-5168-X
- Yoga For Dummies
  0-7645-5117-5

TRAVEL

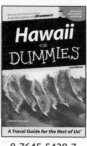

0-7645-5438-7

0-7645-5453-0

Also available:
- Alaska For Dummies
  0-7645-1761-9
- Arizona For Dummies
  0-7645-6938-4
- Cancún and the Yucatán For Dummies
  0-7645-2437-2
- Cruise Vacations For Dummies
  0-7645-6941-4
- Europe For Dummies
  0-7645-5456-5
- Ireland For Dummies
  0-7645-5455-7

- Las Vegas For Dummies
  0-7645-5448-4
- London For Dummies
  0-7645-4277-X
- New York City For Dummies
  0-7645-6945-7
- Paris For Dummies
  0-7645-5494-8
- RV Vacations For Dummies
  0-7645-5443-3
- Walt Disney World & Orlando For Dummies
  0-7645-6943-0

GRAPHICS, DESIGN & WEB DEVELOPMENT

0-7645-4345-8

0-7645-5589-8

Also available:
- Adobe Acrobat 6 PDF For Dummies
  0-7645-3760-1
- Building a Web Site For Dummies
  0-7645-7144-3
- Dreamweaver MX 2004 For Dummies
  0-7645-4342-3
- FrontPage 2003 For Dummies
  0-7645-3882-9
- HTML 4 For Dummies
  0-7645-1995-6
- Illustrator CS For Dummies
  0-7645-4084-X

- Macromedia Flash MX 2004 For Dummies
  0-7645-4358-X
- Photoshop 7 All-in-One Desk
  Reference For Dummies
  0-7645-1667-1
- Photoshop CS Timesaving Techniques
  For Dummies
  0-7645-6782-9
- PHP 5 For Dummies
  0-7645-4166-8
- PowerPoint 2003 For Dummies
  0-7645-3908-6
- QuarkXPress 6 For Dummies
  0-7645-2593-X

NETWORKING, SECURITY, PROGRAMMING & DATABASES

0-7645-6852-3

0-7645-5784-X

Also available:
- A+ Certification For Dummies
  0-7645-4187-0
- Access 2003 All-in-One Desk
  Reference For Dummies
  0-7645-3988-4
- Beginning Programming For Dummies
  0-7645-4997-9
- C For Dummies
  0-7645-7068-4
- Firewalls For Dummies
  0-7645-4048-3
- Home Networking For Dummies
  0-7645-42796

- Network Security For Dummies
  0-7645-1679-5
- Networking For Dummies
  0-7645-1677-9
- TCP/IP For Dummies
  0-7645-1760-0
- VBA For Dummies
  0-7645-3989-2
- Wireless All In-One Desk Reference
  For Dummies
  0-7645-7496-5
- Wireless Home Networking For Dummies
  0-7645-3910-8

HEALTH & SELF-HELP

0-7645-6820-5 *†

0-7645-2566-2

Also available:
- Alzheimer's For Dummies
  0-7645-3899-3
- Asthma For Dummies
  0-7645-4233-8
- Controlling Cholesterol For Dummies
  0-7645-5440-9
- Depression For Dummies
  0-7645-3900-0
- Dieting For Dummies
  0-7645-4149-8
- Fertility For Dummies
  0-7645-2549-2

- Fibromyalgia For Dummies
  0-7645-5441-7
- Improving Your Memory For Dummies
  0-7645-5435-2
- Pregnancy For Dummies †
  0-7645-4483-7
- Quitting Smoking For Dummies
  0-7645-2629-4
- Relationships For Dummies
  0-7645-5384-4
- Thyroid For Dummies
  0-7645-5385-2

EDUCATION, HISTORY, REFERENCE & TEST PREPARATION

0-7645-5194-9

0-7645-4186-2

Also available:
- Algebra For Dummies
  0-7645-5325-9
- British History For Dummies
  0-7645-7021-8
- Calculus For Dummies
  0-7645-2498-4
- English Grammar For Dummies
  0-7645-5322-4
- Forensics For Dummies
  0-7645-5580-4
- The GMAT For Dummies
  0-7645-5251-1
- Inglés Para Dummies
  0-7645-5427-1

- Italian For Dummies
  0-7645-5196-5
- Latin For Dummies
  0-7645-5431-X
- Lewis & Clark For Dummies
  0-7645-2545-X
- Research Papers For Dummies
  0-7645-5426-3
- The SAT I For Dummies
  0-7645-7193-1
- Science Fair Projects For Dummies
  0-7645-5460-3
- U.S. History For Dummies
  0-7645-5249-X

Get smart @ dummies.com®

- **Find a full list of Dummies titles**
- **Look into loads of FREE on-site articles**
- **Sign up for FREE eTips e-mailed to you weekly**
- **See what other products carry the Dummies name**
- **Shop directly from the Dummies bookstore**
- **Enter to win new prizes every month!**